THE
EVERYTHING®
EASY ITALIAN
COOKBOOK

Welcome to the EVERYTHING® Series!

These handy, accessible books give you all you need to tackle a difficult project, gain a new hobby, comprehend a fascinating topic, prepare for an exam, or even brush up on something you learned back in school but have since forgotten.

You can choose to read an Everything® book from cover to cover or just pick out the information you want from our four useful boxes: e-questions, e-facts, e-alerts, and e-ssentials.

We give you everything you need to know on the subject, but throw in a lot of fun stuff along the way, too.

We now have more than 400 Everything® books in print, spanning such wide-ranging categories as weddings, pregnancy, cooking, music instruction, foreign language, crafts, pets, New Age, and so much more. When you're done reading them all, you can finally say you know Everything®!

QUESTION

Answers to common questions

FACT

Important snippets of information

ALERT

Urgent warnings

ESSENTIAL

Quick handy tips

PUBLISHER Karen Cooper

MANAGING EDITOR, EVERYTHING® SERIES Lisa Laing

COPY CHIEF Casey Ebert

ASSISTANT PRODUCTION EDITOR Alex Guarco

ACQUISITIONS EDITOR Hillary Thompson

SENIOR DEVELOPMENT EDITOR Brett Palana-Shanahan

EVERYTHING® SERIES COVER DESIGNER Erin Alexander

THE
EVERYTHING®
EASY ITALIAN COOKBOOK

Dawn Altomari, Culinary Institute of America

Aadamsmedia
Avon, Massachusetts

An Everything® Series Book.
Everything® and everything.com® are registered trademarks of F+W Media, Inc.

Published by
Adams Media, a division of F+W Media, Inc.
57 Littlefield Street, Avon, MA 02322. U.S.A.
www.adamsmedia.com

Contains material adapted and abridged from *The Everything® Mediterranean Cookbook* by Dawn Altomari-Rathjen and Jennifer M. Bendelius, copyright © 2003 by F+W Media, Inc., ISBN 10: 1-58062-869-9, ISBN 13: 978-1-58062-869-3; *The Everything® Italian Cookbook* by Dawn Altomari, copyright © 2005 by F+W Media, Inc., ISBN 10: 1-59337-420-8, ISBN 13: 978-1-59337-420-4; *The Everything® Mediterranean Diet Book* by Connie Diekman and Sam Sotiropoulos, copyright © 2010 by F+W Media, Inc., ISBN 10: 1-4405-0674-4, ISBN 13: 978-1-4405-0674-1; *The Everything® Pie Cookbook* by Kelly Jaggers, copyright © 2011 by F+W Media, Inc., ISBN 10: 1-4405-2726-1, ISBN 13: 978-1-4405-2726-5; *The Everything® Panini Press Cookbook* by Anthony Tripodi, copyright © 2011 by F+W Media, Inc., ISBN 10: 1-4405-2769-5, ISBN 13: 978-1-4405-2769-2; *The Everything® Ice Cream, Gelato, and Frozen Desserts Cookbook* by Susan Whetzel, copyright © 2012 by F+W Media, Inc., ISBN 10: 1-4405-2497-1, ISBN 13: 978-1-4405-2497-4; *The Everything® Coconut Diet Cookbook* by Anji Sandage with Lorena Novak Bull, copyright © 2012 by F+W Media, Inc., ISBN 10: 1-4405-2902-7, ISBN 13: 978-1-4405-2902-3.

ISBN 10: 1-4405-8533-4
ISBN 13: 978-1-4405-8533-3
eISBN 10: 1-4405-8534-2
eISBN 13: 978-1-4405-8534-0

Printed in the United States of America.

10 9 8 7 6 5 4 3 2 1

Library of Congress Cataloging-in-Publication Data
Altomari, Dawn.
 The everything easy Italian cookbook / Dawn Altomari.
   pages cm
 Includes index.
 ISBN 978-1-4405-8533-3 (pb) -- ISBN 1-4405-8533-4 (pb) -- ISBN 978-1-4405-8534-0 (ebook) -- ISBN 1-4405-8534-2 (ebook)
 1. Cooking, Italian. 2. Quick and easy cooking. I. Title.
 TX723.A479 2014
 641.5945--dc23
                                    2014028823

Always follow safety and commonsense cooking protocol while using kitchen utensils, operating ovens and stoves, and handling uncooked food. If children are assisting in the preparation of any recipe, they should always be supervised by an adult.

Photographs © iStockphoto.com by Getty Images.

Cover photos
© StockFood / Eising Studio-Food Photo & Video;
© StockFood / Zouev, Tanya;
© StockFood / Crudo, George;
© StockFood / Loftus, David.

Contents

Introduction

ITALIAN CUISINE IS BELOVED the world over. Famous for their slow-simmered sauces, succulent roasts, fresh homemade pastas, and sinfully creamy gelato, Italian chefs, both modern and traditional, know the secrets behind the acclaimed dishes celebrated in kitchens and restaurants around the globe. Chances are, if you're reading this book, you love Italian cuisine as well—but if you are like most home cooks across America, you don't have as much time to spend in the kitchen as you'd like. Whipping up traditional Italian favorites, such as lasagna, chicken Parmesan, or risotto, isn't an easy feat, especially on busy weeknights and hectic weekends. That's where the magic of *The Everything® Easy Italian Cookbook* comes in. This big collection of recipes brings the flavors, textures, and aromas you love about Italian cuisine to your own home, and for a fraction of the cost and time that traditional Italian recipes require. With the easy-to-follow recipes here, you'll feel as comfortable creating a four-course holiday meal as you will a simple weeknight supper. And you won't sacrifice flavor, either—the recipes here are chef tested and *Nonna* approved.

The purpose of this book is to give you a feel for authentic Italian cuisine. However, compiling a comprehensive collection of recipes to represent the food of Italy is an enormous task. Italy is broken up into several regions, each of which has its own unique character that is dictated by geography and culture. In addition to these regional differences, there is also a distinction between the food of Italy's home kitchens and that of Italian restaurants. From one place to another, you will encounter different spices, different vegetables, and different meats, but they all contribute to the general Italian palate. This book brings together the best flavors of Italian cuisine with step-by-step recipes and readily available ingredients.

In Chapter 1, you will find information to guide you through some specific processes of Italian cooking. There are classic cooking techniques, definitions of particular cooking terms, a list of basic ingredients to have on hand, and much more. Throughout this book, you will find many recipes that are considered "authentic" Italian cuisine, such as Rosemary Pesto (Chapter 3), *Pollo alla Cacciatora* (Chicken Cacciatore) (Chapter 6), Garlic and Olive Bruschetta (Chapter 2), and Anisette Cookies (Chapter 16). You will also see some recipes that are a twist on traditional Italian dishes, like Pear, Goat Cheese, and Prosciutto Panini (Chapter 12), Tiramisu Pie (Chapter 16), and *Gelato alla Nutella* (Hazelnut Nutella Swirl Gelato) (Chapter 16). And there are a few dishes usually associated with other cultures that are given here with traditional Italian ingredients or a typically Italian flair. All come together in an incredible meld of flavor and creativity. Though some of these recipes are easier versions of traditional fare, you can further customize them to your own tastes and the tastes of your family. Add and subtract ingredients to make foods creamier, sweeter, more colorful, or more nutritious. Cooking is all about experimentation!

Above all, remember that classic Italian cooking is about simplicity, quality ingredients, and sharing flavors and dishes with those you love. So grab your favorite ingredients, roll up your sleeves, and prepare to create irresistible meals in no time. *Buon appetito!*

CHAPTER 1

Classic Italian Cuisine Made Easy

Italian cuisine is largely based on family tradition and is characterized by fresh ingredients and simple preparation. Mastering classic Italian cooking does not have to be intimidating or time-consuming; in fact, by learning the basics of regional cuisine and cooking with traditional ingredients, you'll create delicious Italian meals with ease, and feel comfortable adapting recipes to suit your tastes. In this chapter, you'll learn about classic ingredients and cooking styles unique to Italy's separate regions, and broaden your understanding of one of the world's most popular cuisines. With some practice and a little experimentation, you will create incredible Italian favorites in the comfort of your own home.

Regional Differences

Today's Italian cuisine is the result of the slow integration of the many different regional traditions and food customs. When the regions of Italy were unified in the mid-nineteenth century, only about a half million Italians out of the total population of 25 million were able to speak and understand the national language—instead they spoke their own regional dialects.

The same kind of separation was also reflected in the food of each region. However, the slow unification of the regions into one nation and the increased interaction and travel between the different parts of Italy caused both the language and the cooking styles to integrate. While the traditional food customs of each region still exist in the kitchens of Italian homes, restaurants offer the more unified "national" cuisine—a collection of favorites from the various regional cultures.

ESSENTIAL

Extra-virgin olive oil comes from the first pressing of the olives, has the most intense flavor, and is the most expensive. Use this for salads and for dipping breads. Virgin olive oil is from the second pressing. Less expensive than extra-virgin, it can be used for the same purposes. "Olive oil" indicates it is from the last pressing; this is the oil to use for cooking since it does not burn as easily at high temperatures.

Since the history of Italian food is so rooted in the regional cultures, it is interesting to take a look at the main regions of the country and what kinds of food products and dishes each one is known for. The most important regions in Italy to examine for culinary reasons include Abruzzi-Molise, Apulia, Calabria-Lucania, Emilia-Romagna, Liguria, Lombardy, Naples-Campagna, Piedmont, Rome-Lazio, Sardinia, Sicily, Tuscany, Umbria-Marche, and Veneto. These areas can be split up roughly into three categories: northern, central, and southern Italy.

Northern Italy

Emilia-Romagna is one of the most famous regions of Italy when it comes to food. Parmesan cheese—possibly the most famous Italian cheese—comes from the capital city of Parma and the province of Reggio. The trade name Parmigiano-Reggiano is protected by law and should only be used on authentic cheese products produced in this region. Emilia-Romagna is also famous for its pork and pork products, especially a variety of seasoned sausages known as "salumi," including salami, mortadella, prosciutto, pancetta, coppa, zampone, and bologna.

Liguria, which mostly occupies the coastline, is sometimes called "the Italian Riviera." Seafood dishes from Liguria include *cioppino* (seafood stew similar to bouillabaisse), *capon magro* (fish salad), and *baccalà* (dried salt cod). But the most famous dish by far is Genoa's pesto, the traditional sauce made from fresh sweet basil, garlic, pine nuts (*pignoli*) or walnuts, ewe's milk cheese, and olive oil. Traditionally, these ingredients are mixed into a smooth, very aromatic sauce using a mortar and pestle. Pesto is classically served over trenette pasta.

A multitude of Italian dishes are instantly recognizable as having their origins in Milan, the most important city in the region of Lombardy. For example, risotto, minestrone, *costolette* (veal cutlets), and *osso buco* (stew with veal in tomato sauce) are all well-known dishes from this region. You will often see dishes originating from this area referred to as "alla Milanese" (in the style of Milan).

FACT

When the Tuscans were looking for a way to use stale bread, they rubbed cut garlic cloves on the bread slices, brushed them with olive oil, grilled them over hot coals, and sprinkled them with salt. Bruschetta (plural is *bruschette*), which comes from the word *bruscare*, meaning "to toast/roast," can also be prepared in a toaster oven or hot frying pan.

Piedmont is a northern region that shares the Alps with Switzerland and France. The delicate white truffle is the pride of Piedmont and is an important ingredient in many of the dishes of this region. *Fritto misto* (mixed fry), *bagna cauda* (hot garlic dip with anchovy), and *fonduta* (Piedmontese fondue made with fontina cheese) are classic dishes famous in this region.

Food historians say that the more formal Italian cuisine originated in Tuscany (Florence, in particular) in the sixteenth century at the court of the

Medici. Florentine specialties (alla Fiorentina) such as *baccalà* (dried cod), *bistecca* (steak), and *anguilla* (eel) are all examples of the fine art of Tuscan cooking.

The region of Veneto has both mountains and coastline, so the cuisine varies in character according to where you go in the area. Rice and polenta are popular dishes, and the art of cooking fish is also prized among Venetian chefs. Famous dishes are *risi e bisati* (rice with eel), *risi e bisi* (rice and peas), *brodetto di pesce* (Venetian fish soup), *baccalà mantecato* (creamed salt cod), and *fugazza di Pasqua* (Easter bread).

Central Italy

Abruzzi-Molise is a mountainous region that stretches from the Adriatic Sea to the high peaks of the Apennine Mountains. The most famous dish of the region is *maccheroni alla chitarra*—long fresh pasta noodles served with tomato sauce flavored with sweet peppers and pork fat and sprinkled with pecorino cheese. *Chitarra* means "guitar" and refers to the guitar-shaped wooden implement used to cut the fresh pasta. Sheep are raised in the mountains, so lamb is the main meat of this area. Lamb is usually roasted, fried, or cooked *alla cacciatora* (sautéed with red peppers and tomato sauce). The local shepherds are also "masters" of cheese making; pecorino and scamorza (smoked mozzarella) are the two most famous cheese products of the area.

In the region of Rome-Lazio, specialty dishes include *bucatini all'Amatriciana* (pasta in a tomato sauce with onion, pancetta, and a dash of cognac) or *bucatini alla carbonara* (pasta with a creamy egg and cheese sauce), *gnocchi alla Romana saltimbocca* (a fillet of veal rolled in ham and flavored with sage, cooked in butter, and served with a Marsala sauce), and *abbacchio al forno* (roast lamb) or *abbacchio alla cacciatora* (lamb with an anchovy and rosemary sauce).

Sardinia is the second-largest island in Italy (after Sicily). With its rocky terrain the land of Sardinia is not conducive to growing anything. Hence, the region is famous for its bread, which Sardinian women bake lovingly in large ovens. Otherwise, most dishes of note are seafood based. *Burrida* (the famous fish stew of the area), *calamaretti ripieni* (stuffed baby squid), and *spaghetti alla rustica* (country-style spaghetti with anchovy and oregano sauce) are famous Sardinian dishes.

In Umbria-Marche, the cooking is known for its use of the prized black truffle. Specially trained dogs and even pigs with a highly delicate sense of smell are sent out to search for these hidden treasures buried in the soil. Also famous for their pork dishes, Umbrians cook the meat in the oven or roast it on spits. In the classic dish *arrosto alla ghiotta*, a cooking pan or dish is placed under the spit to collect the fat drippings from the roasting meat. White wine, vinegar, lemon slices, sage leaves, and black olives are placed all together in the dish. As the boiling fat drips into the mixture, it releases an aromatic vapor that is infused into the roasting meat as it rises.

Southern Italy

Apulia, which makes up the heel of Italy's "boot," is famous for its pastas and fresh vegetables. Fish and seafood dishes are also common, and oysters, fish soups, mussels, and squid stew are favorites. Apulia is also one of the richest wine-producing regions in Italy.

FACT

There is a product that comes in handy when certain fresh herbs are not in season (or you don't have them on hand). In the freezer section of your local market you can find chopped fresh herbs, such as parsley, basil, cilantro, and oregano, in large spice jars. You can open up the jar, use as much as you need, and pop it back into the freezer.

Most of the region of Calabria-Lucania occupies coastland. For this reason, the population traces its origins back to many different races that once visited the coastal towns, including Greeks, Arabs, Albanians, Spaniards, Normans, and even Turkish pirates. The land away from the coastline is exceedingly fertile, and this region is characterized by vast olive groves and lush plantations of jasmine, lavender, roses, mimosa, sweet peppers, eggplants, and citrus fruits. The famous Italian sausages luganega and soppressata come from here as well. Luganega is made with a mixture of pork spiced with sweet peppers and chili, and soppressata is lean meat and lard seasoned with salt, black pepper, and sweet peppers that are stuffed into casings and hung over a chimney or fire to be smoked. Calabria is also famous for its exports of figs, honey, almonds, and dried fruit.

Pizza and spaghetti are the main attractions in Naples-Campagna. Folklore has it that pizza was born on the streets of Naples two centuries ago when street vendors sold baked wedges of dough with hand-pressed extra-virgin olive oil drizzled on it and topped with chopped garlic. This became known as pizza Napoletana. In 2003, the *Washington Post* reported that "in Naples, pizza makers are trying to get an EU patent on Vera Pizza Napoletana made with dough fermented overnight on marble counters, cooked over a wood fire with a sauce of fresh tomato and buffalo mozzarella."

It makes sense that Sicily, Italy's largest island, is famous for its seafood and fish dishes. Sardines, tuna, and swordfish are central to Sicilian cuisine, and even pasta dishes are cooked with seafood. *Tonno alla cipollata* (tuna fried with onions), *seppia* (cuttlefish served in its own black sauce with pasta), and *pesce spada alla Messina* (swordfish cooked in oil with tomatoes onions, olives, capers, and tomatoes) are classic Sicilian dishes.

The Classic Italian Meal

The "classic" Italian meal is composed of the following elements: a first course (a soup, a pasta, or a risotto), the main course (meat or fish with a vegetable), followed by salad, and ending with the dessert. Of course, this order is not a hard and fast rule. Sometimes the pasta can be a separate course following the first course that is served prior to the main part of the meal. Likewise, the risotto is often used as a side dish to the main meal, instead of as a first course. In many homes the salad may be eaten prior to the main meal instead of after it, and obviously, pasta can often be served as a main dish all on its own. While a formal Italian restaurant may offer the full menu of traditional courses, a family will often customize the order to accommodate their time, mood, or budget.

Basic Ingredients

If you're going to be preparing authentic Italian food, you're going to need several basic ingredients. The fantastic thing about Italian cuisine is the astounding number of different dishes that can be made with a few fundamental items. However, it's important to always use fresh seasonal ingredients —local produce is best, if available. Stock your kitchen ahead of time with the basic nonperishables and make quick specialized trips to the market for fresh produce, meat, and dairy products.

Here is a list of basic ingredients that appear in most Italian recipes:

- **Flour**: there are many varieties besides all-purpose white, such as durum wheat (semolina)
- **Eggs**: freshness is very important—observe dates on cartons and dispose of eggs when the date has passed
- **Milk**
- **Unsalted butter**
- **Fresh fruits**: pears, figs, apples
- **Fresh vegetables**: tomatoes, onions, potatoes
- **Fresh fish and seafood**: cod, shrimp, mussels
- **Fresh meat**: chicken, veal, pork, beef
- **Fresh herbs**: parsley, basil, oregano
- **Olive oils**: pomace, virgin, extra-virgin
- **Spices**: salt, pepper, garlic salt
- **Nuts**: almonds, pecans, walnuts
- **Honey**
- **Sugar**: granulated, brown, confectioners'

In Italian cooking, you will go through a lot of spices, olive oil, and flour in a short time. Always keep extra supplies of these items in your pantry, and find a local market where you can get these basics at affordable prices.

Cooking Techniques

The techniques used in the Italian kitchen are not much different from the basic techniques you would use to prepare any other cuisine. Again, the method of preparation may differ from region to region for the same food, and often the method chosen has to do with the freshness and availability of the particular food item. It is not uncommon to find the method of preparation in the title of a recipe. For example, *Vitello al Forno* (Chapter 5) is veal baked in the oven and *Cavolfiore Fritto* (Chapter 15) is fried cauliflower. There are several different techniques used to make the dishes in this book. Some foods are made in the oven, others are made on the stovetop, and some employ both methods.

On the Stovetop

To bring the contents of a pot to a boil, you must keep the pot on high heat until frothy, popping bubbles arise. You will often need to bring water to a boil and then add food (whether pasta, rice, or vegetables) and lower the burner to medium heat while the food cooks. Simmering is slightly different from boiling. When you are instructed to "simmer" something in a recipe, you are usually heating a liquid or partially liquid mixture at a low to medium-low temperature. A simmer is like a slow, calm boil—there should be small, rolling bubbles instead of frothy, popping ones.

ESSENTIAL

There are a few very basic "nevers" by which a true Italian cook abides. Never overcook pasta. Never buy grated cheese in a jar or plastic container—only use fresh-grated Parmesan or Romano. Never use bottled salad dressing. And of course, *never* buy prepared tomato sauce in a jar or can. Make your own!

Braising (*brasare*, "to braise") indicates first searing the item (browning the outside at a very high heat) and then partially covering it with liquid and simmering at a low heat. Stewing is very similar to braising. When stewing ingredients (*stufare*, "to stew"), you have the option of first searing the item, but it's not required. Then the item is completely covered in liquid and simmered slowly.

When you sauté (*saltare*), you cook an item on the stovetop in a very small amount of fat on high heat. This is a moist cooking technique—the fat used is usually oil or butter. Often the item is lightly dusted with flour, as well, to create a batter or breading. The item is quickly cooked and browned on both sides. Steaming is also a moist cooking technique; it is accomplished by placing food in a perforated container over, not in, rapidly boiling liquid (most commonly water) in a pan with a lid. The lid is kept secure throughout the cooking to trap the steam.

Poaching can be accomplished in a shallow or deep collection of liquid. Items are generally simmered in a flavored liquid (usually stock). *Al cartoccio* means wrapping and cooking food in parchment paper. The more commonly recognized French term for this is *en papillote*. To do this, the food is encased within parchment paper and cooked, either in the oven or in liquid on the stovetop. Sometimes aluminum foil is used in place of the parchment paper.

Frying

Frying (*friggere*, "to fry") can be accomplished several ways. You can pan-fry, deep-fry, or stir-fry food. Pan-frying is similar to sautéing, but items are usually breaded or battered and larger amounts of fat are used in the cooking. Deep-frying is much like sautéing and pan-frying in that items are almost always coated with either flour, breading, or batter. However, the amount of fat utilized is far greater than in either sautéing or pan-frying. The item being cooked is completely submerged in fat and cooked with high, moist heat.

Stir-frying, although not an authentic Italian practice, is a helpful moist cooking technique. Very similar to sautéing, it quickly "fries" items, but there is even less—or no—fat, and items are cut into very small pieces.

In the Oven (*al Forno*)

Roasting (*arrostire*, "to roast") is cooking through indirect heat. Foods that are roasted are often placed on wire racks so that hot air can completely surround and thoroughly cook them. Baking (*cuocere*, "to bake"; or *al forno*, "baked") is similar to roasting. Often dessert mixtures are placed in baking vessels (pans, pie dishes, etc.) and these are placed in the oven. Hot, dry air circulates around the food. Broiling is a dry direct-heat cooking method using high heat, in which the heat comes from above the item. Grilling (*grigliare*, "to grill") is just the opposite: it is dry, direct-heat cooking in which the heat comes from below the item. When broiling or grilling, you can quickly marinate or moisten the product with oil or a vinaigrette before cooking.

Easy Italian Cooking at Home

Now that you've learned the basics of traditional Italian cuisine, it's time to experiment in your own kitchen. Refer back to this chapter for tips and guidance as you start your own Italian culinary adventures. The 300 recipes in this book are broken down into easy-to-follow steps, with fresh ingredients you can find in any grocery store. You'll discover that classic Italian meals don't have to take all day to cook; in fact, many of these easy recipes are perfect for weeknight fare or stress-free entertaining on the weekends.

Each chapter highlights the best of classic Italian cuisine, from traditional sauces to risotto and frittata to fresh takes on sweet Italian desserts. Start slowly by making your own "gravy" and meatballs, served with a tangy antipasto or quick-cooking polenta. Delight your guests with Italian favorites like Classic Chicken Parmesan (Chapter 6), Shrimp Scampi (Chapter 7), or Grilled Rack of Lamb (Chapter 5) at your next dinner party. For the adventurous, there's even a chapter on making your own pasta—surprisingly simple recipes for the freshest, most flavorful spaghetti, linguine, or gnocchi you've ever tasted. With time, quality ingredients, and a little patience, you'll soon master the Italian style.

CHAPTER 2

Appetizers

Clam-Stuffed Portobellos

Portobello mushrooms are not a native Italian variety, but they are used frequently in Italian-American cuisine. Portobellos can be found in most large supermarkets, either loose, packaged whole, or cleaned and sliced.

INGREDIENTS | SERVES 10

1 tablespoon olive oil

5 large portobello mushrooms

1 cup dry white wine (not cooking wine)

2 dozen littleneck clams

4 large slices crusty Italian bread, toasted

6 fresh chives, chopped

1 cup Easy Alfredo Sauce (see Chapter 3)

¼ teaspoon freshly cracked black pepper

Cleaning Mushrooms

Mushrooms should not be washed in water since they absorb liquid like sponges. Instead, use a soft brush or damp paper towel and scrub the mushrooms thoroughly. You simply want to remove any dirt or pebbles that might remain from when the mushrooms were picked.

1. Preheat the oven to 375°F. Lightly grease a large baking dish with the oil. Clean the mushrooms, scrape out the gills, and remove the stems. Finely dice the mushroom stems.

2. Place the mushroom caps stemmed-side up in a baking dish along with the wine. Cover and bake for 8 minutes.

3. Remove the clams from the shells, discard the shells, and clean the clams well. Chop the clam meat. Finely dice the bread.

4. In a large bowl, mix together the diced mushroom stems, clams, bread, chives, and Alfredo sauce.

5. Mound the clam mixture on top of the mushroom caps in the baking dish and sprinkle with the pepper. Cover and bake for approximately 10 minutes.

Fresh Vegetable Dip with Crusty Italian Bread

This is a great recipe to use for entertaining. This dip can be served as an appetizer before a meal or as a snack.

INGREDIENTS | SERVES 10

1 loaf fresh crusty Italian bread
2 medium carrots, grated
2 bunches arugula, chopped
2 medium red onions, minced
½ bulb garlic, minced
1 teaspoon red pepper flakes
1½ cups mayonnaise
1½ cups sour cream

1. Cut the bread into an oval bowl by hollowing out the center piece. Cut the center piece into bite-sized chunks and set aside.

2. In a large bowl, mix together the carrots, arugula, onions, garlic, pepper flakes, mayonnaise, and sour cream.

3. Fill the bread bowl with the dip mixture and serve with the bread chunks for dipping.

Melanzane Marinate (Pickled Eggplants)

This preparation is also great for marinating other vegetables, such as baby onions, carrots, cauliflower, peppers, celery, string beans, or cucumbers. This dish is delicious on its own or served on top of some crusty bread.

INGREDIENTS | SERVES 10

2 medium eggplants
1 medium yellow onion, sliced thin
½ bulb garlic, minced
1 cup granulated sugar
2 cups white wine vinegar
2 bay leaves
5 sprigs fresh thyme

1. Clean and cut the eggplants into long strips.

2. Place all the ingredients into a large stockpot and simmer for 20 minutes.

3. Discard bay leaves and chill mixture before serving. This dish can keep in the refrigerator for 1 month.

Melon and Prosciutto

Similar to the pairing of figs and Gorgonzola, the sweetness of melon and the saltiness of prosciutto are a perfect combination.

INGREDIENTS | SERVES 10

1 large fresh cantaloupe or honeydew melon

½ pound fresh prosciutto, very thinly sliced

1. Wash the melon thoroughly and cut the fruit into 10 wedges.

2. Wrap or drape each wedge with 1 slice of prosciutto and serve.

Appetizer Advice

Appetizers should complement the meal to come, not overpower it. Serve items that have milder but similar flavors to the main dish. Also, don't offer so many appetizers that your guests are full by the time the main meal arrives. Keep appetizers simple and subtle.

Baked Mixed Cheese Hors d'Oeuvres

Serve these appetizers warm out of the oven and top with Fruit Chutney (see Chapter 3) for a hint of sweetness.

INGREDIENTS | SERVES 10

2 tablespoons olive oil, divided

¼ cup Gorgonzola cheese

1½ cups mascarpone cheese (or substitute cream cheese)

¼ cup shredded fontina cheese

½ pasta recipe of choice (see Chapter 13)

1. Preheat the oven to 350°F. Grease a baking sheet with 1 tablespoon of the oil.

2. In a large bowl, mix together the Gorgonzola, mascarpone, and fontina cheeses thoroughly.

3. Roll out the pasta dough to a ½"-thick rectangle. Paint the top of the dough with the remaining oil. Spread the cheese on top of the oiled dough. Carefully roll up the dough like a jellyroll and cut the log into slices.

4. Place the slices on the prepared baking sheet. Bake for 5–8 minutes or until golden brown. Serve.

Dessert "Cheese"

Mascarpone cheese is not really a cheese. It is actually a very rich cream that has been soured with fermenting bacteria. It is made in the Lombardy region, usually in the winter. It is commonly used as a filling in Italian desserts.

Garlic and Olive Bruschetta

For more color and flavor you can add tomatoes to the purée in this recipe.

INGREDIENTS | SERVES 10

1 cup black olives, pitted

½ bulb roasted garlic (see Roasted Garlic Paste recipe in Chapter 3 for garlic-roasting instructions)

¼ bunch fresh parsley, chopped

½ teaspoon kosher salt

½ teaspoon freshly cracked black pepper

2 tablespoons virgin olive oil

1 loaf Italian bread

1. Preheat the oven to 400°F.

2. Purée the olives and garlic in a food processor. Add the parsley, salt, pepper, and oil and blend thoroughly.

3. Slice the bread thinly and lay it out on a baking sheet. Toast the bread in the oven for 10 minutes.

4. Spread the olive purée on the bread and serve.

Spicy Chicken Wings

This Italian version of Buffalo chicken wings makes great party food. Just be sure to put out plenty of napkins for your guests!

INGREDIENTS | SERVES 10

3 sprigs fresh oregano, chopped

½ teaspoon red pepper flakes

2 tablespoons olive oil

2 tablespoons unsalted butter

1 teaspoon freshly cracked black pepper

4 pounds chicken wings

1. In a deep dish, mix together the oregano, red pepper flakes, oil, butter, and black pepper. Add the chicken wings and coat completely in the marinade. Let marinate in the refrigerator for at least 1 hour.

2. Preheat the oven to 400°F.

3. Roast the marinated chicken for 15–20 minutes until thoroughly cooked.

Marinated Beef Skewers

The garlicky, nutty flavor of the marinade lends a unique taste to these beef appetizers.

INGREDIENTS | SERVES 10

2½ pounds sirloin beef

½ cup walnuts

½ bulb roasted garlic (see Roasted Garlic Paste recipe in Chapter 3 for garlic-roasting instructions)

¼ cup olive oil

½ cup dry red wine

1 teaspoon freshly cracked black pepper

1. Thinly slice and skewer the beef. Place the skewers in a single layer in a baking dish large enough for the skewers to lie flat.

2. In a blender, finely grind the walnuts, then peel and add the roasted garlic cloves, oil, wine, and black pepper. Blend completely and pour over the beef skewers in the dish, making sure to coat all the beef completely. Marinate the beef in the refrigerator no longer than 2 hours (the acid in the wine will "cook" the meat if left in too long).

3. Preheat the oven to 400°F. Roast the skewers for 10–15 minutes. Serve hot.

Oregano Pork Ribs

These spicy, finger-licking-good ribs are an interesting variation of the traditional barbecue-sauce version.

INGREDIENTS | SERVES 10

4 cloves garlic, minced

4 sprigs fresh oregano, chopped

3 tablespoons olive oil

1 tablespoon balsamic vinegar

1 teaspoon kosher salt

1 teaspoon freshly cracked black pepper

3 pounds bone-in pork ribs

1. In a small bowl, blend together the garlic, oregano, oil, vinegar, salt, and pepper.

2. Place the ribs in a baking dish and completely coat all the meat in the oil mixture. Let marinate in the refrigerator for 8–12 hours.

3. Preheat the oven to 400°F. Roast the ribs, uncovered, for 45–60 minutes. Serve.

Orange Shrimp

*The extra citrus-flavored sauce used in this recipe can be poured
into a small bowl and set aside for dipping.*

INGREDIENTS | SERVES 10

2 pounds large shrimp
Juice and zest of 3 large oranges
2 shallots, minced
½ teaspoon freshly cracked black pepper
1 teaspoon capers, rinsed
2 tablespoons olive oil

1. Peel and devein the shrimp, but leave the tails on.

2. In a medium bowl, mix together the orange juice, zest, shallots, pepper, capers, and oil.

3. Heat the mixture in a skillet over medium-high heat.

4. Add the shrimp to the pan and quickly cook them in the oil mixture for about 2–3 minutes until opaque in the center.

5. Remove the shrimp from the oil mixture and serve on a platter with a toothpick in each.

Pomodori Ripieni (Stuffed Roma Tomatoes)

*Roma tomatoes are also known as "plum" tomatoes and are smaller and more
oblong in shape than beefsteak tomatoes. They are good for use in stuffing recipes
because they generally have firmer meat, less juice, and fewer seeds.*

INGREDIENTS | SERVES 10

1 teaspoon plus 1 tablespoon olive oil, divided
20 Roma tomatoes
4 sprigs fresh basil, chopped
3 thick slices Italian bread, diced
½ cup shredded provolone cheese
½ teaspoon freshly cracked black pepper

1. Preheat the oven to 400°F. Lightly grease a baking sheet with 1 teaspoon of the oil. Slice the tomatoes in half and scoop out and reserve the insides.

2. In a medium bowl, mix together the tomato insides, basil, bread, cheese, and pepper.

3. Stuff each tomato half with the mixture. Place the tomatoes on the baking sheet, drizzle with the remaining oil, and sprinkle with more pepper if desired. Roast for 8 minutes. Serve immediately.

Sweet Sausage Bread

If you do not have time to make the flatbread recipe, you can substitute any kind of bread. A thinly sliced Italian loaf works well.

INGREDIENTS | SERVES 10

1 recipe Basic Flatbread (see Chapter 9)

1 pound sweet Italian sausage, casings removed

¼ pound fontina cheese, shredded

1. Preheat the oven to 400°F. On a baking sheet, lightly toast the flatbread and cut into small triangles.

2. Spread the toast with the sausage and top with the cheese.

3. Bake for 10–15 minutes and serve hot.

Hearty Artichoke Leaves

The most popular way to eat artichokes in Italy is to stuff them and then braise or bake them. The heart can be boiled, fried, or baked.

INGREDIENTS | SERVES 10

1 tablespoon olive oil

3 large whole artichokes

½ recipe Three-Meat Meatballs (see Chapter 8), unformed and uncooked

1. Preheat the oven to 425°F. Lightly grease a baking sheet with the oil.

2. Remove the outer leaves from the artichokes and snip off the prickly triangular end of each leaf.

3. Quickly blanch the leaves in boiling water and then place in ice water to stop the cooking process.

4. Mound a tablespoonful of the meatball mixture on top of each leaf and place on the greased baking sheet. Roast for 8 minutes and serve.

Gorgonzola Browned Pears

You can substitute apples for pears or substitute any citrus fruit for the oranges in this recipe. This is a great appetizer to experiment with.

INGREDIENTS | SERVES 10

2½ teaspoons olive oil, divided

5 large pears (any variety), cut into wedges

Juice and zest of 2 large oranges

½ cup crumbled Gorgonzola cheese

1 teaspoon honey

½ teaspoon freshly cracked black pepper

1. Preheat the broiler. Lightly grease a baking sheet with 1 teaspoon of the oil.

2. In a large bowl, toss the pears in the remaining oil and the orange juice.

3. Place the pears skin-side down on the prepared baking sheet. Sprinkle the cheese over the pears, then drizzle with the honey. Sprinkle with the orange zest and black pepper.

4. Quickly broil until browned and serve immediately.

Sausage-Filled Shallots

This recipe is just as wonderful made with Vidalia onions, especially if you find the smaller shallots difficult to work with.

INGREDIENTS | SERVES 8

1 teaspoon olive oil

4 medium shallots

½ pound Italian sausage, casings removed

2 cups white table wine

1 bay leaf

½ teaspoon freshly cracked black pepper

1. Preheat the oven to 375°F. Lightly grease a baking sheet with the oil. Carefully peel and slice the shallots in half lengthwise so you can remove the centers of the shallots. Mince the centers.

2. In a medium bowl, mix the shallot centers with the sausage.

3. Place the empty shallot halves in a microwave-safe dish with the wine, bay leaf, and black pepper. Cook for 3 minutes or until the shallots are al dente. Let cool.

4. Stuff the hollowed shallots with the sausage mixture. Place on the prepared baking sheet. Bake for 20 minutes and serve hot.

Frittura di Paranza (Pan-Fried Smelts)

Eat fried smelts like you eat corn on the cob—nibble the flesh off the bone. Serve with green salad.

INGREDIENTS | SERVES 10

¾ pound fresh smelts
1 cup all-purpose flour
1 tablespoon baking powder
1 tablespoon garlic powder
½ cup milk
2 tablespoons olive oil
½ teaspoon kosher salt
½ teaspoon freshly cracked black pepper
½ cup balsamic vinegar (optional)

Balsamic Vinegar

There are various types of Italian vinegar, but perhaps the most famous is balsamic vinegar. Balsamic vinegar is made from reduced wine and aged in special wood barrels for years. Each year's barrels are made of a different type of wood, and the vinegar absorbs the flavor of the wood. Authentic balsamic vinegar ages for a minimum of ten and up to thirty years.

1. Clean the smelts in ice-cold water and pat dry.

2. Sift together the flour, baking powder, and garlic powder onto a plate. Pour the milk into a shallow bowl.

3. Heat the oil over medium heat in a large sauté pan. Dust the smelts with the flour mixture, dip them in the milk, and then dust with the flour again. Carefully place in the oil.

4. Fry the smelts on each side for approximately 3–5 minutes or until browned and thoroughly cooked. Drain on a rack with a paper towel beneath to catch the drippings.

5. Sprinkle with salt and pepper. Drizzle with balsamic vinegar, if desired, and serve hot.

Lobster Capicola

Soaking the skewers in water before threading the food onto them prevents them from burning when placed on the heat.

INGREDIENTS | SERVES 10

1 teaspoon olive oil
5 large lobster tails
10 thin slices capicola

Capicola

Capicola is an Italian ham "cold cut" purchased in the deli section of the supermarket. It is spicier than regular ham and also comes in a "hot" spicy variety. Commonly known as "cappy," capicola can be eaten hot or cold in sandwiches and salads, and used in cooking.

1. Soak 10 wood skewers in water for about 15 minutes. Preheat the oven to 400°F. Lightly grease a baking sheet with the olive oil.

2. Remove the shells from the lobster tails and slice the tails in half lengthwise. Carefully wrap each tail half in 1 slice of the capicola and thread onto a skewer.

3. Place the skewers on the prepared baking sheet. Roast for 5–8 minutes until heated through and the capicola is crispy.

Grilled Pork Skewers

The complementary flavors of pork and apple work perfectly together in this simple but delicious recipe.

INGREDIENTS | SERVES 10

2 pounds thick boneless pork loin
1 teaspoon olive oil
1 teaspoon freshly cracked black pepper
2 cups apple juice
½ teaspoon kosher salt

1. Preheat the grill to high heat. Rub the pork with the oil and season with the pepper.

2. Pour the apple juice into a small saucepan over high heat and reduce the juice by half the volume (about 1 cup).

3. Grill the pork to desired doneness. Transfer to a plate and tent with foil to keep warm. Let rest for about 5 minutes. Cut the pork into large cubes.

4. Serve on small skewers drizzled with the reduced apple juice and sprinkled with salt.

Cheese-Stuffed Prunes

The softness of the prunes and cheese paired with the crunchiness of the nuts in this recipe creates a fun texture.

INGREDIENTS | SERVES 10

2 cups prunes
¾ cup mascarpone cheese
½ cup ricotta cheese
½ cup pecans or walnuts, finely chopped, divided

1. Cut the prunes into hollow halves.

2. In a medium bowl, mix together the cheeses. Stir half the chopped pecans into the cheese mixture.

3. Stuff each prune with the cheese mixture and sprinkle with the remaining pecans. Serve.

CHAPTER 3

Sauces

Old World Gravy (Long-Cooking Tomato Sauce)

You can customize this sauce by adding different meats or poultry. Always brown or thoroughly cook your meat before adding it to the sauce.

INGREDIENTS | MAKES 1 GALLON

1 tablespoon olive oil

2½ pounds pork spare ribs (or any pork meat with bones)

1 pound Italian sausage, casings removed

3 Vidalia onions, diced

1 bulb garlic, minced

6 pounds plum tomatoes, chopped

8 cups stock of choice (see Chapter 4)

1 bunch fresh basil, chopped

½ bunch fresh oregano or marjoram, chopped

½ bunch fresh parsley, chopped

1 teaspoon kosher salt

1 teaspoon freshly cracked black pepper

1. In a large stockpot, heat the oil to medium-high temperature. Add the ribs and sausage and brown for 10 minutes. Add the onions and garlic. Sauté for 5 minutes, then add the tomatoes and stock. Reduce heat to low and simmer for 3 hours, uncovered, stirring occasionally.

2. Add the herbs and spices and simmer for a minimum of 3 more hours, uncovered, stirring occasionally.

3. Adjust seasonings to taste and serve or store as desired. Store in sealed containers and refrigerate for up to 5 days or freeze for up to 3 months.

Gravy or Sauce?

When most Americans hear the word gravy, they think of thick brown sauce that is ladled over turkey, pork, or beef. However, in Italian cooking, "gravy" is the term used for red sauce to be served with meatballs over pasta.

Fra Diavolo (Spicy Old World Gravy)

You will likely see Fra Diavolo sauce offered over lobster or seafood and pasta in restaurants. You can also use this spicy version of Old World Gravy just like regular marinara—over pasta or pasta and meatballs.

INGREDIENTS | MAKES 1 GALLON

1 tablespoon olive oil
1 pound pork bones
1 pound hot Italian pepperoni
1½ pounds Italian sausage, casings removed
4 medium yellow onions, diced
1 bulb garlic, minced
7 pounds plum tomatoes, chopped
1 cup hearty red wine
8 cups Beef Stock (see Chapter 4)
½ bunch fresh parsley, chopped
½ tablespoon red pepper flakes
½ tablespoon freshly cracked black pepper
1 teaspoon garlic powder

1. Heat the oil over medium-high heat in a large stockpot. Add the pork bones, pepperoni, and sausage and brown for 10 minutes. Add the onions and garlic and sauté for 5 minutes. Add the tomatoes, wine, and stock. Reduce heat to low and simmer for 3 hours, uncovered, stirring occasionally.

2. Add the herbs and spices and simmer for 2 more hours, uncovered, stirring occasionally.

3. Adjust seasoning to taste and serve or store as desired. Store in sealed containers and refrigerate for up to 5 days or freeze for up to 3 months.

New World Fresh Sauce

This sauce is called "fresh" because it's made with only the freshest ingredients from the garden and it only needs to simmer for 1 hour—as opposed to the long-cooking traditional gravies.

INGREDIENTS | MAKES 1 GALLON

1 tablespoon olive oil

7 pounds plum tomatoes, chopped

1 bulb garlic, minced

2 shallots, minced

½ bunch fresh basil, chopped

¼ cup pine nuts

½ teaspoon freshly cracked black pepper

1. Heat the oil over medium heat in a large stockpot.

2. Add all the remaining ingredients and stir to combine. Reduce temperature to low and simmer for 1 hour, uncovered. Serve. (Do not store. This sauce should be prepared fresh every time.)

Herb Arithmetic

Dried herbs are stronger than fresh, and powdered herbs are stronger than dried herbs. Here's a tip: ½ teaspoon of powered herb equals ¾–1 teaspoon of crumbled herb equals 2 teaspoons of fresh herb. If a recipe calls for fresh but you only have dried, go ahead and substitute; just be sure you adjust the amount accordingly.

Salsa Besciamella (Béchamel Sauce)

Various flavorings can be stirred in at the end of the cooking process, just before serving. Some examples are tomato paste, cooked shrimp, parsley, capers, or egg (if the sauce will be an ingredient in a baked dish).

INGREDIENTS | MAKES 1 GALLON

½ cup (1 stick) unsalted butter

¼ cup olive oil

¾ cup all-purpose flour

1½ gallons whole milk

½ gallon Chicken Stock or Vegetable Stock (see Chapter 4)

¾ cup fresh-grated pecorino Romano cheese

Aged Cheese

Pecorino Romano is a type of aged cheese sometimes used in recipes that call for Parmesan cheese because it is a less expensive variety. Romano is aged under one year, while Parmesan is aged from eighteen months to five years. Another feature that makes Parmesan more expensive is that it is made only from whole milk that comes from cows that have been exclusively fed fresh grass.

1. Melt the butter in a large saucepan over medium heat, then add the oil. Sprinkle in the flour and stir with a wooden spoon.

2. Whisk in the milk and stock and increase the temperature to medium-high. Simmer until the sauce thickens, about 10 minutes.

3. Remove from heat and stir in the cheese. This sauce is best fresh, but it could be stored in the refrigerator in a sealed container for 1–2 days.

Mozzarella and Ricotta Cheese Sauce

*Both of these cheeses have a high salt content. So, when you are using
this sauce over pasta, do not add salt to the boiling water.*

INGREDIENTS | MAKES 1 GALLON

¼ cup olive oil

¾ cup all-purpose flour

1 gallon Chicken Stock or Vegetable
Stock (see Chapter 4)

1 cup whole milk

1 tablespoon chopped fresh oregano

1 pound mozzarella cheese, shredded
(preferably fresh mozzarella in water)

2 pounds ricotta cheese

1. Heat the oil over medium heat in a large saucepan.
   Sprinkle in the flour and stir with a wooden spoon.

2. Whisk in the stock, milk, and oregano. Simmer until
   the sauce thickens, about 10 minutes.

3. Remove from heat and stir in both cheeses. This sauce
   is best fresh, but it can be stored in a sealed container
   for 2 days in the refrigerator.

Mascarpone Cheese Sauce

*Mascarpone is made from soured cream. It has a creamy, soft texture and is often
used as a filling for sweets and cakes, the most famous being tiramisu.*

INGREDIENTS | MAKES 4 CUPS

½ cup (1 stick) unsalted butter

½ cup all-purpose flour

4 cups whole milk

2 cups light cream

½ pound mascarpone cheese

1. Melt the butter in a large saucepan over medium heat.
   Sprinkle in the flour and stir with a wooden spoon.

2. Whisk in the milk and cream (be careful not to scorch
   the sauce). Simmer until the sauce thickens, about 10
   minutes.

3. Remove from heat and stir in the cheese. Serve. (Do
   not store. This sauce is best made fresh for each use.)

Easy Alfredo Sauce

This rich sauce can be served over pasta or as a dip for focaccia bread or raw vegetables.

INGREDIENTS | MAKES 4 CUPS

6 cups heavy cream
1 cup fresh-grated Parmesan cheese
½ teaspoon freshly cracked black pepper

1. In a large saucepan, bring the cream to a simmer over medium heat. Cook, stirring occasionally, until the cream reduces to 4 cups.

2. Remove from heat, sprinkle in the cheese and pepper, and stir until smooth. This sauce is best fresh, but it can be stored in a sealed container for 2 days in the refrigerator.

Cutting Down on Salt

Cheese sauces can be used on many kinds of dishes. But when using a cheese sauce over pasta, it is a good idea to omit the salt that is usually put in the water to boil the pasta. Although it is a matter of personal taste, the saltiness of the cheese combined with the extra salt in the water might make the dish too salty.

Roasted Garlic Paste

This simple paste has many uses, the most popular of which is making bruschetta.

INGREDIENTS | MAKES 2 CUPS

8 large bulbs garlic
½ cup olive oil

1. Preheat the oven to 400°F. Slice the unpeeled bulbs in half crosswise. Pour the oil into a roasting pan. Place the garlic cut-side down in the pan and cover tightly with a lid or foil.

2. Roast for 10 minutes until the cloves are completely softened.

3. Let cool, then peel each clove. Mash the cloves into a paste.

Cannellini Bean Purée

For variety, you can use other beans in this recipe, such as kidney beans, chickpeas, navy beans, or black beans. Serve this as a flavorful side dish with any kind of meat or as a dip with toasted bread or crackers.

INGREDIENTS | MAKES 2 CUPS

2 cups dry cannellini beans

1½ gallons Vegetable Stock (see Chapter 4), divided

¼ bunch fresh parsley, stems only, chopped

1 bulb garlic, minced

2 bay leaves

½ cup extra-virgin olive oil

½ teaspoon freshly cracked black pepper

1. Soak the beans overnight in ¾ gallon of the stock.

2. The next day, drain the beans and discard the stock.

3. Place the beans in a large stockpot with the remaining stock, the parsley, garlic, and bay leaves. Set the lid ajar and simmer over medium heat about 1½ hours until the beans are thoroughly cooked.

4. Drain and remove the bay leaves. Place the beans into a food processor and purée until smooth. Drizzle with the oil and sprinkle with pepper. Use as desired.

Traditional Pesto

Pesto can stand on its own as a sauce, or you can use just a spoonful to add extra flavor to a number of other dishes—especially stews, soups, and sauces.

INGREDIENTS | MAKES 2 CUPS

2 bunches fresh basil, chopped

½ bulb garlic, chopped

½ cup toasted pine nuts

1 cup extra-virgin olive oil

1. In a food processor, pulse the basil, garlic, and pine nuts until well chopped and blended.

2. Slowly pour in the oil and blend until relatively smooth. Use as desired. (Do not store—pesto should be made fresh for each use.)

Freshness Is Essential

Do not even attempt to make pesto unless you have fresh herbs available. While dried herbs can be substituted in some recipes, only the freshest herbs will suffice in a pesto. Additionally, fresh herbs are the most aromatic, and a plate of steaming pasta with pesto should fill your house with a savory aroma.

Roasted Eggplant Purée

You don't need to peel the eggplant before preparing this recipe. The peel softens during cooking.

INGREDIENTS | MAKES 2 CUPS

1 tablespoon olive oil, divided

2 medium eggplants

8 cloves garlic, minced

¼ bunch fresh oregano, chopped

1 teaspoon freshly cracked black pepper

Freshly Cracked Black Pepper

Like many seeds, a peppercorn's best flavor remains locked inside until it is smashed. If you don't have a pepper mill, take 10 peppercorns and fold them inside wax paper. Place on a flat, hard surface. Use a small skillet or saucepan to apply pressure, pushing with the heel of your hand to break the seeds a few at a time.

1. Preheat the oven to 375°F. Lightly grease a large baking sheet with ½ tablespoon of the oil. Slice the eggplants in half lengthwise.

2. Rub the eggplant halves with the remaining oil and sprinkle with the garlic, oregano, and pepper. Place on the baking sheet and roast for 45 minutes until fork-tender.

3. Let cool, then purée in a food processor. Store in a sealed container and refrigerate for up to 5 days or freeze for up to 3 months.

Walnut Pesto

With any pesto recipe, you can stir ½ cup grated Romano or Parmesan cheese into the sauce just before using for an extra kick of flavor.

INGREDIENTS | MAKES 2 CUPS

2 bunches fresh parsley, chopped
½ bulb garlic, chopped
½ cup walnuts
1 cup extra-virgin olive oil
Zest from 1 large lemon

1. In a food processor, pulse the parsley, garlic, and walnuts until well chopped and blended.

2. Slowly pour in the oil and blend until fairly smooth.

3. Stir in the lemon zest before serving. (Do not store—pesto should be made fresh for each use.)

Freezing Citrus Peels

Save the peels when you use lemons, limes, or oranges for juice or fruit and freeze them in a resealable bag. This way, when a recipe calls for citrus zest, you will have peels on hand, ready to grate or zest, right from the freezer. There's no need to thaw before using.

Oregano-Almond Pesto

If your pesto is too thick, take a tablespoon of the boiling water from your pasta pot and stir it into the pesto to thin it out. This is also a good trick to warm pesto that has been refrigerated.

INGREDIENTS | MAKES 2 CUPS

2 bunches fresh oregano
½ bulb garlic, chopped
½ cup almonds
1 cup extra-virgin olive oil

1. Remove the oregano leaves from the stems and roughly chop the leaves (discard the stems).

2. In a food processor, pulse the oregano, garlic, and almonds until well chopped and blended.

3. Slowly pour in the oil and blend until fairly smooth. Serve. (Do not store—pesto should be made fresh for each use.)

Rosemary Pesto

An important rule with pesto is to make it only when fresh herbs are available. Dried herbs won't give the same flavor or texture. Fresh rosemary adds a fragrant aroma and delicious taste to this spin on traditional pesto.

INGREDIENTS | MAKES 2 CUPS

1 cup chestnuts in shells
1 bunch fresh rosemary
½ bulb garlic, chopped
1 fresh shallot, chopped
1 cup extra-virgin olive oil
½ teaspoon freshly cracked black pepper

1. Preheat the oven to 375°F. Slit the chestnuts with a sharp knife. Place the chestnuts on a baking sheet and roast for 10 minutes. Once the chestnuts are cool enough to handle, shell and roughly chop the nuts.

2. Remove the rosemary needles from the stems (discard the stems).

3. Combine all the ingredients in a food processor and blend until smooth. Serve. (Do not store—pesto should be made fresh for each use.)

Sage Pesto

While pesto is generally used as a sauce over pasta or added to soups or stews for an extra kick, you can also use it to flavor meat. Try rubbing a little of this pesto on pork chops or chicken breasts before cooking.

INGREDIENTS | MAKES 2 CUPS

2 bunches fresh sage
1 Vidalia onion, chopped
½ cup shelled sunflower seeds
1 cup white wine vinegar
½ teaspoon freshly cracked black pepper

Combine all the ingredients in a food processor and blend until smooth.

Brown Sauce

You can add chunks of veal or beef to this sauce for more flavor and texture.

INGREDIENTS | MAKES 4 CUPS

1 teaspoon olive oil

3 medium yellow onions, chopped

2 medium carrots, chopped

2 stalks celery, chopped

2 medium tomatoes, chopped

½ bulb garlic

1 cup dry red wine

1 gallon Beef Stock (see Chapter 4)

1 bay leaf

¼ bunch fresh parsley, chopped

4 sprigs fresh thyme

½ teaspoon freshly cracked black pepper

1. Heat the oil over medium-high heat in a large stockpot. Add the onions, carrots, celery, tomatoes, and garlic. Sauté for about 10 minutes, stirring frequently. Pour in the wine and reduce by half the volume.

2. Add the stock, bay leaf, parsley, thyme, and pepper. Reduce heat and simmer for 2 hours, uncovered. Strain through a fine-meshed sieve and discard the solids. Return the liquid to the pan.

3. Increase heat to high and cook until thickened, about 45–60 minutes, stirring occasionally.

Thickening Agents

Some soups, stews, sauces, and gravies will thicken naturally throughout the cooking process. Lengthy cooking time and starchy ingredients such as potatoes can do the trick. However, with certain recipes, you may want to use thickening agents such as roux, cornstarch or other pure starch (such as potato starch), or tapioca to thicken it up.

Italian Pepperoncini Gremolata

Classic gremolata is used to flavor certain dishes and helps offset the "fatty" flavor of hearty dishes. The most popular dish made with gremolata is osso buco.

INGREDIENTS | MAKES 2 CUPS

Zest of 1 large lemon

1 shallot, minced

2 cups pepperoncini, diced

½ teaspoon freshly cracked black pepper

In a medium bowl, mix together all the ingredients and use as desired. (Do not store—this should be made fresh for each use.)

Minty Fruit Chutney

Only make this chutney when fresh peaches and mint are in season. Use local produce when possible.

INGREDIENTS | MAKES 4 CUPS

5 large peaches, diced

2 sprigs mint, chopped

1 shallot, minced

½ teaspoon freshly cracked black pepper

½ cup peach nectar (or substitute peach juice)

In a medium bowl, mix together all the ingredients until well combined. Use as desired.

Fruit Chutney

A spoonful of this fruit chutney placed on top of a high-fat stewed or braised dish just before serving will ease the "fatty" flavor.

INGREDIENTS | MAKES 2 CUPS

2 medium oranges

5 sprigs fresh rosemary, chopped

5 sprigs fresh mint, chopped

1 cup shelled walnuts, chopped

1 medium yellow onion, diced

1. Zest and juice the oranges, then remove the peel and dice the fruit.

2. In a medium bowl, mix together the zest, juice, chopped fruit, and all the remaining ingredients. Use as desired.

CHAPTER 4

Stocks and Soups

Chicken Stock

You can prepare this broth for use in a specific recipe on the day you plan to cook, or you can make batches ahead of time, let cool completely, and freeze for later use.

INGREDIENTS | MAKES 1 GALLON

5–6 pounds chicken meat with bones

1 tablespoon olive oil

3 medium yellow onions, chopped

3 large leeks (whole), chopped

1 bulb garlic, chopped

4 stalks celery, chopped

6 medium parsnips (or 3 large carrots), chopped

½ bunch fresh parsley or
1 tablespoon dried

5 sprigs fresh thyme or
1 tablespoon dried

2 cups mushrooms (optional), chopped

2 cups dry white wine (not cooking wine)

1½ gallons water

3 bay leaves

½ teaspoon peppercorns

1. Rinse the chicken in cold water and pat dry with paper towels.

2. Heat the oil in a large stockpot over medium heat. Add the chicken and lightly brown it. Add the onions and leeks and let wilt, about 3–4 minutes. Add the garlic, celery, parsnips, parsley, thyme, and mushrooms, if using, and sauté for 5 minutes.

3. Pour in the wine and reduce by half the volume. Add the water, bay leaves, and peppercorns.

4. Bring to a simmer and cook for 4–6 hours, uncovered.

5. Strain the broth through a fine-meshed sieve and discard all the solids. Use immediately or let cool completely and freeze for later use.

Removing Fat from Chicken Stock

It is a good practice to prepare chicken stock one day in advance of using it for a soup recipe. Chilling causes the fat to rise to the top and congeal, so store stock overnight in the refrigerator. The next day, you can remove the thick layer of fat to reveal pure stock.

Beef Stock

Try lining the strainer with cheesecloth before pouring the soup through. In addition to straining out all the solids, this is helpful in removing any fat from the meat.

INGREDIENTS | MAKES 1 GALLON

5–6 pounds beef with bones

1 tablespoon olive oil

5 medium yellow onions, chopped

2 shallots, chopped

1 pound carrots, chopped

1 bunch celery, chopped

1 cup red wine

1½ gallons water

5 sprigs fresh thyme or
1 tablespoon dried

½ bunch fresh parsley or
1 tablespoon dried

3 bay leaves

1. Remove the beef from the bones. Rinse the beef and pat dry with paper towels.

2. Heat the oil in a large stockpot over medium heat. Brown the meat on all sides. Add the onions, shallots, carrots, and celery and sauté for 2 minutes.

3. Add the wine and reduce by half the volume. Add the water, thyme, parsley, and bay leaves. Bring to a simmer and cook for 8 hours, uncovered.

4. Strain the broth through a fine-meshed sieve and discard the solids. Use immediately or let cool completely and freeze for later use.

Vegetable Stock

This basic vegetable stock is easy and great for use in many soup recipes.
Keep some stored in your freezer so you can use it anytime.

INGREDIENTS | MAKES 1 GALLON

4 pounds yellow onions, chopped
1 pound carrots, chopped
1 pound parsnips, chopped
1 bunch celery, chopped
1 bunch fresh parsley
½ bunch fresh thyme
4 bay leaves
1 teaspoon freshly cracked black pepper
2 gallons water

1. Place all the ingredients in a large stockpot and simmer for 2 hours, uncovered.

2. Strain the stock through a fine-meshed sieve and discard the vegetables and herbs. Use or let cool completely and store for later use.

Fish Stock

Do not use oily fish bones like those from salmon or tuna. Light
whitefish bones are a better option for this stock.

INGREDIENTS | MAKES 1 GALLON

4 pounds fish bones
3 large yellow onions, chopped
2 large carrots, chopped
3 stalks celery, chopped
½ bunch fresh parsley
8 sprigs fresh thyme
3 bay leaves
1 teaspoon freshly cracked black pepper
2 gallons cold water

1. Rinse the fish bones in ice-cold water.

2. Place all the ingredients in a large stockpot and bring to a simmer. Cook over medium-low heat for 2 hours, uncovered.

3. Strain the stock through a fine-meshed sieve and discard the solids. Use in recipes as needed or let cool completely and store for later use.

Stracciatella Soup

This is a basic chicken soup, Italian style. You can customize the recipe by substituting certain ingredients—use escarole instead of spinach or try sweet sausage instead of meatballs.

INGREDIENTS | SERVES 10

3 pounds bony chicken pieces (neck, back, wings, etc.)

2 tablespoons olive oil

3 medium yellow onions, chopped

2 medium carrots, chopped

2 stalks celery, chopped

1 bulb garlic

½ bunch fresh parsley

2 sprigs fresh thyme

1 cup Pinot Grigio

8 cups Chicken Stock (see recipe in this chapter)

4 cups water

2 bay leaves

½ teaspoon peppercorns

½ meatball recipe of choice (see Chapter 8)

4 cups fresh spinach leaves

6 large eggs

¼ cup fresh-grated Parmesan cheese

Discarding Solids

When making any chicken-based soup, the reason you discard the chicken and the vegetables after cooking is that their flavor has seeped into the broth. The solids are basically flavorless at this point, so they are discarded.

1. Rinse the chicken pieces in cold water.

2. Heat the olive oil in a large stockpot over medium-high heat. Add the chicken pieces and brown for 5 minutes, stirring occasionally. Add the onions, carrots, celery, and garlic. Brown for 3 more minutes. Add the parsley and thyme.

3. Pour in the wine and reduce by half the volume. Add the stock, water, bay leaves, and peppercorns. Reduce heat and simmer on low for approximately 3 hours, uncovered.

4. Meanwhile, prepare the meatballs and drain on a paper towel. Set aside.

5. Clean the spinach. Steam the spinach in a vegetable steamer or in a large covered pot of boiling water (2" deep) with a colander or strainer for approximately 2 minutes.

6. Strain the soup through a fine-meshed sieve and discard the solids. Return the soup to the pot and heat over medium-high heat. Stir in the eggs and simmer until cooked. Add the meatballs, spinach, and cheese right before serving.

Chicken Orzo Soup

Orzo is a good pasta choice for using in soup. It is a small oval pasta that retains its texture in the hot broth.

INGREDIENTS | SERVES 10

3 pounds bony chicken pieces (neck, back, wings, etc.)

3 medium yellow onions, chopped

2 medium carrots, chopped

2 stalks celery, chopped

½ bulb garlic

½ bunch fresh parsley

3 sprigs fresh thyme

2 bay leaves

10 peppercorns

8½ cups Chicken Stock (see recipe in this chapter), divided

4 cups water

1 cup Pinot Grigio

2 cups fresh mushrooms, sliced

1 teaspoon olive oil

3 cups fresh escarole

2½ cups cooked orzo pasta

¼ cup fresh-grated Romano cheese

1. Rinse the chicken pieces in cold water and pat dry with paper towels.

2. In a large stockpot over low heat, place the chicken pieces, onions, carrots, celery, garlic, parsley, thyme, bay leaves, peppercorns, 8 cups stock, water, and wine. Simmer on low heat for 4 hours, uncovered.

3. Meanwhile, in a large sauté pan over medium heat, sauté the mushrooms with the olive oil. Set aside.

4. Steam the escarole in a large covered sauté pan with the remaining ½ cup of chicken stock. Set aside.

5. Strain the soup through a fine-meshed sieve and discard the solids. Add the mushrooms, escarole, and orzo to the broth just before serving. Sprinkle with the cheese.

Keeping Herbs Fresh

It's easy to prolong the life of your fresh herbs. Simply wrap the stems in plastic wrap and stand them up in a tall glass that is filled halfway with cold water. Store in the refrigerator and use when needed.

Zuppa di Pesce (Fish Soup)

This soup is great served with a loaf of crusty Italian bread. Make sure there is plenty of bread for dipping.

INGREDIENTS | SERVES 10

1 (1½-pound) whole fresh lobster, cooked

¾ pound fresh whitefish

1 dozen large uncooked fresh shrimp with shells

¼ pound fresh sea scallops

¼ pound fresh calamari

1 dozen littleneck clams

3 medium yellow onions, diced

2 medium carrots, diced

2 stalks celery, finely diced

¼ bulb garlic, minced

½ bunch fresh parsley

2 sprigs fresh thyme

2 bay leaves

½ teaspoon peppercorns

6 cups Fish Stock (see recipe in this chapter)

6 cups Old World Gravy (Long-Cooking Tomato Sauce) (see Chapter 3)

¼ cup fresh-grated Parmesan or Romano cheese

1. Rinse all the seafood in ice-cold water. Shell and cut lobster body, tail, and claw meat into bite-sized pieces.

2. In a large stockpot over medium-high heat, place the onions, carrots, celery, garlic, parsley, thyme, bay leaves, and peppercorns. Add the Fish Stock and Old World Gravy and simmer on medium-high heat for 10 minutes, uncovered.

3. Add the whitefish, shrimp, and scallops and simmer for 5 minutes. Add the calamari and clams and simmer for 5 minutes. Add the lobster meat and simmer 1 minute longer to reheat.

4. Remove the herbs and peppercorns. Sprinkle with the cheese and serve.

Minestrone with Meatballs

Minestrone soup can be made with various vegetables, rice or pasta, and almost any kind of meat. Use what is fresh in the market or what you have on hand, and your minestrone will come out different, but delicious, every time.

INGREDIENTS | SERVES 10

1 tablespoon olive oil

3 pounds veal bones and meat

4 medium yellow onions, chopped

2 medium carrots, chopped

½ bulb garlic, chopped

2 stalks celery, chopped

2 cups chopped tomatoes

8 cups water

4 sprigs fresh oregano

½ meatball recipe of choice (see Chapter 8)

½ cup green beans

2½ cups cooked pasta of your choice

⅓ cup fresh-grated Parmesan cheese

1. Heat the oil in a large stockpot on medium heat and brown the veal bones. Add the onion, carrots, garlic, celery, and tomatoes. Add the water and simmer for 3 hours, uncovered.

2. Add the oregano. Simmer for 30 minutes, uncovered.

3. While the soup simmers, make the meatballs and drain on paper towels.

4. In a small covered saucepan, steam the green beans in a small amount of boiling water for 2 minutes; strain.

5. Just before serving, remove the veal bones; add the meatballs, green beans, and pasta to the soup and sprinkle with the cheese.

To Absorb Excess Grease

To absorb excess grease from your soup, drop a lettuce leaf into the simmering broth. As soon as the lettuce soaks up the fat, remove it and throw it away. This trick will not work as well with thicker recipes, such as stews and sauces.

Tomato Soup with Fried Pasta Garnish

Make Parmesan curls by scraping your vegetable peeler against a hard hunk of Parmesan cheese. These curls make a great garnish for many Italian dishes.

INGREDIENTS | SERVES 10

¼ cup olive oil

2 medium yellow onions, diced

1 bulb garlic, minced

8 large tomatoes, cut into wedges

8 cups Vegetable Stock (see recipe in this chapter)

¼ bunch fresh basil, sliced

½ bunch fresh parsley, chopped

½ recipe Deep-Fried Pasta (see Chapter 13)

½ cup Parmesan cheese curls

1 tablespoon capers, rinsed

1 teaspoon freshly cracked black pepper

1. Heat the oil in a large stockpot over medium heat for about 3 minutes. Add the onions and sauté for about 2 minutes. Add the garlic and sauté for about 2 minutes. Add the tomatoes. Reduce heat to low and add the Vegetable Stock. Simmer for 1½ hours, uncovered.

2. Add the basil and parsley and simmer for 30 minutes, uncovered.

3. While the soup simmers, prepare the Deep-Fried Pasta.

4. Serve the soup in individual bowls with clusters of fried pasta. Sprinkle each serving with the Parmesan curls, capers, and pepper.

Basil

Basil is an herb in the mint family and goes particularly well with tomato. Basil is also the main ingredient in pesto sauce. Basil is a good choice if you are picking one or two herbs to grow in a small kitchen garden. Most Italian dishes call for at least a bit of fresh basil.

Lentil Soup

Pancetta is salt-cured pork—the Italian version of bacon. It is usually sold in a large rolled form and can be purchased in Italian delicatessens and some specialty supermarkets.

INGREDIENTS | SERVES 10

2 tablespoons olive oil

½ pound pancetta (or substitute ¼ pound prosciutto or ½ pound bacon), diced

3 medium yellow onions, diced

2 medium carrots, diced

2 stalks celery, chopped

½ bunch fresh parsley, chopped

3 sprigs fresh thyme, stems removed

2 cups dried lentils

12 cups Vegetable Stock (see recipe in this chapter)

2 bay leaves

1. Heat the oil in a stockpot over medium heat for 10 minutes. Lightly brown the pancetta for about 4 minutes.

2. Add the onions and sauté for 1 minute. Add the carrots and celery and sauté for 1 minute. Add the remaining ingredients and simmer for 1 hour, uncovered.

3. Discard the bay leaves and serve.

Why Brown Veggies First?

Why cook vegetables in oil before adding to liquid? Because the rigid cell walls of many veggies lock the flavor and nutrients inside, only lipids can dissolve these walls. Carrots, for example, are high in fat-soluble beta-carotene. To extract this essence, the carrot must first cook slowly in fat or oil to dissolve the cell walls without burning the carrots. If veggies are just thrown in with the liquid, the broth will be bland.

Hearty Fish Soup with Pesto

Although pesto is usually used as a sauce over pasta, it also has many other uses. A dollop in any stew, sauce, or soup will add the fragrant flavor of garlic and basil.

INGREDIENTS | SERVES 10

2 pounds skinless, boneless halibut

3 tablespoons olive oil

4 shallots, diced

3 pounds carrots, diced

2 bunches leeks, diced

½ bunch celery, diced

4 cups Fish Stock (see recipe in this chapter)

2 bay leaves

½ bunch fresh parsley, chopped

About ¾ cup Traditional Pesto (see Chapter 3)

1. Clean and large-dice the fish. Keep chilled until ready to use.

2. Heat the oil in a large stockpot over medium heat. Add the fish, shallots, carrots, leeks, and celery and sauté for 5 minutes.

3. Add the stock and simmer for 1 hour, uncovered. Add the bay leaves and parsley and simmer for 30 minutes, uncovered.

4. While the soup is simmering, prepare the pesto.

5. Discard the bay leaves. Ladle the soup into serving bowls and garnish each with a spoonful of pesto.

Cioppino

This Italian seafood stew is a hearty dish that can be served as a main meal. Accompany a steaming bowl of this with a fresh loaf of Italian semolina bread for dipping.

INGREDIENTS | SERVES 10

2 pounds king crab or snow crab

2 dozen littleneck clams

2 dozen mussels

2 pounds skinless sea bass fillets

1 bunch kale

2 tablespoons olive oil

1 bunch parsnips, chopped

2 bunches fresh leeks, chopped

1 bunch celery, chopped

12 cups Fish Stock (see recipe in this chapter)

5 pounds plum tomatoes, chopped

½ bunch fresh parsley, chopped

4 sprigs fresh thyme, chopped

2 bay leaves

2 tablespoons saffron

1 teaspoon freshly cracked black pepper

1. Clean the shellfish and fish in ice-cold water. Keep chilled. Clean the kale and remove and discard the tough center stalks.

2. Heat the oil in a large stockpot. Add the seafood, parsnips, leeks, and celery. Sauté for 5 minutes. Add the fish stock, tomatoes, parsley, thyme, and bay leaves. Simmer for 30 minutes, uncovered.

3. Discard the bay leaves. Add the kale, saffron, and pepper just before serving.

Saffron

Saffron is one of the most expensive food ingredients in the world. In Italy it grows in the Abruzzi region and can be purchased in either threads or powdered form. Saffron is used to give both flavor and color to food and must be used sparingly, not only because of the expense but because too much of it will make the food taste slightly medicinal.

Pasta e Fagioli (Pasta and Bean Soup)

You can presoak the beans overnight to make the cooking faster, or you can use a good brand of imported Italian canned chickpeas (see step 3 of the recipe).

INGREDIENTS | SERVES 10

1 pound dried chickpeas

4 gallons Vegetable Stock (see recipe in this chapter), divided

2 tablespoons olive oil

4 shallots, finely chopped

1 bulb garlic, finely chopped

2 celeriac (celery root), finely chopped

2 pounds plum tomatoes, chopped

½ bunch fresh parsley, chopped

2 cups cooked bite-sized pasta of choice

½ cup fresh-grated Asiago cheese

1 teaspoon freshly cracked black pepper

Shocking Pasta

When a soup recipe calls for pasta, never add the uncooked pasta to the pot to cook along with the soup. Instead, cook it separately, and shock it with cold water as soon as you drain it. It should be cooked only al dente, because it will cook more in the hot soup. Add it to the soup just before serving.

1. Sort through the chickpeas, discarding any stones. In a large stockpot, simmer the peas in 2 gallons of the stock for approximately 2–3 hours until the beans are tender. Drain.

2. Heat the oil in a large stockpot over medium heat. Sauté the shallots, garlic, and celeriac for 3 minutes. Add the tomatoes and sauté for 1 minute. Add the remaining stock, the chickpeas, and the parsley. Let simmer for 1 hour, uncovered.

3. Just before serving, stir in the pasta (and beans, if using canned). Sprinkle each serving with the cheese and pepper.

Bean and Sausage Soup

To make it easier to cut the raw sausages in this recipe, freeze them for about 30 minutes before you slice them. Just let them thaw a little before cooking.

INGREDIENTS | SERVES 10

2 pounds hot Italian sausage

1 tablespoon olive oil

3 medium yellow onions, finely sliced

2 gallons Beef Stock (see recipe in this chapter)

2 pounds cooked cannellini beans

About ⅔ cup store-bought roasted red pepper purée

About ⅛ cup Roasted Garlic Paste (see Chapter 3)

4 sprigs thyme, stems discarded

1. Cut the sausage into slices about ½" thick.

2. Heat the oil over medium heat in a large stockpot. Add the sausages and brown them for 3 minutes. Add the onions and cook for 1 minute (do not brown the onions).

3. Add the stock and simmer on low heat for 1 hour, uncovered. Add the beans and simmer for 30 minutes, uncovered.

4. Ladle the soup into bowls. Garnish each serving with about 1 tablespoon of the red pepper purée, ½ teaspoon of the garlic paste, and a few thyme leaves.

Dandelion Egg Drop

Dandelion greens are hard to find but worth the effort for this dish. However, you can substitute any green (kale, escarole, spinach) if your local market does not carry dandelion greens.

INGREDIENTS | SERVES 10

6 large eggs

1 tablespoon olive oil

1 bunch leeks, sliced

2 gallons Chicken Stock (see recipe in this chapter)

2 pounds fresh dandelion greens, sliced

⅓ cup fresh-grated Romano cheese

1 teaspoon freshly cracked black pepper

1. Beat the eggs in a small bowl and keep chilled.

2. Heat the oil over medium heat in a large stockpot. Add the leeks and let wilt for 2 minutes. Add the stock and let simmer for 30 minutes, uncovered.

3. Add the dandelion greens and beaten eggs and stir constantly for 2 minutes. Remove from heat.

4. Sprinkle each serving with the grated cheese and black pepper.

Garlic Soup

Garlic Soup is great with homemade crostini. To make your own crostini, cut off the crust from day-old Italian or semolina bread. Slice the bread very thinly, and either fry in oil or butter, or brush the slices with olive oil and toast in the oven.

INGREDIENTS | SERVES 10

1 tablespoon olive oil

2 shallots, minced

½ bunch celery, thinly sliced

1 cup Roasted Garlic Paste (see Chapter 3)

2 gallons Vegetable Stock (see recipe in this chapter)

4 sprigs fresh parsley, minced

1. Heat the oil in a stockpot over medium heat for about 2 minutes. Add the shallots and celery. Whisk in the garlic paste and sauté for 1 minute. Add the stock and simmer for 1 hour, uncovered.

2. Sprinkle each serving with the parsley and serve the crostini on the side.

Wonderful Wooden Spoons

When cooking soups, stews, and sauces, the most intense, delicious flavors often concentrate on the bottom of the pot. Wooden spoons gently loosen soluble concentrated juices from the bottom of the pan, without scraping up metal shavings or burned solids. They are also gentle on your metal cookware.

Vegetable Soup with Rigatoni

Rigatoni adds texture and body to this traditional vegetable soup. You could easily add shredded chicken or cooked mini-meatballs to add protein to the dish.

INGREDIENTS | SERVES 10

¼ cup olive oil, divided

4 large white onions, finely diced

½ pound parsnips, finely diced

½ pound carrots, finely diced

1 bulb garlic, minced

1 bunch celery, chopped

1 bunch fresh parsley, chopped

6 sprigs fresh thyme, stems discarded

2 bay leaves

4 cups vegetable juice (such as V8)

4 cups Vegetable Stock (see recipe in this chapter)

1 teaspoon freshly cracked black pepper

½ pound cooked rigatoni

Season to Taste

If something seems to be missing from your soup, it's usually salt! Salt brings out the flavor of soups. Unless you have specific health issues requiring you to limit your salt intake, season for ideal flavor. Don't stop adding spices until it tastes perfect.

1. Heat 1 tablespoon of the oil over medium-high heat in a large stockpot. Add the onions, parsnips, and carrots. Sauté for about 5 minutes or until lightly browned, stirring constantly. Reduce heat to medium and add the garlic and celery. Sauté for 5 minutes.

2. Add the parsley, thyme, bay leaves, juice, stock, and black pepper. Reduce heat to medium-low and simmer for 1½ hours, uncovered.

3. Fifteen minutes before the soup is finished, add the cooked rigatoni and heat through.

4. Remove the bay leaves and ladle the soup into serving bowls. Serve hot.

Pasta with Rich Broth

Pastina is tiny star-shaped pasta that can be added to soups or cooked on its own and served with butter and grated cheese. Pastina with butter and cheese is a great dish for kids.

INGREDIENTS | SERVES 10

2 pounds chicken or turkey (bone-in)

½ teaspoon freshly cracked black pepper

1 tablespoon olive oil

2 gallons Chicken Stock (see recipe in this chapter)

2 bunches fresh escarole, sliced

3 cups uncooked pastina

½ cup fresh-grated Asiago cheese

1. Rinse the chicken and pat dry with paper towels. Season with the black pepper.

2. Heat the oil in a large stockpot over medium heat. Add the chicken and brown on all sides.

3. Add the stock and simmer for 2 hours, uncovered. Strain the broth through a fine-meshed sieve and discard the solids.

4. Bring the strained broth to a simmer. Add the escarole and pastina to the broth. Cook for about 3 minutes until the pastina is al dente.

5. Sprinkle each serving with the Asiago cheese.

Chilled Beet Soup

The natural sweetness of beets makes this a tasty soup. Always take special care when puréeing hot liquids—it is safer to cool them first.

INGREDIENTS | SERVES 10

2 pounds fresh beets, with tops

1 gallon Vegetable Stock (see recipe in this chapter)

8 sprigs fresh thyme, stems discarded, divided

1 cup plain yogurt

1 large white onion, finely diced (optional)

1 teaspoon freshly cracked black pepper (optional)

Parsley, to garnish (optional)

1. Peel and chop the beets.

2. In a large stockpot over medium heat, simmer the beets in the stock with half the thyme for 1½ hours, uncovered. Let cool slightly, add the remaining thyme, and carefully purée.

3. Ladle the soup into serving bowls. Garnish each with a dollop of the yogurt and sprinkle the onion, pepper, and parsley over the top, if using.

Pork Soup

Browning the bones and meat before adding the stock is an important step when making a meat soup. The small bits of meat that stick to the pan during the browning process help flavor the broth.

INGREDIENTS | SERVES 10

2½ pounds pork meat (bone-in)

1 tablespoon olive oil

2 gallons Beef Stock (see recipe in this chapter)

1 cup dry red wine

½ bulb garlic, minced

½ bunch fresh oregano, stems discarded

2 cups fresh spinach leaves

1 teaspoon freshly cracked black pepper

1. Remove the pork from the bones and finely dice the meat.

2. Heat the oil in a large stockpot over medium-high heat. Add the pork meat and bones and brown for about 10 minutes.

3. Reduce heat and add the stock, wine, garlic, and oregano. Simmer for 2 hours, uncovered.

4. About 30 minutes before the broth is finished, steam the spinach for 1 minute in a covered saucepan with ½ cup boiling water.

5. Remove the bones from the soup. Just before serving, add the spinach and sprinkle with pepper.

CHAPTER 5

Meat

Sweet and Spicy Pork

Serve this delicious pork with risotto or polenta and a steamed vegetable of choice.

INGREDIENTS | SERVES 10

1 pound pork meat

1 pound Italian pork sausage, uncooked

1 tablespoon olive oil

2 pounds red bell peppers, seeded and cut into chunks

2 shallots, finely sliced

½ bulb garlic, minced

2 stalks celery, sliced

1 teaspoon minced fresh ginger (or ¼ teaspoon ground)

Zest and juice of 2 medium oranges

3 sprigs fresh thyme, stems discarded

1 bay leaf

½ teaspoon kosher salt

½ teaspoon freshly cracked black pepper

1. Thickly dice the pork and cut the sausage into 1½" pieces.

2. Heat the oil in a large skillet over medium-high heat. Brown the pork and sausage on all sides. Add the bell peppers, shallots, garlic, celery, and ginger. Reduce heat to medium and sauté for 5 minutes.

3. Add the orange juice and zest, thyme, and bay leaf. Season with salt and pepper and simmer for 20 minutes, uncovered. Discard the bay leaf and serve hot.

Leg of Lamb

A large Dutch oven with a rack works best for cooking the lamb in this dish. However, you can use any large baking dish with a rack. Just wrap the lamb in foil to prevent the herbs from burning.

INGREDIENTS | SERVES 10

1 bulb garlic

3 sprigs fresh rosemary

3 sprigs fresh mint

1 cup shelled walnuts, finely chopped

⅓ cup olive oil, divided

1 (5-pound) leg of lamb

1 teaspoon kosher salt

1 teaspoon freshly cracked black pepper

1 cup Pinot Noir (or other red drinking wine of choice)

1. Preheat the oven to 350°F. Mince half the garlic. Cut each of the remaining garlic cloves in half. Mince half the rosemary and mint.

2. In a food processor, blend the minced garlic and minced herbs with the walnuts and half the oil.

3. Pierce the lamb with a sharp knife in several places. Insert 1 piece of the garlic, 1 rosemary leaf, and 1 mint leaf in each cut. Rub the herb-nut mixture on the outside of the lamb and season with salt and pepper.

4. Grease a rack with the remaining oil and set in the bottom of a Dutch oven or a baking pan with a tight-fitting lid. Pour the wine into the bottom of the pan. Place the lamb on the rack.

5. Cover the pan tightly and bake for 1½ hours. Remove the lid and cook to desired doneness.

Fresh-Baked Pork and Potatoes

This dish is great to serve to guests for a holiday meal. Try it out this Christmas or New Year's Day.

INGREDIENTS | SERVES 10

1 bulb garlic

5 large Idaho potatoes

1 (5-pound) pork roast (bone-in)

8 sprigs fresh oregano, stems discarded

1 teaspoon kosher salt

1 teaspoon freshly cracked black pepper

1 tablespoon olive oil

2 medium white onions, cut into large wedges

Potato Tips

To keep potatoes from budding, place an apple in the potato bag. For really smooth mashed potatoes, press cooked potatoes through a "ricer," which looks like an over-sized garlic press, then fold in the milk, butter, and seasonings by hand. The ricer gets rid of lumps without overworking the potato into a glutinous gob. For a more homestyle (lumpy) texture, use either a stiff whisk or potato masher to smash spuds.

1. Preheat the oven to 375°F. Cut the garlic cloves in half. Scrub the potatoes and leave whole.

2. Pierce the pork with a sharp knife in several places and insert a piece of garlic and an oregano leaf in each cut. Season with salt and pepper. Place the pork roast on an oiled rack set in a Dutch oven or a baking pan with a tight-fitting lid. Cover and roast for 1¼–1¾ hours.

3. Remove the pork with the rack. Pour the oil into the pan and add the potatoes and onions. Return the pork to the pan, without the rack. Add any remaining herbs and stir.

4. Roast, uncovered, for about 1 hour until the potatoes are fork-tender and the pork is cooked through.

Marinated Venison Roast

*In order to properly marinate the venison in this recipe, you'll
have to start preparation one day ahead of time.*

INGREDIENTS | SERVES 10

3 Vidalia onions, chopped

2 shallots, chopped

1 bulb garlic, chopped

½ bunch fresh parsley, chopped

5 sprigs fresh thyme, chopped or
½ teaspoon dried

1 tablespoon ground cinnamon

2 bay leaves

1 teaspoon freshly cracked black pepper

1 cup robust red wine

2 cups Beef Stock (see Chapter 4)

1 (5-pound) venison roast

1 tablespoon olive oil

1. Combine all the ingredients except the venison and the oil in a large container with a lid or in a resealable plastic bag. Mix well. Add the venison to the mixture, turning the meat to coat completely with the marinade. Refrigerate for at least 8 hours or up to 1 day.

2. When ready to cook, preheat the oven to 350°F. Heat a heavy-bottomed ovenproof pan with a lid (such as a Dutch oven) on the stovetop over medium-high heat and add the oil. Remove the meat from the marinade, place in the pan, and sear until browned on all sides. Pour in the marinade and bring to a boil. Immediately cover and place the pan in the oven.

3. Braise for 2½ hours. Remove the pan from the oven and place it on the stovetop. Transfer the venison to a pan with a rack, place back in the oven, and bake for 30 more minutes.

4. While the meat roasts, reduce the marinade by half the volume over high heat on the stovetop. Once the meat is cooked, drizzle the reduced marinade over the top and serve.

Spiced Oxtails

These oxtails must marinate in the refrigerator the night before.

INGREDIENTS | SERVES 10

3½ pounds oxtails

2 medium yellow or white onions, diced

1 shallot, minced

½ bulb garlic, minced

2 bay leaves

½ teaspoon ground cloves

1½ teaspoons ground cinnamon

½ teaspoon ground nutmeg

½ teaspoon freshly cracked black pepper

2 tablespoons olive oil

1 cup dry red wine (not cooking wine)

4 cups Beef Stock (see Chapter 4)

1. In a large lidded container or a large zip-top bag, mix the oxtails with the onions, shallot, garlic, bay leaves, and spices. Cover and refrigerate overnight.

2. Preheat the oven to 350°F. Heat the olive oil to medium-high heat in a large Dutch oven (or heavy-bottomed ovenproof pot with a lid). Add the oxtails and sear on all sides. Add the wine and reduce by half the volume. Pour in the stock and bring to a boil.

3. Cover the pan and place in the oven. Braise for about 2½ hours until cooked through. Serve hot.

Italian Meatloaf

*This version of meatloaf, layered with spinach and mashed potatoes, is
a bit more elegant and complex than standard meatloaf.*

INGREDIENTS | SERVES 10

1 teaspoon olive oil

3 pieces Basic Flatbread (see Chapter 9), cubed

1 medium yellow onion, chopped

1 shallot, chopped

4 cloves garlic, minced

¼ cup pecans, chopped

3 sprigs fresh thyme, stems discarded

1½ pounds ground beef

1 large egg, lightly beaten

¼ cup dried currants

1 teaspoon ground cinnamon

¼ teaspoon red pepper flakes

1½ cups Roasted Garlic Smashed Potatoes (see Chapter 15)

2 cups steamed spinach

1. Preheat the oven to 375°F. Grease a loaf pan with the oil. In a small bowl, soak the flatbread cubes in 2 cups water, then squeeze out the liquid.

2. In a large bowl, mix together the soaked flatbread, onions, shallot, garlic, pecans, thyme, beef, egg, currants, cinnamon, and pepper flakes.

3. Layer the smashed potatoes, spinach, and beef mixture in the prepared pan. Press firmly.

4. Bake for 45 minutes, uncovered. Drain off excess grease and let cool slightly. Remove from loaf pan, slice, and serve.

Osso Buco with Polenta Dumplings

This version of osso buco is topped off with polenta dumplings instead of the more familiar gremolata.

INGREDIENTS | SERVES 10

5 pounds veal shanks

2 tablespoons olive oil

5 medium parsnips or carrots, chopped

2 bulbs celeriac (celery root) or 5 stalks celery, chopped

2 large leeks, chopped

5 shallots, thinly sliced

1 bulb garlic, thinly sliced

3 pounds plum tomatoes, chopped

½ cup red wine

3 cups Beef Stock (see Chapter 4)

3 bay leaves

4 sprigs fresh thyme, chopped

½ bunch fresh parsley, chopped

½ recipe Basic Polenta (see Chapter 11), cooked

½ teaspoon kosher salt

½ teaspoon freshly cracked black pepper

1. Preheat the oven to 350°F. Rinse the veal shanks and pat dry with paper towels.

2. Heat the oil over medium-high heat in a heavy-bottomed ovenproof pot with a tight-fitting lid (such as a Dutch oven). Add the shanks and sear them on all sides. Add the parsnips, celeriac, leeks, shallots, and garlic. Sauté for 5 minutes. Add the tomatoes and stir.

3. Pour in the wine and reduce by half the volume. Add the stock. Reduce heat to medium and bring to a simmer. Cover the pan and place in the oven. Braise for 4 hours, then add the herbs and simmer 30 more minutes.

4. Remove the pan from the oven and place on the stovetop over medium-high heat. Drop in heaping tablespoonfuls of the polenta. Cover and cook for 15–20 minutes. Remove bay leaves.

5. Sprinkle to taste with salt and pepper. Ladle into bowls and serve.

Mama Theresa's Beef Braciola

*Braciola makes a great leftover. Don't worry if you make too much
for dinner—just reheat it for lunch the next day.*

INGREDIENTS | SERVES 10

½ pound capicola, thinly sliced

½ pound salami, thinly sliced

¼ pound pepperoni, thinly sliced

4 pounds beef braciola, thinly sliced

1 medium white onion, chopped

½ bulb garlic, minced

2 large hard-boiled eggs, chopped

¼ pound fontina cheese, shredded

½ bunch fresh parsley, chopped

1 teaspoon freshly cracked black pepper

2 tablespoons olive oil

1 cup Syrah (or other hearty red wine of choice)

4 cups Old World Gravy (Long-Cooking Tomato Sauce) (see Chapter 3)

1. Finely chop the capicola, salami, and pepperoni slices.

2. Lay out the beef and sprinkle with the onion, garlic, chopped meats, eggs, shredded cheese, parsley, and pepper. Carefully roll up the meat and tie with butcher's twine.

3. Heat the oil over medium-high heat in a large skillet. Sear the tied meat on all sides. Reduce heat and add the wine. Simmer, uncovered, for 90 minutes.

4. In a small saucepan, warm the tomato sauce. Serve the braciola with the tomato sauce over the top.

Pork Terrine

This dish is delicious served with a baked apple. To prepare the apple: Core and slice off the top of the apple. Sprinkle with cinnamon. Place in a microwave-safe dish with a small amount of water and lemon juice, and cover with plastic wrap. Heat on high for about 5 minutes.

INGREDIENTS | SERVES 10

½ teaspoon olive oil

1½ pounds boneless pork

3 large Idaho baking potatoes, thinly sliced

½ bulb garlic, minced

½ bunch fresh oregano, stems discarded

2 plum tomatoes, chopped

1 medium eggplant, sliced lengthwise

½ teaspoon freshly cracked black pepper

¼ cup fresh-grated Romano cheese

Imported Is Best

When using canned tomatoes in a recipe that calls for fresh tomatoes, it is worth the extra expense and effort of seeking out and purchasing tomatoes imported from Italy. Look for cans of tomatoes that are labeled with "San Marzano." This means that they are grown in the San Marzano region of Italy and are known to be top-quality tomatoes.

1. Preheat the oven to 375°F. Lightly grease a loaf pan with the oil. Cut the pork into ½"-thick slices.

2. Line the prepared pan with the pork, then add the potatoes, garlic, oregano, tomatoes, eggplant, black pepper, and Romano.

3. Cover with aluminum foil and roast for 45 minutes. Remove from the oven and uncover. Carefully drain off grease. Return to the oven. Roast, uncovered, for 20 minutes.

4. Remove from the oven and let cool thoroughly. Serve at room temperature or reheat as desired.

Vitello al Forno (Baked Veal)

If you have some leftover rice or risotto in the house, feel free to use it in place of the brown rice called for in this recipe.

INGREDIENTS | SERVES 10

4 tablespoons olive oil, divided
2 medium red bell peppers
2 medium yellow bell peppers
1 medium white onion, sliced
1½ pounds boneless veal, thinly sliced
1½ cups cooked brown rice
6 fresh sprigs marjoram, chopped
½ cup shredded fontina cheese
½ teaspoon freshly cracked black pepper

1. Preheat the oven to 375°F. Lightly grease a loaf pan with 1 tablespoon of the oil.

2. Toss the peppers and onions in the remaining oil. Place on a large baking sheet. Roast in the oven for 10–20 minutes until the onion is softened and the "skin" of the peppers blisters. Remove from the oven and immediately seal the peppers in a plastic bag (this makes it easier to remove the skin). Place the onions on paper towels to drain. Gently remove the skins from the peppers. Cut the peppers in half and remove the stems and seeds.

3. Layer the veal, peppers, rice, onions, marjoram, cheese, and black pepper in the prepared loaf pan.

4. Cover with aluminum foil and roast for 45 minutes. Remove from the oven and uncover. Carefully drain off grease. Return to the oven and roast, uncovered, for 20 minutes.

5. Remove from the oven and let cool thoroughly. Slice and serve at room temperature or reheat as desired.

Lamb Loaf

This is a delicious variation of the classic meatloaf. Even if you don't like regular meatloaf, give this a try. Its flavor may surprise and delight you.

INGREDIENTS | SERVES 10

2 tablespoons olive oil, divided

1 recipe Basic Pasta (see Chapter 13), unformed and uncooked

1¾ pounds lamb, cut into large cubes

½ bulb garlic, minced

⅓ bunch fresh mint, chopped

½ cup walnuts, finely chopped

½ teaspoon freshly cracked black pepper

1. Preheat the oven to 350°F. Grease a loaf pan with 1 tablespoon of the oil.

2. Roll out the pasta dough on a floured surface into a sheet a few inches longer and wider than the top of the loaf pan.

3. Layer the lamb, garlic, mint, and walnuts in the loaf pan and sprinkle with black pepper. Gently place the pasta dough over the top and tuck firmly around the ingredients. Drizzle with the remaining olive oil. Cover with aluminum foil and bake for about 45 minutes.

4. Let cool thoroughly. Slice and serve at room temperature or reheat as desired.

Stuffed Pork Roast

The fennel and apples impart a wonderful fresh flavor to this pork roast. This dish makes a great autumn meal.

INGREDIENTS | SERVES 10

3 boneless shoulder pork roasts

1 pound raw sausage mixture of choice

1 bulb fennel with tops, thickly sliced

1 medium white onion, thinly sliced

2 Granny Smith apples (or other tart variety), thinly sliced

½ teaspoon freshly cracked black pepper

1. Preheat the oven to 375°F. Cut open the roasts (lay out meat to layer ingredients on top).

2. Lay out the roasts and layer with the sausage mixture, fennel, onion, and apples. Roll and tie securely with butcher's twine.

3. Place on a rack in a large roasting pan. Sprinkle with pepper. Cover and roast for 2 hours; then uncover and roast for ½–1 hour longer until the pork is thoroughly cooked. Untie, slice, and serve.

Grilled Rack of Lamb

Simple but delicious, this recipe depends on just the pure taste of the roast lamb with some basic seasoning. Serve with Roasted Garlic Smashed Potatoes (see Chapter 15).

INGREDIENTS | SERVES 10

5 pounds rack of lamb

½ bulb garlic, minced

2 tablespoons olive oil

½ teaspoon freshly cracked black pepper

1 teaspoon coarse salt

Grilling Indoors

If you use your outdoor grill all summer, you are probably a little lost once the winter weather rolls in. However, there's a solution: Grill pans provide that same grilled flavor and can be used indoors on your stovetop. Just remember to allow the grill pan to get hot before placing the food on it, just as you would with an outdoor grill.

1. "French" the ends of the lamb rack by cutting away suet, fat, etc., from the bone ends just past the "center" chop area. Scrape the bones clean and cover the bare bones with foil. Preheat the grill.

2. In a small bowl, mix together the garlic, oil, pepper, and salt.

3. Thoroughly rub the lamb with the prepared garlic oil.

4. Grill the lamb on all sides to desired doneness (anywhere from 10–20 minutes) and serve.

Easter Pizza Casserole

Pot cheese, or farmer's cheese, is a mild white cheese made of curds from soured skim milk. If pot cheese is unavailable, you can substitute goat cheese.

INGREDIENTS | SERVES 10

Crust
¼ cup butter
1½ cups all-purpose flour
3 tablespoons cold water
¼ cup olive oil

Casserole
6 large eggs
2 cups heavy cream
¾ cup pot cheese
1 tablespoon olive oil
½ pound Italian pork sausage, sliced into ½" coins
½ pound cooked ham, diced
3 medium white onions, thinly sliced
1 head fresh broccoli, rough chopped into bite-sized pieces

1. Prepare the crust: In a large bowl, combine all the crust ingredients. Mix by hand or in an electric mixer with a dough hook at medium speed until a ball forms. Wrap the dough in plastic wrap and let rest for 30 minutes in the refrigerator.

2. Once rested, roll out the dough on a floured surface into a large rectangle. Place the dough in the bottom of a large baking pan.

3. Prepare the casserole: Preheat the oven to 375°F.

4. In a large bowl, beat the eggs. Add the cream and cheese. Set aside.

5. Heat the oil to medium temperature in a large sauté pan. Add the sausage, ham, and onions and cook for 8 minutes. Add the broccoli and cook for 3 more minutes. Remove from heat and drain on paper towels.

6. Place the ham and sausage mixture on top of the crust. Pour in the egg mixture. Bake for 1 hour, uncovered. Serve.

Chuck Steak Pot Roast

*This hearty winter dish goes wonderfully with Browned Risotto Patties
(see Chapter 11). The combination creates quite a feast!*

INGREDIENTS | SERVES 10

1 tablespoon olive oil

1 (4-pound) beef chuck roast

4 medium yellow onions, chopped

1 pound carrots, chopped

1 bunch celery, chopped

4 tomatoes, chopped

1 cup Cabernet Sauvignon

1 gallon Beef Stock (see Chapter 4)

1 bunch fresh parsley, chopped

3 sprigs fresh thyme, chopped

1 bay leaf

"Sweating" Onions

Sweating onions means to cook them in a small amount of oil or butter over moderate heat, covered. This cooking method breaks down the rigid cell walls and allows the juices to escape without burning, which releases the full flavor of the onions. Many Italian recipes include this step.

1. Preheat the oven to 375°F.

2. Heat the oil over medium-high heat in a heavy-bottomed ovenproof pot with a tight-fitting lid (such as a Dutch oven). Add the roast and sear the meat on all sides. Add the onions, carrots, and celery and sauté for 5 minutes. Add the tomatoes.

3. Pour in the wine and reduce by half the volume. Add the stock. Reduce heat to medium and bring to a simmer. Cover the pan and place in the oven. Braise for 4 hours.

4. Add the parsley, thyme, and bay leaf. Simmer for 30 more minutes with the lid ajar. Serve.

Baked Smoked Ham

The fruity glaze contrasts nicely with the salty ham. For a different taste, substitute another juice, such as orange.

INGREDIENTS | SERVES 10

1 (5-pound) smoked ham
¼–½ cup cloves
½ cup apple juice
½ cup honey
½ cup Dijon mustard

1. Preheat the oven to 350°F. Score the outside of the ham from one end to the other, making lines about an inch apart. Repeat in the opposite direction, making a diamond pattern on the ham.

2. Place the ham in a large baking dish. Insert a clove at every corner where the scored lines intersect. (The round part of the cloves should be sticking out of the ham.)

3. In a medium bowl, mix together the juice, honey, and mustard. Spoon the glaze over the ham.

4. Cover and bake for 1½ hours. Uncover and bake for 30 more minutes. Remove the cloves before serving.

Vitello alla Francese (French-Style Veal)

Francese refers to a style of cooking meat or poultry cutlets with a lemon-based sauce.

INGREDIENTS | SERVES 10

4 large eggs, lightly beaten
½ cup fresh-grated Parmesan cheese
¼ teaspoon freshly cracked black pepper
½ bunch fresh parsley, chopped, divided
3½–4 pounds veal cutlets
½ cup all-purpose flour
¼ cup olive oil
Zest and juice of 4 large lemons
½ cup cold unsalted butter

1. In a medium bowl, combine the egg, cheese, pepper, and half of the parsley.

2. Dust the cutlets with the flour. Dip the cutlets in the egg mixture, dip back in the flour, and shake off excess flour.

3. Heat the oil over medium heat in a large sauté pan. Sauté the veal on one side and turn. Add the lemon zest, juice, and cold butter. Sauté the veal until fully cooked.

4. Serve sprinkled with the remaining parsley.

Vitello Brasato (Braised Veal)

*Never completely cover a braising dish. Instead, leave the lid ajar on
the pot. Serve this veal with polenta or a potato dish.*

INGREDIENTS | SERVES 10

2 tablespoons olive oil

2½ pounds boneless veal, cut into large cubes

2 medium yellow onions, cut into wedges

3 medium carrots, sliced

3 stalks celery, sliced

1½ pounds plum tomatoes (or 2½ cups canned), chopped

½ bulb garlic, minced

2 cups dry red wine (not cooking wine)

2 cups Beef Stock (see Chapter 4)

2 bay leaves

½ bunch fresh parsley, chopped

3 sprigs fresh thyme, chopped

3 sprigs fresh marjoram or oregano, chopped

½ teaspoon freshly cracked black pepper

1. Preheat the oven to 350°F.

2. Heat the oil over medium-high heat in a large skillet. Add the veal and brown for 8 minutes. Add the onions and carrots and sauté for 3 minutes. Add the celery, tomatoes, and garlic and sauté for 2 minutes.

3. Pour in the wine and reduce by half the volume.

4. Add the stock, herbs, and pepper. Cover partially and simmer on medium low heat for 2 hours. Serve hot.

Braising Meat

Braising is a popular cooking method in Italian cuisine. For braising, you must use a deep pot with a heavy bottom, just big enough for the meat to fit in. If the pot is too big, the liquid will evaporate too quickly. The liquid should only cover the meat halfway, never completely. Always leave the cover ajar on the pot. Braising requires careful attention and a long cooking time.

Pork with Leeks and Celery

Only use the white ends of the leeks and not the green stalks for this dish.

INGREDIENTS | SERVES 4

1 medium onion, finely chopped

½ cup extra-virgin olive oil

2 pounds pork shoulder, chopped into cubes

½ cup white wine

2 cups water

2 pounds leeks, chopped

1 cup finely chopped celery

1 cup tomatoes, diced and sieved (fresh or canned)

1 teaspoon dried oregano

½ teaspoon salt

½ teaspoon freshly ground pepper

Choosing Tomatoes

In season, use ripe vine tomatoes. Off-season, use quality canned rather than greenhouse tomatoes. Tomatoes should be aromatic; tomatoes with no aroma will have no taste. Avoid tomatoes with leathery, dark patches; this is a sign of blossom-end rot.

1. In a deep-walled pot over medium-high heat, sauté the onion in olive oil until slightly soft, about 3–5 minutes. Add the pork and brown thoroughly.

2. Add the wine to the pot; bring to a boil then cover and simmer for 15 minutes, stirring regularly. Remove the pork; cover to keep warm and set aside.

3. Add the water to the pan along with the leeks and celery; bring to a boil and simmer 30 minutes over medium heat.

4. Return the pork to the pot along with the tomatoes, oregano, salt, and pepper; stir well. Bring to a boil and then continue to simmer until sauce is reduced and thickened, approximately 8–10 minutes. Serve immediately.

Braised Lamb Shoulder

Serve this dish with rice, plain spaghetti, or fried potatoes.

INGREDIENTS | SERVES 4

1½–2 pounds lamb shoulder

½ cup extra-virgin olive oil

½ cup hot water

2 cups tomato, diced and sieved (fresh or canned)

2 bay leaves

4 garlic cloves, minced

1 cinnamon stick

1 tablespoon dried thyme

½ teaspoon salt

½ teaspoon freshly ground pepper

1. Wash the meat well and cut into small pieces; include the bones.

2. Heat the olive oil in a pot over medium-high heat, add the lamb, and brown on all sides.

3. Add the water, tomatoes, bay leaves, garlic, cinnamon, thyme, salt, and pepper. Cover, bring to a boil, then turn the heat down to medium-low.

4. Simmer for 1½ hours, stirring occasionally. Remove the bones, cinnamon stick, and bay leaves before serving.

CHAPTER 6

Poultry

Chicken Scaparelli

Serve this dish with a crisp salad and a loaf of crusty Italian bread for a delicious, well-balanced meal.

INGREDIENTS | SERVES 10

5 pounds bone-in chicken, cut into serving pieces (breasts, wings, thighs, legs)

¼ cup olive oil

3 Vidalia onions, finely chopped

½ bulb garlic, finely chopped

2 medium parsnips, finely chopped

1 medium carrot, finely chopped

2 stalks celery, finely chopped

¼ bunch fresh oregano, leaves chopped and stems discarded

¼ bunch fresh marjoram, leaves chopped and stems discarded

2 sprigs fresh thyme, leaves chopped and stems discarded

½ bunch fresh parsley, chopped

½ teaspoon coarse salt

½ teaspoon freshly cracked black pepper

1. Preheat the oven to 375°F. Clean the chicken in ice-cold water. Pat dry with paper towels and remove the skin if desired.

2. Pour the oil into a large roasting pan and add all the ingredients. Stir to combine and cover the pan.

3. Roast for 1 hour. Uncover and roast for 20 more minutes. Serve immediately.

Cut the Fat

One way to reduce the fat in chicken recipes is to remove the skin from the chicken before cooking. This will lower the amount of fat in the chicken by more than half, leaving you with a much healthier but still delicious meal.

Pollo alla Cacciatora (Chicken Cacciatore)

Cacciatora *literally translates as "hunter's style." It connotes a dish made with chopped tomatoes, mushrooms, herbs, and garlic sauce. Serve this dish with cooked pasta, polenta, risotto, or mashed potatoes.*

INGREDIENTS | SERVES 10

5 pounds bone-in chicken, cut into serving pieces (breasts, thighs, wings, legs)

1 tablespoon olive oil

3 medium yellow onions, sliced

½ bulb garlic, minced

2 stalks celery, sliced

12 plum tomatoes, cut into wedges

1 pound fresh mushrooms, halved

1 cup red wine

½ bunch fresh parsley, chopped

2 cups Beef Stock (see Chapter 4)

1 tablespoon dried oregano

1 tablespoon dried basil

2 bay leaves

½ teaspoon freshly cracked black pepper

1. Clean the chicken in ice-cold water and pat dry with paper towels.

2. Heat the oil over medium-high heat in a large heavy-bottomed pan. Add the chicken pieces and brown them on all sides for about 5 minutes.

3. Reduce heat to medium and add the onions, garlic, celery, tomatoes, and mushrooms. Stir, and sauté for 2 minutes.

4. Pour in the wine and reduce by half the volume. Add the remaining ingredients, and reduce heat to low. Simmer, uncovered, for 2 hours.

Turkey Tetrazzini

Don't throw away leftover Thanksgiving turkey! This recipe is a great way to use up those pesky leftovers.

INGREDIENTS | SERVES 10

1 tablespoon olive oil

3 pounds boneless turkey meat, cooked

¾ cup melted unsalted butter, divided

1 pound mushrooms, sliced

½ cup all-purpose flour

1 cup Chicken Stock (see Chapter 4), chilled

1 cup whole milk

½ cup fresh-grated Parmesan cheese

½ pound cooked pasta of choice

¼ cup plain bread crumbs

Clarifying Butter

Fresh butter smokes and burns when added to a hot pan, so why do so many recipes suggest sautéing in butter? Because "clarified" butter is an ideal sauté medium. Fresh butter is an emulsion of butterfat, water, and milk proteins. Slowly heating whole butter divides these elements, enabling you to skim off the clarified butterfat, which is a clear, golden oil. This oil tolerates the high cooking temperatures needed to brown foods in a hot pan.

1. Preheat the oven to 350°F. Lightly grease a large casserole dish with the oil. Cut the turkey into thick cubes.

2. Heat ½ cup of the butter over medium heat in a large saucepan. Sauté the turkey until lightly golden. Add the mushrooms and sauté for 2 minutes.

3. Add the flour to the pan and mix with a wooden spoon or whisk until the flour and butter in the pan form a roux (paste). Whisk in the stock and cook until the mixture begins to thicken. Whisk in the milk and cook until the mixture thickens into a sauce.

4. Remove from heat and stir in the cheese and pasta. Transfer the mixture to the prepared casserole dish.

5. Mix together the remaining melted butter and the bread crumbs in a small bowl. Sprinkle over the top of the casserole. Bake for 20 minutes, uncovered. Serve hot.

Pollo Rustico (Rustic Chicken)

This country-style roasted chicken goes well with any risotto, green vegetable, or salad.

INGREDIENTS | SERVES 10

1 (5-pound) whole chicken

2 tablespoons olive oil

½ pound Italian pork sausage, unformed and uncooked

2 medium red bell peppers, seeded and halved

2 medium yellow bell peppers, seeded and halved

2 medium white onions, cut into wedges

2 sprigs fresh rosemary, stems discarded

1 sprig fresh sage, leaves torn in half

½ teaspoon freshly cracked black pepper

1. Preheat the oven to 350°F. Clean the chicken thoroughly in cold water and pat dry with paper towels. Remove any excess loose fat.

2. Pour the oil into the bottom of a large roasting pan. Put the chicken in the pan. Scatter the sausage, peppers, onions, and herbs around the chicken. Sprinkle with pepper.

3. Cover the pan and place in the oven. Cook for 30 minutes. Uncover and stir. Increase heat to 425°F. Roast, uncovered, for 20 more minutes or until the chicken is golden brown and the juices run clear. Remove from the oven, loosely cover with foil, and let rest for 10 minutes before carving.

Classic Chicken Parmesan

Yes, you can make this Italian restaurant favorite in your own kitchen!
Leftovers make a nice "sub" sandwich on Italian bread.

INGREDIENTS | SERVES 10

3½ pounds skinless, boneless chicken

3 large eggs

1 cup plain bread crumbs

¾ cup all-purpose flour

2 tablespoons olive oil

2 cups Old World Gravy (Long-Cooking Tomato Sauce) (see Chapter 3), divided

2 teaspoons dried basil

2 teaspoons dried oregano

1 teaspoon freshly cracked black pepper

1 pound mozzarella or provolone cheese, shredded

¼ cup sliced scallions, to garnish

1. Preheat the oven to 375°F. Rinse the chicken in ice-cold water and pat dry with paper towels.

2. Beat the eggs in a shallow bowl. Place the bread crumbs in a separate shallow bowl. Place the flour in a third bowl. Lightly dust the chicken with the flour. Dip in the egg, then coat in the bread crumbs.

3. Heat the oil over medium-high heat in a large sauté pan. Add the breaded chicken and quickly brown on each side, remove, and drain on paper towels.

4. Ladle ½ cup of the Old World Gravy in the bottom of a baking pan. Place the chicken in the pan in a single layer. Top with the remaining sauce and season with the basil, oregano, and pepper. Top with the cheese.

5. Bake for 20 minutes. Garnish with chopped scallions. Serve with pasta.

Ricotta Chicken Breasts

Serve with Bread Salad and Wilted Kale with Dried Currants and Walnuts (see Chapters 14 and 15).

INGREDIENTS | SERVES 10

1 tablespoon olive oil

10 large chicken breasts (bone-in, with wings attached if possible), cut in half

2 large eggs

½ bunch fresh basil, chopped

2½ cups ricotta cheese

½ teaspoon freshly cracked black pepper

1. Preheat the oven to 375°F. Grease a baking pan with the oil. Rinse the chicken breast halves in ice-cold water.

2. In a medium bowl, beat the eggs. Add the basil, cheese, and pepper and mix well.

3. Form a "pocket" under the breast skin of each chicken breast by poking a small hole in the back area of the breast near the wing joint and gently lifting the skin with your finger. Stuff an even amount of the cheese mixture into each pocket with a pastry bag or spoon.

4. Place the chicken skin-side up in the prepared baking pan and roast for 1 hour, uncovered. Serve hot.

Turkey Piccata

This "piccata" style of cooking meat very quickly in a pan with butter and lemon can also be used with chicken or veal.

INGREDIENTS | SERVES 10

3–4 pounds boneless turkey meat

2 tablespoons olive oil

½ cup all-purpose flour

2 tablespoons capers, rinsed

Zest and juice of 2 large lemons

1 cup Chicken Stock (see Chapter 4)

½ bunch fresh parsley, chopped

½ teaspoon freshly cracked black pepper

1. Slice the turkey into serving-sized portions.

2. Heat the oil over medium heat in a large sauté pan. Dust the turkey with the flour and shake off excess. Add the turkey to the pan and brown the turkey pieces on one side, then turn.

3. Add the capers, lemon zest and juice, and the stock. Cook for 6–10 minutes longer until browned and cooked through.

4. Sprinkle with the parsley and pepper and serve.

Turkey with Mascarpone Sauce

Because of the rich sauce, this should be served with bland sides, such as Basic Risotto or Basic Polenta (see Chapter 11) and a steamed vegetable.

INGREDIENTS | SERVES 10

1 tablespoon olive oil

4–5 pounds boneless turkey

½ teaspoon freshly cracked black pepper

2 medium white onions, chopped

2 cups Mascarpone Cheese Sauce (see Chapter 3)

1. Preheat the oven to 400°F. Grease a large roasting pan with the oil. Slice the turkey into thin portions and season with pepper.

2. Place the onions in the prepared pan and top with the turkey. Cover and roast for 20 minutes. Uncover and continue to roast 10–15 minutes longer.

3. While the turkey cooks, heat the cheese sauce in a small saucepan.

4. Place the turkey and onions on a platter and drizzle with some sauce. Serve the remaining sauce on the side at the table.

Asiago Pollo con Prosciutto (Asiago Chicken with Prosciutto)

Be sure there is little or no salt in the stock you use for this dish. The prosciutto and Asiago cheese already provide plenty of salt.

INGREDIENTS | SERVES 10

3 pounds skinless, boneless chicken breasts

½ pound thinly sliced prosciutto

½ pound Asiago cheese, grated

1 teaspoon freshly cracked black pepper

2 tablespoons olive oil

½ cup Chicken Stock (see Chapter 4)

1 cup Oregano-Almond Pesto (see Chapter 3)

1. Rinse the chicken in cold water and pat dry with paper towels. Carefully slit the thickest part of each breast to form a pocket. Cut the sliced prosciutto into thin strips.

2. Carefully stuff each breast pocket with the prosciutto and cheese. Sprinkle the outside of the breasts with pepper.

3. Heat the oil over medium-high heat in a large sauté pan. Add the chicken and brown it on each side. Pour in the stock and reduce heat to medium-low temperature. Cover and cook for about 20 minutes until the chicken is thoroughly cooked. Serve with the pesto spooned over the top of the chicken (do not heat pesto).

Layered Duck

Grilling the duck and then baking it with the vegetables is a two-step process, but the final outcome of this dish is definitely worth the extra effort.

INGREDIENTS | SERVES 10

2 tablespoons olive oil, divided

3 pounds skinless, boneless duck meat

½ teaspoon freshly cracked black pepper

2 large baked potatoes

2 large carrots, grated

½ cup Rosemary Pesto (see Chapter 3)

Choosing Carrots

There are two main choices when it comes to carrots. You can either buy "horse" carrots, the large variety that must be peeled, or "baby" carrots, which usually come peeled, prewashed, and packaged in a bag. Horse carrots tend to be sweeter and juicier than baby carrots, which tend to be bland unless very fresh.

1. Preheat the grill to medium-high temperature and preheat the oven to 325°F. Lightly grease a loaf pan with 1 tablespoon of the oil. Lightly rub the outside of the duck with the remaining oil and season with pepper. Peel the potatoes and cut into thick slices.

2. Brown the duck on both sides on the grill. Thinly slice the duck meat on the bias. Place the duck meat in the bottom of the prepared loaf pan. Layer the carrots, potatoes, and pesto on top (in that order).

3. Cover and bake for 10 minutes. Serve hot.

Chicken Marsala

Authentic Chicken Marsala is finished with a small amount of the wine and does not necessarily have mushrooms.

INGREDIENTS | SERVES 10

3½ pounds skinless, boneless chicken breasts

2 large eggs

½ cup all-purpose flour

¼ cup olive oil

2 cups fresh mushrooms, sliced

½ bulb garlic, minced

1 cup Marsala wine

½ cup cold unsalted butter, cut into pats

1. Rinse the chicken and pat dry with paper towels. Place between layers of plastic wrap and pound until thin.

2. Beat the eggs in a shallow bowl. Place the flour in a separate shallow bowl. Dust the chicken with the flour. Dip the chicken in the eggs and return to the flour. Shake off excess flour.

3. Heat the oil over medium-high heat in a large sauté pan. Add the chicken and brown on one side. Turn over and add the mushrooms and garlic. Pour in the wine and reduce to half the volume.

4. Add the pats of cold butter and stir into the sauce. Serve the chicken with the sauce.

Chicken Fricassee

This Italian version of stewed chicken is a favorite dish in many Italian and Italian-American homes.

INGREDIENTS | SERVES 10

3 pounds boneless chicken

3 tablespoons olive oil

2 medium white onions, chopped

1 bulb garlic, minced

20 plum tomatoes, chopped

1 cup Merlot

4 cups Chicken Stock (see Chapter 4)

½ bunch fresh parsley

10 sprigs fresh thyme

2 bay leaves

1 tablespoon fennel seeds

1 teaspoon freshly cracked black pepper

¼ cup fresh-grated Parmesan cheese

1. Rinse the chicken in cold water and pat dry with paper towels.

2. Heat the oil over medium-high heat in a large Dutch oven (or other heavy-bottomed pan with a lid). Add the chicken and brown it on all sides. Add the onion and garlic and lightly brown, about 2–3 minutes. Add the tomatoes and stir for 2 minutes.

3. Pour in the wine and reduce by half the volume. Add the stock, herbs, and spices. Reduce heat to low.

4. Cover and simmer for 90 minutes. Remove the bay leaves and serve sprinkled with the cheese.

Grilled Duck Breast with Fruit Salsa

Duck breast has the best flavor when cooked rare to medium-rare. For this recipe, try using Moulard duck breast.

INGREDIENTS | SERVES 6

1 medium plum, diced

1 large peach, diced

1 large nectarine, diced

1 medium red onion, diced

3 sprigs mint, minced

½ teaspoon freshly cracked black pepper, or to taste

1 tablespoon olive oil

1 teaspoon chili powder

1½ pounds boneless duck breast

1. Preheat the grill.

2. In a medium bowl, toss together the fruit, onion, mint, and pepper.

3. In a small bowl, mix together the oil and chili powder. Coat the duck breast with the oil and cook to desired doneness on grill.

4. Slice the duck on the bias and serve with spoonful of salsa.

Chicken Sausage Patties

These can be made smaller in ball or patty form for appetizers. Serve with spicy chutney for an added kick.

INGREDIENTS | MAKES 24 PATTIES

3 pounds ground turkey

1 medium yellow onion, finely minced

½ cup finely chopped Italian parsley

1 tablespoon chopped fresh sage or 2 teaspoons dry sage

6 cloves garlic, minced

1 tablespoon minced fresh ginger or 2 teaspoons dry ground ginger

2 teaspoons red pepper flakes

1 teaspoon ground clove

1 teaspoon white pepper

4 tablespoons olive oil

1. In a large mixing bowl, combine all the ingredients except the oil; mix well by hand.

2. Form into 24 equal-sized patties that are approximately 2" × 1".

3. Heat the oil in a large sauté pan. Sauté over medium heat for approximately 5 minutes on each side until cooked through.

Rosemary Chicken Thighs and Legs with Potatoes

To save time and effort, you can purchase minced garlic in jars from most supermarkets.

INGREDIENTS | SERVES 6

2 pounds chicken thighs and legs
6 sprigs rosemary
1 medium leek, sliced
8 cloves garlic, minced
6 small red potatoes
1 tablespoon olive oil
½ teaspoon freshly cracked black pepper
¼ cup capers

1. Preheat the oven to 375°F.

2. Remove the skin from the chicken. Remove the top 2" portion of each rosemary sprig for garnish; remove the needles from the rest of the rosemary sprigs and discard the stems.

3. Toss all the ingredients except the pepper and capers in a large baking dish. Place in the oven and roast for 1 hour or until the juices run clear from the chicken. Remove from the oven, season with pepper, and sprinkle with capers. Serve.

Pesto-Baked Chicken

To keep the pesto from burning, loosely cover it with foil.

INGREDIENTS | SERVES 6

1 (4–5 pound) whole chicken
¼ cup all-purpose flour
½ cup Traditional Pesto (see Chapter 3)
1 teaspoon olive oil
1 teaspoon freshly cracked black pepper
1 teaspoon kosher salt
2 cups New World Fresh Sauce (see Chapter 3)

1. Preheat the oven to 375°F.

2. Remove the skin from the chicken and cut the chicken into serving pieces (breasts, wings, thighs, legs).

3. Place the flour in a small bowl. Place the pesto in a separate bowl. Toss the chicken parts in the flour, then dredge in pesto.

4. Place the chicken on an oiled rack in a roasting pan. Season with pepper and salt and bake for 1–1½ hours.

5. While the chicken bakes, heat the New World Fresh Sauce in a medium saucepan. Serve the warmed sauce over the chicken.

Roast Chicken

A good way to save time when crushing several cloves of garlic is to use a rolling pin placed over all the cloves at once.

INGREDIENTS | SERVES 6

2 (3-pound) frying chickens
1 teaspoon salt
1 teaspoon pepper
4 cloves garlic, crushed
3 tablespoons olive oil
⅓ cup lemon juice
½ cup water

1. Preheat the oven to 425°F.

2. Rub the chicken with salt, pepper, and crushed garlic. Place in a large roasting pan breast-side up. Brush all over with the oil.

3. Roast for 20 minutes, then reduce heat to 325°F and continue roasting for 50–60 minutes.

4. To test doneness, twist a leg joint. If it moves easily, it is done. Pour the lemon juice over the chicken and transfer to platter; keep warm.

5. To make the gravy, transfer the roasting pan to a burner if it is stovetop-safe, or pour the drippings into a saucepan; add the water to the pan and bring to a boil, stirring constantly until reduced by half. Slice the chicken and serve with gravy.

Chicken with Egg Noodles and Walnuts

If you have a nut allergy, don't worry: the walnuts are really an optional element and not necessary for the success of this dish.

INGREDIENTS | SERVES 4–6

1 (4–5 pound) whole chicken
½ cup extra-virgin olive oil
1 medium onion, diced
¼ cup butter
2 cups tomato pulp, minced and sieved
4 cups boiling water
1 tablespoon fresh mint, chopped
1 teaspoon salt
1 teaspoon pepper
1 pound egg noodles
½ cup crushed walnuts
Grated Parmesan cheese, for garnish (optional)

1. Wash the chicken well inside and out and pat dry with a paper towel. Cut into sections.

2. Heat the oil in a large sauté pan over medium-high heat. Add the onion and sauté it slightly; add the butter and chicken and sauté thoroughly on all sides.

3. Add the tomatoes, boiling water, mint, salt, and pepper. Bring to a boil; cover and simmer over medium-low heat 30 minutes.

4. Add the egg noodles and crushed walnuts; give a good stir. Cover and continue to simmer another 30 minutes.

5. Stir before serving hot with some grated Parmesan cheese over each helping.

Chicken Livers in Red Wine

For a nice (and sweet!) variation on this recipe, you can try using a fortified wine, such as port wine or Marsala. Serve this dish over mashed potatoes.

INGREDIENTS | SERVES 4

1 pound chicken livers
1 cup chicken broth
½ cup butter
1 small onion, diced
1 tablespoon all-purpose flour
½ cup red wine
½ teaspoon salt
½ teaspoon pepper
2 tablespoons fresh parsley, finely chopped

1. Wash the chicken livers thoroughly and drain well before using.

2. Bring the broth to a boil in a small pan and then let simmer over low heat.

3. Melt the butter over medium-high heat in another frying pan. Add the onion and slightly sauté, about 2–3 minutes. Turn up to high heat, add the chicken livers, and cook for 3–5 minutes, stirring constantly to avoid browning.

4. Sprinkle the flour over top of the livers and butter; continue to stir well to form a sauce in the bottom of the pan. Stir constantly to avoid clumping.

5. Slowly add the hot broth to the pan with the livers, stirring constantly. Slowly add the wine; continue to simmer and stir for several minutes. Reduce heat to low; cook another 5–10 minutes to thicken the sauce.

6. Season with salt and pepper and serve hot with chopped parsley as a garnish.

CHAPTER 7

Fish and Seafood

Aragosta con Burro all'Aglio (Lobster with Garlic Butter)

*It's best to keep it simple when it comes to lobster. Some light seasoning
and melted butter is enough to complement the natural flavor.*

INGREDIENTS | SERVES 10

20 long wooden skewers

10 small lobster tails

½ pound unsalted butter

½ bulb garlic, minced

½ bunch fresh parsley, chopped

½ teaspoon kosher or sea salt

½ teaspoon freshly cracked black pepper

Feast of the Seven Fishes

Christmas Eve is one of the most important religious holidays in Italy, and fish and seafood are the focus of the meal. Tradition demands that at least seven different fish dishes are prepared seven different ways and served at Christmas Eve dinner. Some think the tradition has its origin in the seven sacraments, but that is just speculation.

1. Soak the skewers for at least 20 minutes in water. Remove the lobster meat from the shells. Rinse the meat in ice-cold water and pat dry. (Reserve the shells and freeze for use in another recipe, if desired.) Skewer each tail with 2 skewers (one at each end), then wrap the skewer ends in foil to prevent burning. Preheat the grill (or broiler) to medium-high heat.

2. Melt the butter in small sauté pan over medium heat. Reduce heat to medium-low and add the garlic. Sauté for 5 minutes.

3. Grill the lobster for about 3 minutes on each side.

4. Drizzle the lobster with the garlic butter and sprinkle with the parsley, salt, and pepper. Serve.

Scallops Alfredo

Make sure you use very fresh scallops for this dish. Do not use bay scallops, as they will overcook.

INGREDIENTS | SERVES 5

2 tablespoons olive oil, divided

1 pound sea scallops

2 tablespoons unsalted butter

4 tablespoons all-purpose flour

½ cup dry white wine (not cooking wine)

1 cup Fish Stock (see Chapter 4)

1 cup heavy cream

½ cup shredded fontina cheese

½ teaspoon freshly cracked black pepper

1. Preheat the broiler on high. Lightly grease a large baking pan with 1 tablespoon of the oil. Rinse the scallops in cold water and pat dry with paper towels.

2. Melt the butter in a large saucepan over medium heat and add the remaining oil. Add the scallops and sauté for 1 minute. Stir in the flour and continue to stir for 1 minute.

3. Pour in the wine and stock and simmer for 8–10 minutes. Whisk the mixture constantly until thickened.

4. While scallops simmer, reduce the heavy cream by half the volume in a small saucepan over medium-high heat.

5. Remove the scallops from heat, whisk in the cream, and stir in the cheese.

6. Ladle the scallops mixture into the prepared baking pan. Sprinkle with pepper and brown quickly under the broiler.

Red Snapper with Peppers

Serve this dish with Basic Risotto (see Chapter 11) and fresh crusty Italian bread.

INGREDIENTS | SERVES 10

5 small red snapper fillets

3 sprigs fresh thyme

¼ cup barley flour (or substitute all-purpose flour)

2 tablespoons olive oil

1 medium red bell pepper, seeded and finely sliced

1 medium yellow bell pepper, seeded and finely sliced

1 medium red onion, finely sliced

3 cloves garlic, finely sliced

½ teaspoon freshly cracked black pepper

¼ cup wine vinegar

1. Gently clean the fish in ice-cold water and pat dry with paper towels. Remove the leaves from 2 sprigs of thyme and discard the stems (reserve 1 sprig for garnish).

2. Lightly flour the fillets. Heat the oil over medium heat in a large sauté pan. Add the fish, sauté for 2 minutes, and turn. Add the peppers, onions, garlic, thyme leaves, black pepper, and vinegar.

3. Cover and cook for 5–10 minutes until the fish is flaky and the peppers are lightly cooked. Serve on a platter garnished with the thyme sprig.

How to Tell If Fish Is Fresh

For one thing, fresh fish has virtually no smell. With whole fish, the body should be rigid and the flesh firm. The skin should not be dry and the scales should be shiny and tightly connected to the body. With fillets, the flesh should be white or rosy, with iridescent reflections.

Citrus-Braised Halibut

Since the citrus flavor is very strong in this dish, the best choice for a side is Basic Risotto (see Chapter 11).

INGREDIENTS | SERVES 10

1 (1¾-pound) halibut fillet

2 tablespoons olive oil

¼ cup all-purpose flour

1 large yellow onion, cut into wedges

3 cloves garlic, halved

Zest and juice of 4 large oranges

½ bunch fresh parsley, stems discarded

3 sprigs fresh thyme, stems discarded

½ cup Fish Stock (see Chapter 4)

½ cup dry white wine (not cooking wine)

1 bay leaf

1 teaspoon capers, rinsed

½ teaspoon freshly cracked black pepper

1. Preheat the oven to 350°F. Rinse the halibut with ice-cold water and pat dry with paper towels. Cut into large chunks.

2. Heat the oil over high heat in a Dutch oven or other heavy-bottomed ovenproof pan with a lid. Dust the fish with the flour, add it to the pan, and sear until brown on both sides.

3. Add all the remaining ingredients except the capers and pepper. Bring to a quick boil, cover, and place the pan in the oven. Braise for 20 minutes or until the fish flakes.

4. Place the fish on a serving platter and drizzle with the pan juices. Sprinkle with the capers and pepper. Serve with cooked parsley and thyme from the pan for garnish.

Cod Parmesan

Serve this dish with a simple side of pasta, risotto, or a steamed vegetable and some fresh Italian bread.

INGREDIENTS | SERVES 10

3 tablespoons olive oil, divided

10 (6-ounce) thick pieces fresh cod fillet

2 pounds plum tomatoes, diced

½ bunch fresh basil, sliced

¼ cup Roasted Garlic Paste (see Chapter 3)

1 teaspoon freshly cracked black pepper

2 egg whites

½ cup durum wheat (semolina) flour

¼ cup all-purpose flour

2 teaspoons baking powder

½ pound provolone cheese, thinly sliced

1. Preheat the oven to 400°F. Lightly grease a baking pan with 1 tablespoon of the oil. Rinse the fish in ice-cold water and thoroughly dry with paper towels.

2. In a medium mixing bowl, combine the tomatoes, basil, garlic paste, and pepper. Set aside.

3. In a small bowl, whisk the egg whites. In separate bowl, sift together the flours and baking powder. Dip the fish in the flour, then in the egg whites, then back in the flour.

4. Heat the remaining oil over medium heat in a large sauté pan. Add the fish and lightly brown on both sides. Place the fish in the prepared baking pan. Top with the cheese. Bake for about 10 minutes, or until the cheese browns and the fish flakes.

5. To serve, place the fish on serving plates and top each with 2 heaping tablespoons of the tomato mixture.

Grilled Fish and Seafood Primavera

A good fish market will clean shrimp and other fresh seafood for you if you order in advance. This will save you some work in the kitchen.

INGREDIENTS | SERVES 10

½ pound large fresh shrimp

1 pound fresh tuna

½ pound fresh sea scallops

½ bulb garlic, minced

¼ cup olive oil

1 medium eggplant, sliced lengthwise into 1½"-thick slices

2 medium red bell peppers, cut in half, seeds removed

2 stalks celery

2 medium white onions, sliced into ½"-thick slices

½ cup Fish Stock (see Chapter 4)

½ cup dry white wine (not cooking wine)

¼ pound cold unsalted butter

3 sprigs fresh basil, sliced

1 pound cooked pasta of choice

½ cup fresh-grated Romano cheese

1 teaspoon freshly cracked black pepper

Fish and Seafood

Fish and seafood are staple foods in Italy. Italians seem to prefer fish to any other food. Remember that Italy is basically a peninsula and is surrounded by water on three sides. The most common cooking methods in Italy are roasting and grilling. Fish "stews" such as *Zuppa di Pesce* are also popular, and stuffed fish dishes are common as well.

1. Preheat the grill to medium-high heat. Peel and devein the shrimp. Thoroughly clean the shrimp, tuna, and scallops with ice-cold water. Pat dry with paper towels and keep chilled.

2. In a large bowl, mix together the garlic and oil. Dip the shrimp, tuna, scallops, eggplant, bell peppers, celery, and onions in the oil. Shake off excess oil.

3. Grill the oiled seafood and vegetables for about 5–8 minutes, turning every 1–2 minutes until the vegetables are al dente and the shellfish is cooked. Continue to grill the tuna to desired doneness.

4. Cut the eggplant, peppers, and celery into strips. Cut the onion rings in half. Thinly slice the tuna.

5. In a small saucepan, add the stock and wine and bring to a boil. Boil for 2 minutes. Remove from heat and stir in the butter.

6. In a large bowl, mix together all the ingredients and serve.

Orange-Poached Salmon with Prosciutto

You can "moist bake" or poach fillets in the oven instead of the usual method of poaching on the stovetop in a pot of simmering liquid.

INGREDIENTS | SERVES 10

1 teaspoon olive oil

2 pounds salmon fillet

4 large oranges

¼ pound prosciutto, very thinly sliced

½ bulb garlic, minced

½ cup raisins

½ teaspoon freshly cracked black pepper

1. Preheat the oven to 375°F. Lightly grease a large baking dish with the oil. Rinse the salmon in cold water and pat dry with paper towels. Cut the salmon into 10 equal serving portions. Keep chilled.

2. Zest and juice 2 of the oranges. Cut the remaining 2 oranges into slices ½" thick.

3. Lay out the prosciutto on a clean surface. Place a salmon fillet on top of each slice. Sprinkle with the garlic and orange zest. Place 2 orange slices on top of each fillet and sprinkle with the raisins. Wrap the prosciutto around the salmon, enclosing the stuffing. Place the prosciutto bundles in the prepared baking dish. Pour in the orange juice. Sprinkle with pepper.

4. Cover and poach in the oven for 20–30 minutes until the fish flakes. Serve.

Fish Casserole

This is a simple dish that can be served at room temperature or chilled.

INGREDIENTS | SERVES 10

1 tablespoon olive oil

1½ pounds salmon fillet

1½ pounds cod fillet

1 large white onion, finely chopped

2 cups Italian Pepperoncini Gremolata (see Chapter 3)

½ loaf crusty Italian bread, finely chopped

2 large eggs, beaten

2 cups Mozzarella and Ricotta Cheese Sauce (see Chapter 3)

Pesce Fritto (Fried Fish)

Olive oil is the best medium for frying fish. With the exception of anchovy, fish for frying should not weigh more than 3 ounces. Fish should be dipped in milk, water, or egg, and then coated in flour before frying. After frying, drain off excess fat by placing on paper towels.

1. Preheat the oven to 400°F. Grease a loaf pan with the oil.

2. Line the prepared loaf pan with the salmon, allowing excess to hang over one side. Place layers of the cod, onion, Pepperoncini Gremolata, and bread in the pan. Repeat layers and pour the beaten eggs over the top. Wrap the excess salmon over the top and press down to compress all the ingredients.

3. Pour the cheese sauce over the top. Cover with foil and bake for 30 minutes. Uncover and bake for 10 more minutes.

4. Remove from the oven and let rest for 30 minutes. Serve.

Hearty Cioppino

The saffron makes this a wonderfully fragrant seafood stew.
Serve with fresh Italian bread and a crisp salad.

INGREDIENTS | SERVES 10

1 pound mussels
½ pound fresh sea scallops
½ pound fresh large shrimp
½ pound fresh halibut fillet
½ pound fresh cod fillet
10 Roma tomatoes, quartered
1 cup Old World Gravy (Long-Cooking Tomato Sauce) (see Chapter 3)
2 cups Fish Stock (see Chapter 4)
1½ teaspoons saffron thread
2 large white onions, cut into wedges
½ pound parsnips, cut into wedges
½ bunch celery, cut into chunks
½ bunch fresh parsley, finely chopped
1 teaspoon freshly cracked black pepper

1. Clean the mussels and scallops in ice-cold water. Scrub and debeard the mussels. Remove the tough muscle from the scallops. Peel, devein, and clean the shrimp. Cut the halibut and cod into large chunks.

2. Place the tomatoes, tomato sauce, stock, saffron, onions, parsnips, celery, parsley, and black pepper in a large stockpot. Simmer with the lid ajar for 1½ hours.

3. Fifteen minutes before cooking time is complete, add all the seafood.

4. Discard any unopened mussels before serving.

Shrimp Quality

Size doesn't generally affect taste and texture when it comes to shrimp; freshness and origin do. The best, sweetest shrimp are from Ecuador and South America. Most shrimp are frozen within hours of being caught; otherwise, they lose their firm texture and sweet flavor. Stores thaw just what they think they will sell that day.

Seafood Bake

Only use fresh seafood whenever possible. Frozen seafood rarely retains all of its original texture and flavor.

INGREDIENTS | SERVES 10

2 tablespoons olive oil, divided

½ pound crabmeat

½ pound sea scallops

½ recipe Basic Risotto (see Chapter 11)

2 medium red bell peppers, seeded and minced

½ bunch chives, finely sliced

1 teaspoon freshly cracked black pepper

1. Preheat the oven to 375°F. Lightly grease a loaf pan with 1 tablespoon of the oil. Pick through the crabmeat to remove any shells. Thinly slice the scallops.

2. Spread a thin layer of risotto in the prepared loaf pan; then alternate layers of crab, bell pepper, scallops, chives, black pepper, and risotto. Repeat the process 2 more times, ending with a top layer of risotto.

3. Drizzle the top with the remaining oil and cover with foil. Bake for 25 minutes. Uncover and cook for 10 more minutes until the top is browned. Serve sprinkled with more black pepper if desired.

Pasta con Alici (Pasta with Anchovy Sauce)

Anchovy are bluish green in color, except for the silver stomach, and they do not have scales. They can be marinated, fried, or baked.

INGREDIENTS | SERVES 10

1½ tablespoons olive oil

2 tablespoons cold unsalted butter

3 large cloves garlic, minced

¼ cup anchovy fillets

Zest and juice of 1 large lemon

½ cup dry white wine (not cooking wine)

1 cup Fish Stock (see Chapter 4)

1 pound linguine, cooked al dente

½ bunch fresh parsley, chopped

½ teaspoon freshly cracked black pepper

1. Heat the oil over medium heat in a medium-sized saucepan. Add the butter and garlic and sauté 2 minutes. Add the anchovies and toss in the oil for 1 minute.

2. Add the lemon juice and wine and let reduce for 1 minute. Add the stock. Cook for 5 minutes.

3. Add the pasta and toss thoroughly. Sprinkle with the parsley, lemon zest, and pepper. Serve in heated bowls.

Baccalà in Saffron Marinara Broth

This unique dish is very fragrant because of the saffron. Serve with plenty of Italian bread for dipping.

INGREDIENTS | SERVES 10

1½ pounds *baccalà* (salted cod)

1 tablespoon olive oil

2 shallots, minced

½ bulb garlic, minced

1 pound plum tomatoes, chopped

1 teaspoon saffron threads

½ cup dry white wine (not cooking wine)

1 cup Fish Stock (see Chapter 4)

2 tablespoons fresh-grated Parmesan cheese

½ bunch fresh parsley, chopped

½ teaspoon freshly cracked black pepper

Baccalà

Baccalà, or salt cod, is a common dish in Italy. Fresh whole cod is boned and its sides salt-cured and preserved in wood barrels. Before cooking, soften the cod by pounding on it with a wooden mallet or pestle. Soak the softened fish in cold water for a minimum of 2 days (4–5 days is better) to remove the salt. Change the water 3 times a day, and gently rinse the fish each time under clean water.

1. Lightly pound the *baccalà* to soften. Soak the *baccalà* in ice-cold water in a large plastic container for at least 2 days (4 days is better) in the refrigerator. Pour off the water every 8–12 hours, rinse the fish, and add fresh ice-cold water. Pat the fish dry.

2. Heat the oil to medium heat in a large saucepan. Add the fish, shallots, garlic, and tomatoes. Sauté for 5 minutes. Add the saffron and wine; let the wine reduce by half the volume.

3. Pour in the stock and cook for approximately 20 minutes, uncovered.

4. Serve in shallow bowls sprinkled with the cheese, parsley, and pepper.

Shrimp Scampi

Shrimp scampi must be served right from the stove for the best texture. If it has to sit, the shrimp becomes slightly soggy as it soaks up the sauce.

INGREDIENTS | SERVES 10

1 pound medium-sized shrimp (20–30 count)
2 tablespoons olive oil
1 teaspoon freshly cracked black pepper
½ bulb garlic, minced
Zest and juice of 1 large lemon
½ cup dry white wine (not cooking wine)
½ cup Fish Stock (see Chapter 4)
¼ cup cold unsalted butter
½ bunch fresh parsley, chopped

1. Peel and devein the shrimp (leave the tails intact). Rinse in cold water and pat dry with paper towels.

2. Heat the oil over medium heat in a large sauté pan. Season the shrimp with pepper and add to the hot oil. Sauté for 1 minute, stirring constantly.

3. Add the garlic, then lemon juice and wine, stirring constantly. Sauté for 1 minute, then add the stock. Cook for 3 minutes.

4. Add the cold butter, stir until melted, and remove from heat. Sprinkle with the lemon zest and parsley and serve.

Cozze al Vino (Mussels in White Wine Broth)

Serve this with bruschetta (sliced Italian bread rubbed with garlic and olive oil and toasted). Bruschetta is great for sopping up the broth in this dish.

INGREDIENTS | SERVES 10

3 dozen fresh mussels
2 tablespoons olive oil
2 shallots, minced
½ bulb garlic, minced
3 sprigs fresh thyme, chopped, divided
3 sprigs fresh basil, chopped, divided
3 sprigs fresh parsley, chopped, divided
1 bay leaf
2 tablespoons unsalted butter
1 cup dry white wine (not cooking wine)
1 cup Fish Stock (see Chapter 4)
½ teaspoon freshly cracked black pepper

1. Thoroughly clean the mussels.

2. Heat the oil over medium heat in a large saucepan. Add the mussels, shallots, garlic, half the herbs, the bay leaf, butter, wine, and stock.

3. Cover and simmer for 8–10 minutes until the mussels open. (Discard any mussels that do not open.)

4. Remove from heat. Serve sprinkled with the remaining herbs and black pepper.

Salmon and Haddock Terrine

Start a day in advance for this recipe, which creates a beautiful plate for presentation. You can also use a chutney or salsa with this.

INGREDIENTS | SERVES 6

1 tablespoon olive oil
¾ pound fresh salmon fillet
¾ pound haddock fillet
1 medium eggplant
½ teaspoon freshly cracked black pepper
½ teaspoon kosher salt
1 head arugula
2 roasted red peppers
3 cloves garlic, thinly sliced

1. Preheat the oven to 375°F. Grease a loaf pan with the olive oil. Rinse the fish in ice-cold water and pat dry.

2. Cut the eggplant in half lengthwise, place on a baking pan, and roast for 20 minutes.

3. Season the fish with black pepper and salt. In the prepared pan, layer the salmon, cooled eggplant, arugula, haddock, red pepper, garlic, then more arugula, and top with eggplant.

4. Wrap the pan tightly with foil and bake for 20 minutes. Unwrap and press down on the layered ingredients; rewrap tightly and bake for 10–20 minutes longer until thoroughly cooked. Remove from the oven and let cool overnight.

5. To serve, unmold from loaf pan. Slice and serve.

Oven-Stewed Sea Bass

You can use any type of bass or other hearty fish in this recipe.

INGREDIENTS | SERVES 6

1½ pounds sea bass
2 medium yellow onions, sliced
1 parsnip, sliced
1 stalk celery, chopped
2 Idaho baking potatoes, chopped
1 medium summer squash, chopped
1 medium red pepper, seeded and chopped
1½ cups Fish Stock (see Chapter 4)
1 cup dry red wine
2 sprigs thyme, leaves only
2 bay leaves
½ teaspoon freshly cracked black pepper
½ teaspoon Old Bay Seasoning

1. Preheat the oven to 350°F. Rinse the fish in ice-cold water and pat dry.

2. In a medium-sized baking dish, layer the onions, parsnip, celery, potatoes, squash, red pepper, and fish in that order. Add the stock, wine, thyme, bay leaves, black pepper, and Old Bay Seasoning.

3. Cover and bake for 20–30 minutes until the vegetables are al dente and the fish flakes.

Lemon Sole with Capers

If you are searching for something to serve with this dish, consider crème fraîche; it makes for a very nice accompaniment.

INGREDIENTS | SERVES 6

1½ pounds sole
½ teaspoon freshly cracked black pepper
1 teaspoon fresh-grated lemon zest
3 cloves garlic, minced
1 teaspoon olive oil
3 sprigs fresh dill, leaves only, chopped
½ teaspoon capers

1. Preheat the oven broiler.

2. Place the sole on a broiler pan; sprinkle with pepper, zest, and garlic and drizzle with the oil. Place under the broiler for 3 minutes, then turn carefully and broil for 1 minute longer.

3. Remove from the broiler and top with the dill and capers.

Pan-Fried Trout

Serving fish with or without the head is up to the discretion of the cook.
Finicky guests may appreciate your removing the heads, however.

INGREDIENTS | SERVES 6

¼ cup all-purpose flour

2 tablespoons cornmeal

½ teaspoon garlic powder

½ teaspoon freshly cracked black pepper

2 egg whites

1 tablespoon cold water

6 small trout

¼ cup olive oil

¼ bunch fresh parsley, chopped

½ teaspoon kosher salt, or to taste

1. In a shallow bowl, mix together the flour, cornmeal, garlic powder, and pepper. In another shallow bowl, beat together the egg whites and water. Dust the trout with the flour mixture, dip in the egg mixture, and then in the flour mixture again. Shake off any excess.

2. Heat the oil over medium heat in large skillet. Cook the trout on each side for approximately 5 minutes until it is golden brown and thoroughly cooked.

3. Remove the trout from the pan and thoroughly drain on a rack covered with paper towels. Sprinkle with parsley and salt before serving.

Baked Tuna

Archaeologists have discovered evidence of extensive tuna fishing operations in the Mediterranean as early as 6000 B.C.

INGREDIENTS | SERVES 4

4 center-cut tuna fillets, 6–8 ounces each (2 pounds total)

¼ cup extra-virgin olive oil, divided

1 large yellow onion, sliced

1 large green pepper, diced

2 cloves garlic, minced or pressed

2 tablespoons chopped parsley

1 teaspoon dried marjoram (or ½ teaspoon dried oregano)

½ teaspoon salt

½ teaspoon freshly ground pepper

2 cups peeled tomatoes, finely minced (canned tomatoes are fine)

½ cup water

1. Preheat the oven to 400°F.

2. Wash the tuna steaks well and set aside.

3. In a large frying pan, heat 2 tablespoons olive oil on medium-high heat. Sauté the onion and green pepper until soft.

4. Add the garlic, parsley, marjoram, salt, and pepper; stir over heat another minute or so.

5. Add the tomatoes and water; bring to a boil. Lower heat to medium-low and simmer for 15–20 minutes.

6. Place the tuna steaks in a baking dish along with the remaining olive oil, making sure to coat the tuna with the oil; pour the sauce over top. Bake uncovered for 45 minutes.

7. Serve immediately, spooning some sauce over each portion and garnishing with chopped fresh parsley, if desired.

CHAPTER 8

Meatballs

Basic Beef Meatballs

These classic meatballs are great served over pasta or as appetizers. If served as appetizers, smaller bite-sized meatballs work best.

INGREDIENTS | SERVES 10

5 thick slices day-old or toasted Italian bread

½ bulb garlic, minced

¼ bunch fresh parsley, chopped

1½ pounds lean ground beef

1 large egg, lightly beaten

¼ cup fresh-grated Parmesan or Romano cheese

½ teaspoon freshly cracked black pepper

Using Bread

Day-old or two-day-old Italian bread is ideal to use for meatball and meat stuffing mixtures. If slightly stale bread is unavailable, you can simply toast some fresh bread, or use bread crumbs instead.

1. Soak the bread in water for 1 minute. Thoroughly squeeze out all the liquid.

2. In a large mixing bowl, combine all the ingredients. Form the mixture into balls about 2"–3" in size.

3. Bake or fry the meatballs: To bake, preheat the oven to 375°F. Place the meatballs in a lightly greased baking pan and cover. Bake for 30 minutes. Uncover and brown for 5–10 minutes. To fry, heat about 1 tablespoon olive oil over medium heat in a skillet. Fry for 30 minutes, uncovered, stirring occasionally until cooked through.

4. Transfer the meatballs to paper towels to drain. Serve the meatballs plain, with sauce, or over pasta.

Three-Meat Meatballs

You can form your meatballs into any shape and size you like. However, if you make large meatballs, allow for more cooking time.

INGREDIENTS | SERVES 10

5 thick slices day-old or toasted Italian bread

2 sprigs fresh oregano, chopped

4 sprigs fresh parsley, chopped

2 shallots, minced

½ bulb garlic, minced

¾ pound ground veal

¾ pound lean ground pork

¾ pound lean ground beef

1 large egg, lightly beaten

¼ cup fresh-grated Parmesan or Romano cheese

½ teaspoon freshly cracked black pepper

1. Soak the bread in water for 1 minute. Thoroughly squeeze out all liquid.

2. In a large mixing bowl, combine all the ingredients. Form into balls about 2"–3" in size.

3. Bake or fry the meatballs: To bake, preheat the oven to 375°F. Place the meatballs in a lightly greased baking pan and cover. Bake for 30 minutes. Uncover and brown for 5–10 minutes. To fry, heat about 1 tablespoon olive oil over medium heat in a skillet. Fry for 30 minutes, uncovered, stirring occasionally until cooked through.

4. Transfer the meatballs to paper towels to drain. Serve plain, with sauce, or over pasta.

Chicken Meatballs

These meatballs are lower in fat and cholesterol than others. Make some of these in addition to regular meatballs so dieting family members can also enjoy the meal.

INGREDIENTS | SERVES 10

5 thick slices day-old or toasted Italian bread

2 shallots, minced

½ bulb garlic, minced

1 cup mushrooms, sliced

Zest and juice of 1 medium lemon

¼ bunch fresh parsley, chopped, divided

2 pounds ground chicken

2 large egg whites

½ teaspoon freshly cracked black pepper

1½ tablespoons olive oil

¼ cup dry white wine (not cooking wine)

2 tablespoons cold unsalted butter

Substituting Onions

Onions can be used in many recipes in place of leeks, shallots, and even scallions, unless otherwise specified. You can also vary the type of onion you use in most recipes. Red onions have a strong, sweet flavor, while yellow and white onions are much milder varieties.

1. Soak the bread in water for 1 minute. Thoroughly squeeze out all the liquid.

2. In a large mixing bowl, thoroughly combine the bread, shallots, garlic, mushrooms, lemon zest, half the parsley, the chicken, egg whites, and black pepper. Form into 2" balls.

3. Heat the oil over medium heat in a large sauté pan. Add the meatballs and cover. Sauté for about 20 minutes until cooked through, turning occasionally to lightly brown on all sides.

4. Pour in the lemon juice and wine. Simmer uncovered until the liquid is reduced by half the volume. Reduce heat to low and add the cold butter and remaining parsley. Stir for 1 minute and serve.

Pork and Apple Meatballs

The addition of apple to these meatballs gives them a slightly sweet flavor. These are great to serve as part of an autumn meal.

INGREDIENTS | SERVES 10

1 tablespoon olive oil

5 thick slices day-old or toasted Italian bread

1 medium yellow onion, finely chopped

3 large tart apples, finely diced

2 sprigs fresh oregano, chopped

2 pounds lean ground pork

1 egg, lightly beaten

¾ cup chopped walnuts

½ teaspoon freshly cracked black pepper

1. Preheat the oven to 375°F. Lightly grease a baking sheet with the oil. Soak the bread in water for 1 minute. Thoroughly squeeze out all the liquid.

2. In a large mixing bowl, thoroughly combine all the ingredients. Form the mixture into 2" balls.

3. Place the meatballs on the prepared baking sheet. Bake for about 30 minutes until thoroughly cooked and golden brown.

4. Transfer the meatballs to paper towels to drain. Serve as desired.

Turkey and Fig Balls

For a fun variation on the classic Thanksgiving turkey, try serving these meatballs as part of the holiday feast.

INGREDIENTS | SERVES 10

5 thick slices day-old or toasted Italian bread

½ cup dried figs, chopped

1 medium yellow onion, diced

2 sprigs fresh sage, chopped or 1 tablespoon dried

2 pounds ground turkey

1 large egg, lightly beaten

½ cup chopped pecans

½ teaspoon freshly cracked black pepper

1. Soak the bread in water for 1 minute. Thoroughly squeeze out all the liquid.

2. In a large mixing bowl, thoroughly combine all the ingredients. Form the mixture into balls about 2"–3" in size.

3. Bake or fry the meatballs: To bake, preheat the oven to 375°F. Place the meatballs in a lightly greased baking pan and cover. Bake for 30 minutes. Uncover and brown for 5–10 minutes. To fry, heat about 1 tablespoon olive oil over medium heat in a skillet. Fry for 30 minutes uncovered, stirring occasionally until cooked through.

4. Transfer the meatballs to paper towels to drain. Serve plain, with sauce, or over pasta.

Veal and Date Balls

If you do not have dates on hand, raisins can be substituted. However, it's a good idea to have dates in the house. They complement many different kinds of meat.

INGREDIENTS | SERVES 10

5 thick slices day-old or toasted Italian bread

1 medium yellow onion, finely chopped

2 sprigs fresh oregano, chopped

2 sprigs fresh thyme, chopped

½ cup dried dates, finely diced

¼ cup pine nuts, finely diced

1 tablespoon olive oil

1½ pounds ground veal

½ pound Italian pork sausage, unformed and uncooked

1 large egg, lightly beaten

½ teaspoon freshly cracked black pepper

Dates

Dates can be purchased either semidry/fresh, or dried. The semidry/fresh type is softer and less sweet than the dried, and needs to be stored in the refrigerator, unlike dried dates. Dates originated in North African and Middle Eastern cuisine, but because of the proximity of these areas to southern Italy, dates are used in some Italian cuisine as well.

1. Soak the bread in water for 1 minute. Thoroughly squeeze out all the liquid. Peel and finely chop the onion.

2. In a large mixing bowl, combine all the ingredients. Form the mixture into balls about 2"–3" in size.

3. Bake or fry the meatballs: To bake, preheat the oven to 375°F. Place the meatballs in a lightly greased baking pan and cover. Bake for 30 minutes. Uncover and brown for 5–10 minutes. To fry, heat about 1 tablespoon olive oil over medium heat in a skillet. Fry for 30 minutes uncovered, stirring occasionally until cooked through.

4. Transfer the meatballs to paper towels to drain. Serve plain, with sauce, or over pasta.

Polpette con Pollo e Orzo (Chicken Meatballs with Orzo)

The arugula and goat cheese in these meatballs makes them special, but in a pinch, you could use parsley and another soft cheese, such as fontina, instead.

INGREDIENTS | SERVES 10

½ small bunch fresh arugula, chopped

½ bulb garlic, minced

½ pound goat cheese, crumbled

1½ pounds ground chicken

1 cup cooked orzo pasta

1 large egg, lightly beaten

½ teaspoon freshly cracked black pepper

1. In a large mixing bowl, combine all the ingredients. Form the mixture into balls about 2"–3" in size.

2. Bake or fry the meatballs: To bake, preheat the oven to 375°F. Place the meatballs in a lightly greased baking pan and cover. Bake for 30 minutes. Uncover and brown for 5–10 minutes. To fry, heat about 1 tablespoon olive oil over medium heat in a skillet. Fry for 30 minutes uncovered, stirring occasionally until cooked through.

3. Transfer the meatballs to paper towels to drain. Serve plain, with sauce, or over pasta.

Venison Meatballs

If you don't have venison available, you can substitute beef.

INGREDIENTS | SERVES 10

5 thick slices day-old or toasted Italian bread

¼ bunch fresh parsley, chopped

½ bulb garlic, minced

1½ pounds ground venison meat

½ pound Italian pork sausage, unformed and uncooked

1 large egg, lightly beaten

¾ cup dried currants or raisins

½ cup chopped pine nuts

½ teaspoon freshly cracked black pepper

1. Soak the bread in water for 1 minute. Thoroughly squeeze out all the liquid.

2. In a large mixing bowl, combine all the ingredients. Form the mixture into balls about 2"–3" in size.

3. Bake or fry the meatballs: To bake, preheat the oven to 375°F. Place the meatballs in a lightly greased baking pan and cover. Bake for 30 minutes. Uncover and brown for 5–10 minutes. To fry, heat about 1 tablespoon olive oil over medium heat in a large skillet. Fry for 30 minutes uncovered, stirring occasionally until cooked through.

4. Transfer the meatballs to paper towels to drain. Serve plain, with sauce, or over pasta.

Meatless Balls

Vegetarians and meat eaters alike will enjoy these. Serve them over pasta, as you would meatballs, or as appetizers.

INGREDIENTS | SERVES 10

2 tablespoons olive oil

3 large carrots, shredded

3 medium yellow onions, shredded

3 stalks celery, shredded

½ bulb garlic, minced

3 sprigs fresh oregano, chopped

2 cups cooked or canned cannellini beans, mashed

1 cup Basic Risotto (see Chapter 11)

2 large eggs, lightly beaten

½ teaspoon freshly cracked black pepper

1. In a large mixing bowl, combine all the ingredients. Form the mixture into balls about 2"–3" in size.

2. Bake or fry the veggie balls: To bake, preheat the oven to 375°F. Place the balls in a generously greased baking pan and cover. Bake for 15 minutes. Uncover and brown for 5–10 minutes. To fry, heat about 1 tablespoon olive oil over medium heat in a skillet. Fry for 15–20 minutes uncovered, stirring occasionally until cooked through.

3. Transfer the veggie balls to paper towels to drain. Serve plain, with sauce, or over pasta.

Soaking Beans

Soaking dried beans in water overnight makes them cook more quickly, but soaking is usually not necessary. Tiny beans like lentils never require soaking. Soaked beans tend to break apart more during cooking, which is fine for soup but not for bean salad. To soak beans, submerge them in at least 3 inches of water in a container large enough to allow the beans to expand, and refrigerate.

Rosemary Chicken Meatballs

Don't throw away leftover mashed potatoes! This recipe gives you a great chance to use them.

INGREDIENTS | SERVES 10

2 shallots, minced

½ bulb garlic, minced

3 sprigs rosemary, chopped

2 pounds ground chicken

1 large egg, lightly beaten

½ cup fresh-grated Parmesan cheese

1 cup mashed potatoes

½ teaspoon freshly cracked black pepper

1. In a large mixing bowl, combine all the ingredients. Form the mixture into balls about 2"–3" in size.

2. Bake or fry the meatballs: To bake, preheat the oven to 375°F. Place the meatballs in a lightly greased baking pan and cover. Bake for 30 minutes. Uncover and brown for 5–10 minutes. To fry, heat about 1 tablespoon olive oil over medium heat in a large skillet. Fry for 30 minutes uncovered, stirring occasionally until cooked through.

3. Transfer the meatballs to paper towels to drain. Serve plain, with sauce, or over pasta.

Agnello Polpette (Lamb Meatballs)

Serve this with Spelt Pasta (see Chapter 13), oil and balsamic vinegar, and Roasted Garlic Paste (see Chapter 3).

INGREDIENTS | SERVES 10

5 thick slices day-old or toasted Italian bread

3 shallots, minced

½ bulb garlic, minced

4 sprigs mint, chopped

1½ pounds ground lamb

½ pound Italian pork sausage, unformed and uncooked

1 large egg, lightly beaten

½ teaspoon freshly cracked black pepper

1. Soak the bread in water for 1 minute. Thoroughly squeeze out all the liquid.

2. In a large mixing bowl, combine all the ingredients. Form the mixture into balls about 2"–3" in size.

3. Bake or fry the meatballs: To bake, preheat the oven to 375°F. Place the meatballs in a lightly greased baking pan and cover. Bake for 30 minutes. Uncover and brown for 5–10 minutes. To fry, heat about 1 tablespoon olive oil over medium heat in a skillet. Fry for 30 minutes uncovered, stirring occasionally until cooked through.

4. Transfer the meatballs to paper towels to drain. Serve plain, with sauce, or over pasta.

Eggplant Meatballs

You can roast the eggplant ahead of time to make for easy mixing. Just be sure to cool the eggplant before you work with it.

INGREDIENTS | SERVES 10

1 tablespoon olive oil

1 large eggplant

2 shallots, minced

3 cloves garlic, minced

¼ bunch fresh parsley, chopped

½ cup shredded mozzarella cheese

¾ pound ground beef

½ pound Italian pork sausage, unformed and uncooked

3 thick slices day-old or toasted Italian bread

½ teaspoon freshly cracked black pepper

1 large egg

Meatball Appetizers

Although you might not think of meatballs as a dish for entertaining, they make wonderful appetizers. Most meatball recipes can be adapted for use as appetizers by making the meatballs smaller, drizzling a pesto sauce over the top, inserting toothpicks, and placing them on a serving platter.

1. Preheat the oven to 375°F. Lightly grease a baking sheet with the oil.

2. Slice the eggplant lengthwise. Place cut-side down on the prepared baking sheet. Roast for 40 minutes. Let cool completely and then mash.

3. In a large mixing bowl, combine all the ingredients. Form the mixture into balls about 2"–3" in size.

4. Bake or fry the meatballs: To bake, preheat the oven to 375°F. Place the meatballs in a lightly greased baking pan and cover. Bake for 30 minutes. Uncover and brown for 5–10 minutes. To fry, heat about 1 tablespoon olive oil over medium heat in a skillet. Fry for 30 minutes uncovered, stirring occasionally until cooked through.

5. Transfer the meatballs to paper towels to drain. Serve plain, with sauce, or over pasta.

Meatballs in Egg-Lemon Sauce

Ground beef, pork, or lamb can easily be used as a substitute for the veal in this recipe.

INGREDIENTS | SERVES 6

2 pounds lean ground veal
2 medium onions, finely diced
½ cup dry bread crumbs
1 large egg, beaten
¼ cup extra-virgin olive oil, divided
¼ cup fresh mint, finely chopped
¼ cup fresh parsley, finely chopped
1 teaspoon dried oregano
½ teaspoon salt
½ teaspoon pepper
4 cups beef or veal stock
2 large eggs
Juice of 1 medium lemon

1. Preheat the oven to 400°F.

2. In a large mixing bowl, combine the meat, onions, bread crumbs, beaten egg, 2 tablespoons olive oil, mint, parsley, oregano, salt, and pepper; mix together well with your hands.

3. Using your fingers, take up small pieces of meat mix and fashion them into meatballs about the size of golf balls. Place in rows in a baking dish greased with the remaining olive oil. Bake 30–40 minutes until cooked.

4. In a stockpot, bring the stock to a boil. Add the meatballs; cover and simmer 10 minutes.

5. Beat the 2 remaining eggs in a mixing bowl; slowly add lemon juice and some of the hot stock in slow streams as you beat them to achieve a frothy mix.

6. Pour the egg-lemon mix into the pot with the meatballs. Cover and simmer another 2–3 minutes. Serve immediately.

Coconut Meatballs

These delicious meatballs fried in coconut oil are served with rice and a yummy coconut mushroom sauce.

INGREDIENTS | SERVES 6

2 pounds ground beef

1 large onion, diced

2 cloves garlic, pressed

2 large eggs

½ teaspoon sea salt

1 teaspoon ground cumin

1 teaspoon coriander

¼ teaspoon cayenne

½ teaspoon oyster sauce

1 cup coconut milk, divided

3 tablespoons coconut oil

½ cup portobello mushrooms, chopped

1 teaspoon potato starch flour

1 tablespoon cold water

2 teaspoons fresh chopped parsley, or to taste

Coconut Milk, Coconut Cream, and Creamed Coconut

When working with coconut recipes, it can be confusing when you see ingredients like coconut water, coconut milk, coconut cream, and creamed coconut. Each of these ingredients is different, but unless you work with coconut recipes a lot, you might not know the difference. Coconut water is the clear liquid inside the coconut. Coconut milk is made by blending the coconut meat with water and then straining out the "milk." The coconut cream will rise to the top of the coconut milk and can be skimmed off, much like cream from fresh whole cow's milk. To make creamed coconut, strain the liquid out of the coconut cream by passing it through several layers of cheesecloth or a fine sieve.

1. In a large bowl, combine the ground beef, onion, garlic, eggs, salt, cumin, coriander, cayenne, oyster sauce, and 4 tablespoons of coconut milk until well mixed. Shape into 1" balls.

2. In a heavy-bottomed skillet, heat the coconut oil over medium heat and cook the meatballs until browned, about 5 minutes.

3. Remove the meatballs from the skillet and add the mushrooms. Cook for 2–3 minutes, then add the remaining coconut milk. Stir, scraping the bottom of the skillet to loosen the meat juices from the bottom of the pan.

4. In a small bowl, mix the potato starch flour and cold water. Whisk into the coconut milk mixture; bring to a simmer. Cook for another 2–3 minutes, or until the sauce begins to thicken.

5. Serve the meatballs with rice and top with the coconut mushroom sauce and parsley.

Garlic Knots (Chapter 9)

Traditional Pesto (Chapter 3)

Melon and Prosciutto (Chapter 2)

Roasted Red Peppers (Chapter 15)

Basic Beef Meatballs (Chapter 8)

Chicken Marsala (Chapter 6)

Chilled Beet Soup (Chapter 4)

Limoncello Gelato (*Gelato di limoncello*)
(Chapter 16)

Fresh Mozzarella and Tomato Salad (Chapter 14)

Espresso Gelato (*Gelato di espresso*) (Chapter 16)

Asparagus–Egg White Frittata (Chapter 10)

Cheese Tortellini (Chapter 13)

Classic Fettuccine Alfredo (Chapter 13)

Cannellini Bean Salad (Chapter 14)

Classic Chicken Parmesan (Chapter 6)

Baked Smoked Ham (Chapter 5)

Spinach Pasta (Chapter 13)

Spicy Chicken Wings (Chapter 2)

Basil, Mozzarella, and Tomato Panini (Chapter 12)

Classic Biscotti (Chapter 16)

Basic Risotto (Chapter 11)

Traditional Lasagna (Chapter 13)

Pecan Broccoli (Chapter 15)

Hearty Cioppino (Chapter 7)

CHAPTER 9

Flatbreads, Pizza, and Focaccia

Basic Flatbread

Iodized salt is better to use in baking recipes. It dissolves faster, so you won't end up with gritty dough.

1. Sift together the flour and salt. Mix the flour and water in a mixer using a large dough hook for 3 minutes or until the ingredients are incorporated and the dough is formed. Let the dough rest for 1 hour in the refrigerator.

2. Form the dough into small balls. On a floured surface, use a floured rolling pin to roll out each ball into a circle about ½" thick.

3. For stovetop preparation, lightly grease a medium skillet with the oil and heat over medium heat. For oven preparation, preheat the oven to 400°F and lightly grease a baking sheet with the oil.

4. Lightly brown the bread until thoroughly cooked, about 5 minutes per side.

Whole-Wheat Flatbread

You can use all whole-wheat flour for more nutritious dough, but using a bit of all-purpose white flour makes for easier handling.

Knife Know-How

Serrated-edge "bread" knives are great for cutting crumbly things that would crush under the pressure of a smooth blade. But for clean slices, especially when carving cooked meats, there's no substitute for a razor-sharp slicing knife.

1. Sift together the flours and salt. Mix the flour and water in a mixer using a large dough hook for 3 minutes or until the ingredients are incorporated and the dough is formed. Let the dough rest for 1 hour in the refrigerator.

2. Form the dough into small balls. On a floured surface, use a floured rolling pin to roll out each ball into a circle about ½" thick.

3. For stovetop preparation, lightly grease a medium skillet with the oil and heat over medium heat. For oven preparation, preheat the oven to 400°F and lightly grease a baking sheet with the oil.

4. Lightly brown the bread until thoroughly cooked, about 5 minutes per side.

Chickpea Flatbread

Chickpea flour is found in the international or Middle Eastern section of grocery stores and specialty markets.

INGREDIENTS | SERVES 10

2 cups chickpea flour
2 cups all-purpose flour
½ teaspoon iodized salt
1–1¼ cups cold water
1 teaspoon olive oil

1. Sift together the flours and salt. Mix the flour and water in a mixer using a large dough hook for 3 minutes or until the ingredients are incorporated and the dough is formed. Let the dough rest for 1 hour in the refrigerator.

2. Form the dough into small balls. On a floured surface, use a floured rolling pin to roll out each ball into a circle about ½" thick.

3. For stovetop preparation, lightly grease a medium skillet with the oil and heat over medium heat. For oven preparation, preheat the oven to 400°F and lightly grease a baking sheet with the oil.

4. Lightly brown the bread until thoroughly cooked, about 5 minutes per side.

Onion Flatbread

This onion-flavored bread is great for dipping in soups or eating as a snack. For a snack, it doesn't need more than a light toasting and a bit of butter.

INGREDIENTS | SERVES 10

3½ cups all-purpose flour

½ teaspoon iodized salt

1–1¼ cups cold water

1 large yellow onion, minced

1 teaspoon olive oil

How Long Do You Need to Knead?

Developing a feel for how much to knead your dough comes with time and experience. If you overwork it, you overdevelop the gluten in the dough, making it tough. This causes the bread to have a chewy, unpleasant texture. A few quick motions should be all the kneading your dough needs.

1. Sift together the flour and salt. Mix the flour and water in a mixer, using a large dough hook for 3 minutes or until the ingredients are incorporated and the dough is formed. Add the onion and incorporate into the dough. Let the dough rest for 1 hour in the refrigerator.

2. Form the dough into small balls. On a floured surface, use a floured rolling pin to roll out each ball into a circle about ½" thick.

3. For stovetop preparation, lightly grease a medium skillet with the oil and heat over medium heat. For oven preparation, preheat the oven to 400°F and lightly grease a baking sheet with the oil.

4. Lightly brown the bread until thoroughly cooked, about 5 minutes per side.

Roasted Garlic Flatbread

Flatbread is often served with soup, cheese, or salad. You could get a little more creative and use this or the other flatbread recipes as a crust for pizza toppings.

INGREDIENTS | SERVES 10

2¾ cups whole-wheat flour

1 cup all-purpose flour

½ teaspoon iodized salt

½ cup Roasted Garlic Paste (see Chapter 3)

1–1¼ cups cold water

1 teaspoon olive oil

1. Sift together both flours and the salt. Mix the garlic paste with the sifted flour. Mix the flour mixture and water in a mixer using a large dough hook for 3 minutes or until the ingredients are incorporated and the dough is formed. Let the dough rest for 1 hour in the refrigerator.

2. Form the dough into small balls. On a floured surface, use a floured rolling pin to roll out each ball into a circle about ½" thick.

3. For stovetop preparation, lightly grease a medium skillet with the oil and heat over medium heat. For oven preparation, preheat the oven to 400°F and lightly grease a baking sheet with the oil.

4. Lightly brown the bread until thoroughly cooked, about 5 minutes per side.

Herbed Flatbread

Only use fresh herbs in this recipe. Dried herbs will not give the flavor needed to season this bread.

3 cups whole-wheat flour
1 cup all-purpose flour
½ teaspoon iodized salt
1–1¼ cups cold water
¼ bunch fresh herb of choice, chopped
1 teaspoon olive oil

1. Sift together the flours and salt. Mix the flour and water in a mixer using a large dough hook for 3 minutes or until the ingredients are incorporated and the dough is formed. Add the herb and incorporate into the dough. Let the dough rest for 1 hour in the refrigerator.

2. Form the dough into small balls. On a floured surface, use a floured rolling pin to roll out each ball into a circle about ½" thick.

3. For stovetop preparation, lightly grease a medium skillet with the oil and heat over medium heat. For oven preparation, preheat the oven to 400°F and lightly grease a baking sheet with the oil.

4. Lightly brown the bread until thoroughly cooked, about 5 minutes per side.

Saffron Flatbread

Chop the saffron threads well before incorporating them. If you prefer to use powdered saffron, use about ¼ teaspoon, or about half the amount of threads called for. Powdered saffron does dissolve better than saffron threads.

INGREDIENTS | SERVES 10

4 cups all-purpose flour
½ teaspoon saffron threads
½ teaspoon iodized salt
1–1¼ cups cold water
1 teaspoon olive oil

1. Sift together the flour, saffron, and salt. Mix the flour and water in a mixer using a large dough hook for 3 minutes or until the ingredients are incorporated and the dough is formed. Let the dough rest for 1 hour in the refrigerator.

2. Form the dough into small balls. On a floured surface, use a floured rolling pin to roll out each ball into a circle about ½" thick.

3. For stovetop preparation, lightly grease a medium skillet with the oil and heat over medium heat. For oven preparation, preheat the oven to 400°F and lightly grease a baking sheet with the oil.

4. Lightly brown the bread until thoroughly cooked, about 5 minutes per side.

Cornmeal Flatbread

Each culture has its own version of flatbread. This one, made with cornmeal, is similar to a Mexican tortilla.

INGREDIENTS | SERVES 10

2 cups cornmeal (or corn flour)

2 cups all-purpose flour

½ teaspoon iodized salt

1–1¼ cups cold water

1 teaspoon olive oil

1. Sift together the cornmeal, flour, and salt. Mix the flour mixture and water in a mixer using a large dough hook for 3 minutes or until the ingredients are incorporated and the dough is formed. Let the dough rest for 1 hour in the refrigerator.

2. Form the dough into small balls. On a floured surface, use a floured rolling pin to roll out each ball into a circle about ½" thick.

3. For stovetop preparation, lightly grease a medium skillet with the oil and heat over medium heat. For oven preparation, preheat the oven to 400°F and lightly grease a baking sheet with the oil.

4. Lightly brown the bread until thoroughly cooked, about 5 minutes per side.

Barley Flatbread

Barley flour is made from ground barley, which is a whole grain. Barley is a common ingredient in soups, and this bread is great for dipping!

INGREDIENTS | SERVES 10

3 cups barley flour
1 cup all-purpose flour
½ teaspoon iodized salt
1–1¼ cups cold water
1 teaspoon olive oil

1. Sift together the flours and salt. Mix the flour and water in a mixer using a large dough hook for 3 minutes or until the ingredients are incorporated and the dough is formed. Let the dough rest for 1 hour in the refrigerator.

2. Form the dough into small balls. On a floured surface, use a floured rolling pin to roll out each ball into a circle about ½" thick.

3. For stovetop preparation, lightly grease a medium skillet with the oil and heat over medium heat. For oven preparation, preheat the oven to 400°F and lightly grease a baking sheet with the oil.

4. Lightly brown the bread until thoroughly cooked, about 5 minutes per side.

Fried Dough

This is a classic Italian street vendor's treat. Fried dough is delicious with any of a number of sweet toppings, including powdered sugar, honey, and jam.

INGREDIENTS | SERVES 10

1 (¼-ounce) packet dry active yeast

¼ cup warm water (should not exceed 115°F)

4 large eggs

¼ cup melted unsalted butter

1 pound all-purpose flour

1 teaspoon granulated sugar

¼ teaspoon iodized salt

2 cups vegetable oil

Confectioners' sugar, for garnish

Yeast

When dissolving yeast in warm water to use in a baking recipe, you must take care that the water is not too hot. If the water is over 115°F, it will kill the yeast and the bread will not rise. The same result will occur if the yeast you use is not fresh. Always check the package for freshness dates and storing instructions.

1. In a small bowl, stir together the yeast and the water and let stand for about 5 minutes until foamy.

2. In a medium-sized bowl, beat the eggs and stir in the slightly cooled melted butter.

3. Sift together the flour, sugar, and salt in a large bowl.

4. Combine the egg mixture with the dissolved yeast mixture.

5. Combine the wet and dry ingredients in a mixer using a dough hook until fully incorporated and the dough forms into a ball.

6. Cover and let rise for 1 hour in a warm place. Punch down the dough and knead it. Form the dough into flat 4" circular pieces (½" thick), cover, and let rise in a warm place again for 30 minutes.

7. Heat the oil over medium-high heat in a large skillet. Fry the dough pieces one at a time until browned and cooked through. Transfer the fried dough to paper towels to drain. Let cool slightly, then sprinkle with confectioners' sugar and serve.

Easter Egg Bread

This tasty bread is a tradition for Easter Sunday dinner, and the colored eggs make it a visual treat as well.

INGREDIENTS | SERVES 10

1 (¼-ounce) dry active packet yeast

¼ cup warm water (should not exceed 115°F)

1½ cups scalded milk (100°F–115°F)

¼ cup unsalted butter

5 cups all-purpose flour

½ cup granulated sugar

½ teaspoon iodized salt

3 colored hard-boiled eggs

1. In a small bowl, combine the yeast and the water and let stand for about 5 minutes until foamy.

2. Once the scalded milk has cooled, place in a medium bowl and stir in the butter.

3. In a large bowl, sift together the flour, sugar, and salt (you may need to add more or less flour depending on the level of humidity).

4. Mix together all the ingredients except the colored eggs in a mixer with a dough hook at medium speed for about 5 minutes until the dough forms into a ball. Let the dough rest in a warm place for about 1 hour until it rises.

5. Preheat the oven to 375°F. Punch down the dough and form into desired shape (loaf or braid). Press the eggs into the top of the dough, allowing no more than ⅓ of each egg to show. (If too much of each egg is showing, it could crack or explode from the heat of the oven.)

6. Bake for about 1 hour until the bread is golden brown.

Crusty Egg Bread

This is a great bread to serve as part of a brunch buffet, or with a pot of soup and a crisp salad.

INGREDIENTS | SERVES 10

2 teaspoons olive oil

1 loaf whole-grain Italian bread

10 thin slices prosciutto

1 cup mascarpone cheese

1 shallot, minced

10 large eggs, beaten

¼ bunch fresh chervil, chopped

½ teaspoon freshly cracked black pepper

1. Preheat the oven to 350°F. Lightly grease a baking sheet with the olive oil. Slice the bread into 10 thick (1½"–2") slices, then hollow out part of the center of each (leaving approximately 1" in diameter, including crust) to form a shallow bread cup. Reserve the centers for another use.

2. Cut the prosciutto into thin ⅛"–¼" strips.

3. Lay out the bread cups on the prepared baking sheet. Place 1½–2 tablespoons mascarpone in each, then add the shallot. Pour in the eggs, filling the bread cups to the top but being careful not to let them overflow. Top with the prosciutto.

4. Bake for about 10–15 minutes until the eggs are set and lightly brown.

5. Sprinkle with the chervil and pepper and serve.

Garlic and Herb Focaccia

This focaccia is great with soup or salad for a light lunch. Serve warm with freshly grated Parmesan cheese.

INGREDIENTS | SERVES 10

2 teaspoons olive oil, divided

1 (¼-ounce) dry active packet yeast

½ cup warm water (should not exceed 115°F)

6 cups all-purpose flour

¼ teaspoon salt

2 cups water

½ bunch fresh basil, chopped

3 cloves garlic, minced

Focaccia Dough

There is a quick trick you can use to customize your focaccia dough. To make it crispier, drizzle a little olive oil on the crust before baking. To make the bread softer, brush the crust with oil immediately after it comes out of the oven.

1. Lightly grease a 13" × 9" baking pan with 1 teaspoon of the olive oil.

2. In a small bowl, stir together the yeast and warm water and let stand for about 5 minutes until foamy.

3. In a medium bowl, sift together the flour and salt (you may need more or less flour depending on the level of humidity—use more in a humid environment to keep the dough from becoming too sticky).

4. Mix together the flour, dissolved yeast mixture, and the water by hand or in a mixer with a dough hook at slow speed for 3–5 minutes until the dough forms into a ball. Remove the dough from the bowl, cover with a clean kitchen towel, and let rest on a floured surface for 1 hour.

5. While the dough rests, combine the basil and garlic with the remaining oil.

6. Place the dough in the prepared pan, either leaving it as a ball or forming it as desired. Use your fingers to gently push the garlic and basil into the bread, evenly distributing them over the entire surface. Cover with a kitchen towel and let rise in a warm place for about 1 hour.

7. Preheat the oven to 425°F. Bake the bread for 1 hour until lightly brown.

Whole-Wheat Focaccia

This focaccia dough can be used for deep-dish and Sicilian pizza recipes.
Just add various pizza toppings and bake until lightly brown.

INGREDIENTS | SERVES 10

1 teaspoon olive oil

1 (¼-ounce) packet dry active yeast

2½ cups warm water (should not exceed 115°F)

5 cups whole-wheat flour

2 cups all-purpose flour

Pinch salt

1 cup water

Focaccia Variations

Cooked vegetables or herbs can be added to the focaccia recipe to make different flavored breads. Also, you can shape focaccia dough into any shape you like. Create long rolls for sub sandwiches or tight balls for bread to serve with dinner.

1. Lightly grease a 13" × 9" baking pan with the olive oil.

2. In a small bowl, stir together the yeast and warm water and let stand for about 5 minutes until foamy.

3. In a large bowl, sift together the flours and salt.

4. Mix together the flour, dissolved yeast mixture, and water by hand or in a mixer with a dough hook until the dough forms into a ball. Remove from the mixing bowl and cover with a clean kitchen towel. Let rise in a warm place for about 45 minutes.

5. Knead the dough for 3 minutes, place in the prepared pan, and cover with a towel. Let rise again for about 30 minutes. Either leave the dough as a ball or form as desired.

6. Preheat the oven to 425°F. Bake for 45 minutes until lightly brown.

Basic Cheese Pizza

This recipe has as many variations as your imagination allows.
Experiment with different toppings and combinations.

INGREDIENTS | SERVES 10

1 tablespoon olive oil, divided

1 recipe Basic Flatbread (see recipe in this chapter), unformed and uncooked

1 cup Old World Gravy (Long-Cooking Tomato Sauce) (see Chapter 3)

1 cup shredded provolone cheese

1 cup shredded mozzarella cheese

½ bulb garlic, minced

½ teaspoon dried oregano

½ teaspoon dried basil

½ teaspoon dried marjoram

½ teaspoon freshly cracked black pepper

1. Preheat the oven to 425°F. Lightly grease 2 pizza pans with ½ tablespoon of the oil.

2. Roll out the dough on a floured surface into 2 large circles. Place the rolled dough on the pizza pans.

3. Ladle the sauce over the dough, spreading it out evenly over the surface. Top with the cheeses and sprinkle with the garlic, herbs, and pepper. Drizzle with the remaining oil.

4. Bake for 15–20 minutes until the cheese is melted and the dough is cooked through.

Sicilian Pizza

The oblong shape makes this traditional Sicilian Pizza. Try topping
this with sliced olives and fresh sage or rosemary.

INGREDIENTS | SERVES 10

1 tablespoon olive oil, divided

1 recipe Whole-Wheat Focaccia dough (see recipe in this chapter), uncooked

1½ cups Old World Gravy (Long-Cooking Tomato Sauce) (see Chapter 3)

1½ cups shredded mozzarella cheese

¼ cup fresh-grated Romano cheese

4 sprigs fresh basil, chopped

4 sprigs fresh oregano, chopped

½ teaspoon freshly cracked black pepper

1. Preheat the oven to 425°F. Lightly grease an oblong pan with ½ tablespoon of the oil.

2. Roll out the dough on a floured surface into a 2"-thick rectangle and place in the prepared pan. Allow to rise again for 30 minutes.

3. Ladle the sauce over the dough, spreading it out evenly over the entire surface. Top with cheese and sprinkle with the herbs and pepper. Drizzle with the remaining oil.

4. Bake for 20–25 minutes.

Frisedda

Frisedda originates in the Puglia section of Italy. This twice-baked bread can be served as is, or soaked in water and seasoned with oil, fresh tomato, oregano, and salt.

INGREDIENTS | SERVES 10

1 tablespoon olive oil, divided

1 recipe Whole-Wheat Focaccia dough (see recipe in this chapter), uncooked

1. Preheat the oven to 400°F. Lightly grease a baking sheet with ½ tablespoon of the oil.

2. Roll out the dough on a floured surface, separate it into 3" balls, and roll out the balls slightly. Poke a hole in the center of each to form a bagel shape. Allow to rise for 30 minutes.

3. Place the bread on the prepared pan. Bake for 15 minutes.

4. Slice in half crosswise and lay the halves cut-side up on the pan. Drizzle the halves with the remaining oil. Return to the oven for 10 minutes until toasted golden.

Bread Sticks

This Italian classic is great for dipping in tomato sauce, Alfredo sauce, or just extra-virgin olive oil with pepper.

INGREDIENTS | SERVES 10

1 tablespoon olive oil, divided

1 recipe Basic Flatbread (see recipe in this chapter), unformed and uncooked

1. Preheat the oven to 400°F. Lightly grease a baking sheet with ½ tablespoon of the oil.

2. Roll out the dough on a floured surface until about 1" thick and cut into 6"-long strips.

3. Place strips on the prepared baking sheet, drizzle with the remaining oil, and bake for 15–20 minutes.

Garlic Knots

*Serve these in a linen-lined basket at dinner. They are especially
great for sopping up sauce after a hearty pasta meal.*

INGREDIENTS | SERVES 4

1 tablespoon olive oil, divided

1 recipe Whole-Wheat Focaccia dough
(see recipe in this chapter), uncooked

1 bulb garlic, minced

½ teaspoon freshly cracked black
pepper

1 teaspoon dried parsley (optional)

¼ cup fresh-grated Parmesan cheese
(optional)

Garlic

Aglio is the Italian word for "garlic." It is a
staple that appears extensively, both
cooked and raw, in Italian cuisine. It is one
of the oldest known cultivated plants and is
closely related to the onion. The bulb, or
head, is a cluster of cloves connected at
the root end and held together by papery
skin. Store in an open container, in a cool,
dark, dry place. Unpeeled garlic will stay
fresh for 3–4 weeks.

1. Lightly grease a baking sheet with ½ tablespoon of the oil.

2. Roll out the dough on a floured surface to 1" thick and cut into 12" strands. Tie each strip loosely into a knot, stretching gently if necessary to make four (4") knots. Place the knots on the prepared pan, cover with a clean kitchen towel, and let rise in a warm place.

3. Preheat the oven to 425°F. Sprinkle the dough knots with the remaining oil, then sprinkle with the garlic, pepper, and parsley.

4. Bake for 15–20 minutes. Sprinkle with the cheese if using and serve.

CHAPTER 10

Frittatas

Basic Frittata

All of the frittata recipes in this book call for potatoes. Potatoes are a common ingredient in frittatas, but they're not a necessity. You can vary these recipes according to your tastes and moods.

INGREDIENTS | SERVES 10

5 large russet potatoes
10 large eggs
½ cup whole milk
¼ cup shredded mozzarella cheese
2 tablespoons olive oil
2 medium yellow onions, sliced
½ teaspoon freshly cracked black pepper

Italian Omelet

The frittata is the Italian version of the omelet. Once you know how to make the basic frittata, there are many ways you can vary the recipe by adding ingredients. You can make frittatas with almost any type of vegetable, cheese, meat, or fish.

1. Preheat the oven to 375°F. Peel the potatoes if desired and thinly slice them.

2. In a medium bowl, beat the eggs. Whisk in the milk and cheese.

3. Heat the oil over medium heat in a large ovenproof frying pan. Add the potatoes and onions. Cover and cook for 3 minutes. Turn the potatoes, cover, and cook for 3 more minutes. Continue cooking and turning the potatoes every 3–5 minutes until tender and lightly browned.

4. Pour in the egg mixture and mix thoroughly.

5. Place the pan in the oven and bake uncovered until the egg is thoroughly cooked and set, about 15–20 minutes. Serve sprinkled with black pepper.

Bell Pepper Frittata

This is the Italian version of the Western omelet. You can use Idaho or red potatoes in this recipe.

INGREDIENTS | SERVES 10

4 large russet potatoes
10 large eggs
½ cup whole milk
¼ cup fresh-grated Parmesan cheese
3 tablespoons olive oil
2 medium red bell peppers, diced
2 medium green bell peppers, diced
1 medium yellow bell pepper, diced
2 Vidalia onions, diced
½ teaspoon freshly cracked black pepper

1. Preheat the oven to 375°F. Peel the potatoes if desired. Thinly slice the potatoes.

2. In a large bowl, beat the eggs. Whisk in the milk and cheese.

3. Heat the oil over medium heat in a large ovenproof frying pan. Add the potatoes. Cover and cook for 3 minutes. Turn the potatoes, cover, and cook for 3 more minutes. Add the peppers and onions, stir, and cover. Continue cooking and turning the potatoes every 3–5 minutes until tender and lightly browned.

4. Pour in the egg mixture and mix thoroughly.

5. Place the pan in the oven and bake uncovered until the egg is set, about 15–20 minutes. Serve sprinkled with black pepper.

Four-Cheese Frittata

Serve this frittata warm with fresh, crusty Italian bread and a leafy green salad on the side.

INGREDIENTS | SERVES 10

5 medium red potatoes
10 large eggs
½ cup whole milk
½ cup shredded mozzarella cheese
½ cup part-skim ricotta cheese
¼ cup mascarpone cheese
¼ cup fresh-grated Parmesan cheese
2 tablespoons olive oil
3 Vidalia onions, sliced
¼ bunch fresh parsley, chopped
½ teaspoon freshly cracked black pepper

1. Preheat the oven to 375°F. Peel the potatoes if desired. Thinly slice the potatoes.

2. In a large bowl, beat the eggs. Whisk in the milk and cheeses.

3. Heat the oil over medium heat in a large ovenproof sauté pan. Add the potatoes and onions. Cover and cook for 3 minutes. Turn the potatoes, cover, and cook for 3 more minutes. Continue cooking and turning the potatoes every 3–5 minutes until tender and lightly browned.

4. Pour in the egg and cheese mixture and mix thoroughly.

5. Place the pan in the oven and bake uncovered until the egg is set, about 15–20 minutes. Serve sprinkled with the parsley and black pepper.

Grilled Vegetable Frittata

The vegetables can be grilled ahead of time and set aside until you're ready to prepare the rest of the dish.

INGREDIENTS | SERVES 10

¼ cup, plus 1 teaspoon olive oil, divided

6 shallots, minced

1 large eggplant, cut into 1"-thick slices

2 medium zucchini, cut into 1"-thick slices

2 medium red bell peppers, seeded and halved

2 medium red onions, cut into 1"-thick slices

12 large eggs

½ cup whole milk

¼ cup fresh-grated Asiago cheese

½ teaspoon freshly cracked black pepper

Zucchini

Zucchini is a wonderfully versatile squash that can be grown in almost any climate. It is good when small and still has many uses as it grows large. Many cooks use it instead of eggplant because it adds a subtle flavor and a great deal of substance to a dish. It also works much like tofu, soaking up the other flavors.

1. Preheat the oven to 350°F. Lightly grease a baking dish with 1 teaspoon oil. Preheat the grill to medium temperature.

2. Mix together the shallots and ¼ cup oil in a shallow bowl large enough to dip the vegetable slices in. Dip the vegetables in the oil mixture and shake off excess. Grill for 2 minutes on each side. Remove and drain on a rack with paper towels underneath to catch the drippings.

3. Slice the grilled vegetables into bite-sized pieces. Layer the vegetables in the prepared baking dish.

4. In a large bowl, beat the eggs. Whisk in the milk and cheese. Pour the egg mixture over the vegetables.

5. Bake for about 20 minutes uncovered until the egg is set. Serve sprinkled with black pepper.

Sun-Dried Tomato and Fresh Basil Frittata

Sun-dried tomatoes are prepared at the end of July or the start of August, when the sun is very hot. They are cut in half, liberally salted, and left out in the sun for 4 or 5 days. You can dry your own tomatoes in a 200°F oven for 8 hours.

INGREDIENTS | SERVES 10

4 medium red potatoes

10 large eggs

½ cup whole milk

2 tablespoons olive oil

2 shallots, minced

½ cup sun-dried tomatoes (rehydrated with 1 cup water)

½ bunch fresh basil, sliced, divided

½ cup shredded mozzarella cheese

1 teaspoon freshly cracked black pepper, divided

Mozzarella Cheese

Mozzarella is a cheese that is commonly associated with Italian cooking. It has a texture that is soft and elastic, and its taste is sweet and milky. The best way to buy it is fresh, in water. It comes in various shapes and sizes, such as large and small balls.

1. Preheat the oven to 350°F. Peel the potatoes if desired. Thinly slice the potatoes.

2. In a large bowl, beat the eggs. Whisk in the milk.

3. Heat the oil over medium heat in an ovenproof frying pan. Add the potatoes. Cover and cook for 3 minutes. Turn the potatoes, cover, and cook for 3 more minutes. Add the shallots, stir, and cover. Continue cooking and turning the potatoes every 3–5 minutes until tender and lightly browned.

4. Pour in the egg mixture. Stir in the tomatoes, ¾ of the basil, the cheese, and ½ teaspoon black pepper.

5. Cover the pan and place it in the oven. Bake for 15 minutes. Uncover and bake for 5 minutes until the egg is set. Serve sprinkled with the remaining basil and black pepper.

Asparagus–Egg White Frittata

This frittata is a very healthy option, especially for those who are trying to lower cholesterol intake.

INGREDIENTS | SERVES 10

2 tablespoons olive oil, divided

1 pound fresh asparagus

1 large tomato

1 (5–6 ounce) package mushrooms

18 large egg whites

1 yellow onion, minced

½ cup shredded Parmesan cheese

½ teaspoon freshly cracked black pepper (optional)

Preparing Asparagus

The best way to trim the ends of asparagus spears is to gently hold each end of the spear and bend until the spear breaks. Just don't throw away the ends. You can freeze the "woody" ends for later use in vegetable stock.

1. Preheat the oven to 350°F. Lightly grease a large baking pan with 1 tablespoon of the oil. Clean the asparagus and break off the tough ends. Dice the tomato. Wipe the mushrooms clean with a damp cloth and thinly slice.

2. In a large bowl, whip the egg whites with an electric mixer until stiff peaks form.

3. Heat the remaining oil over medium heat in a large frying pan. Add the onions, stir, and cover. Cook for 3–5 minutes until the onions are soft.

4. Meanwhile, blanch the asparagus in boiling water for about 3 minutes until just tender. Shock in ice water and drain.

5. Place alternating layers of the onions, asparagus, tomatoes, and mushrooms in the prepared baking pan. Pour the egg whites over the top to cover all the ingredients. Sprinkle with the cheese.

6. Bake for 15–20 minutes uncovered until the egg is thoroughly cooked. Serve with black pepper sprinkled over the top if desired.

Baked Potato and Mascarpone Frittata

*The mascarpone makes this a very rich frittata. You will likely only be able to
eat a small amount at a time, so don't add too many side dishes.*

INGREDIENTS | SERVES 10

1 tablespoon olive oil

6 medium baking potatoes, baked
and cooled

6 large eggs

1 bunch scallions, sliced

1 cup mascarpone cheese

4 plum tomatoes, finely chopped

¼ bunch fresh parsley, chopped

½ teaspoon freshly cracked black
pepper

1. Preheat the oven to 350°F. Lightly grease a large baking pan with the oil. Peel the potatoes and slice lengthwise into 1"-thick rounds.

2. In a medium bowl, beat the eggs.

3. Arrange the potato slices in an even layer in the prepared baking pan. Sprinkle with the scallions and dot with dollops of the mascarpone. Pour the eggs over the top.

4. Bake for 20–30 minutes uncovered until the egg is set. Top with the tomatoes, parsley, and black pepper.

Pasta Frittata

The peppery taste of the arugula enhances the flavor of the goat cheese and eggs in this dish.

INGREDIENTS | SERVES 10

1 tablespoon olive oil

1 pound penne pasta

10 large eggs

½ cup whole milk

2 cups fresh arugula

3 shallots, minced

5 plum tomatoes, sliced lengthwise

½ pound goat cheese

½ teaspoon freshly cracked black
pepper

4 scallions, thinly sliced

1. Preheat the oven to 350°F. Grease a large baking pan with the oil. Cook the pasta until al dente according to package directions and drain.

2. In a large bowl, beat the eggs. Whisk in the milk.

3. Layer the pasta, arugula, shallots, tomatoes, and goat cheese in the prepared baking pan. Pour in the egg mixture and sprinkle with pepper.

4. Cover and bake for 20 minutes. Uncover and bake until the egg is set, about 10 more minutes. Top with the scallions and serve.

Cipolla Frittata (Onion Frittata)

You can use Spanish or yellow onions in this recipe instead of Vidalia onions, if you prefer.

INGREDIENTS | SERVES 10

¼ pound sliced Genoa salami or soppressata
¼ pound sliced pepperoni
2 medium red potatoes
10 large eggs
½ cup whole milk
2 tablespoons olive oil
2 Vidalia onions, sliced into rings
1 medium red onion, sliced into rings
1 leek, sliced thick
¾ cup ricotta
½ bunch scallions, thinly sliced
½ teaspoon freshly cracked black pepper

1. Preheat the oven to 350°F. Finely dice the sliced salami and pepperoni. Peel the potatoes if desired. Thinly slice the potatoes.

2. In a large bowl, beat the eggs. Whisk in the milk.

3. Heat the oil over medium heat in a large ovenproof frying pan. Add the potatoes and the Vidalia and red onions. Cover and cook for about 20 minutes, turning occasionally until the potatoes and onions are just tender. Add the leeks, cover, and cook for 3 minutes. Remove from heat.

4. Dot with dollops of the ricotta and sprinkle the salami and pepperoni over the top. Pour in the egg mixture.

5. Place the pan in the oven and bake for 15–20 minutes uncovered until the egg is set. Top with the scallions and black pepper and serve.

Toasted Italian Bread Frittata

This dish is great to prepare ahead of time and serve as part of a brunch when entertaining.

INGREDIENTS | SERVES 10

1 large loaf crusty Italian bread
2 tablespoons olive oil, divided
12 large eggs
½ cup whole milk
2 medium yellow onions, thinly sliced
½ pound pancetta, finely diced
½ pound provolone, shredded
3 sprigs fresh basil, sliced, divided
½ teaspoon freshly cracked black pepper

1. Preheat the broiler. Slice the bread into 2"-thick slices and toast in the oven until golden brown. Cut or tear the bread into large cubes.

2. Change the oven setting to Bake and preheat to 375°F. Lightly grease a large baking pan with 1 tablespoon of the oil.

3. In a large bowl, beat the eggs. Whisk in the milk.

4. Heat the remaining oil in a large ovenproof frying pan. Sauté the onions for 3 minutes. Add the pancetta and cook for 1 minute. Sprinkle in the cheese, ½ of the basil, and the bread. Immediately pour in the egg mixture, stir, and cover.

5. Cover the pan and place in the oven. Bake for 20 minutes. Uncover and bake for 5–10 minutes until the egg is set. Sprinkle with the remaining basil and black pepper and serve.

Risotto Frittata

*This is a great recipe for using your leftover risotto from last night's dinner.
Of course, you can also make the risotto fresh for the recipe.*

INGREDIENTS | SERVES 10

1 tablespoon olive oil
10 large eggs
1 cup whole milk
6 sprigs fresh oregano, chopped
3 cups Basic Risotto (see Chapter 11)
3 cups cooked or canned cannellini beans
½ teaspoon freshly cracked black pepper

1. Preheat the oven to 350°F. Lightly grease a large baking pan with the oil.

2. In a large bowl, beat the eggs. Whisk in the milk and chopped oregano.

3. In a separate bowl, mix together the risotto and beans. Drop spoonfuls of the risotto-bean mixture into the prepared baking pan. Pour in the egg mixture.

4. Cover and bake for 15 minutes. Uncover, and bake for 5–10 minutes until the egg is set.

5. Sprinkle with black pepper. Serve hot.

Smashed Potato and Capicola Frittata

*To make smashed potatoes: Simmer 5 thoroughly cleaned, large potatoes in
water until al dente. Drain, and heat the potatoes in a hot pan or oven until
dry. "Smash" the potatoes with ¼ cup milk and ¼ cup butter.*

INGREDIENTS | SERVES 10

1 tablespoon olive oil
½ pound thinly sliced capicola
3 large eggs
7 large egg whites
1 cup whole milk
8 cups smashed potatoes (about 5 potatoes)
3 shallots, minced
½ bunch fresh parsley, chopped
½ teaspoon red pepper flakes (optional)

1. Preheat the oven to 350°F. Lightly grease a large baking dish with the oil. Cut the sliced capicola into thin strips.

2. In a large bowl, beat together the eggs and egg whites. Whisk in the milk.

3. In another large bowl, mix together the smashed potatoes, shallots, parsley, and egg mixture. Pour into the prepared baking dish. Sprinkle with red pepper flakes if using.

4. Cover and bake for 20 minutes. Uncover and bake for 5–10 minutes until the egg is set.

Beef and Tomato Frittata

This is a great summertime frittata. Serve it for breakfast or lunch when you have company.

INGREDIENTS | SERVES 10

10 large eggs

½ cup whole milk

1 cup shredded mozzarella cheese

3 sprigs fresh marjoram or oregano, chopped, divided

1 tablespoon olive oil

1½ pounds lean ground beef

5 large red potatoes, peeled and thinly sliced

1 teaspoon freshly cracked black pepper, divided

2 medium onions of choice, diced

6 plum tomatoes, cut into wedges

1. Preheat the oven to 350°F.

2. In a large bowl, beat the eggs. Whisk in the milk, cheese, and half the chopped marjoram.

3. Heat the oil over medium heat in a large ovenproof frying pan. Add the beef and potatoes and sprinkle with ½ teaspoon black pepper. Cover and cook for 30 minutes, stirring occasionally. Add the onions and the remaining marjoram and cook for 5 minutes.

4. Thoroughly drain off all the grease. Add the tomatoes, pour in the egg mixture, and stir to mix.

5. Cover the pan and place in the oven. Bake for 15 minutes. Uncover and bake for 5–10 minutes until the egg is set.

6. Sprinkle with remaining pepper. Serve hot.

Sausage and Pepper Frittata

This dish of sausage, peppers, onions, and eggs goes well with fresh, crusty Italian bread. It can be served for brunch, lunch, or dinner.

INGREDIENTS | SERVES 10

10 large eggs
½ cup whole milk
¼ cup fresh-grated Asiago cheese
3 tablespoons olive oil
1 pound Italian sausage,
cut into ½"-thick slices
4 large red potatoes,
cut into ½"-thick slices
5 medium green bell peppers, sliced
into thin strips
2 large yellow onions, diced
½ teaspoon freshly cracked black
pepper

When to Grease a Pan

Some recipes ask you to grease a pan before baking the ingredients, while others don't. The reason is that dishes with a fair amount of fat in them, such as those with cheeses, will create their own layer of grease on the bottom. Those that are primarily made up of flour or have a lot of lean vegetables will have a tendency to stick to a baking dish if it isn't greased.

1. Preheat the oven to 375°F.

2. In a large bowl, beat the eggs. Whisk in the milk and cheese.

3. Heat the oil over medium heat in a large ovenproof frying pan. Add the sausage and potatoes. Cover and cook for 5 minutes. Turn the sausage and potatoes and cover. Continue cooking, turning the sausage and potatoes and stirring occasionally until the sausage is cooked and the potatoes are tender. Add the peppers and onions and stir. Cover and cook for 5 minutes.

4. Pour in the egg mixture and stir to mix.

5. Place the pan in the oven. Bake for 15–20 minutes until the egg is set. Sprinkle with black pepper and serve.

Shrimp Frittata

This frittata is excellent for serving to company at any summertime gathering.

2 pounds large shrimp

1 pound whole leeks

5 large eggs

5 large egg whites

1 cup whole milk

1 tablespoon olive oil

¼ pound bacon, diced

3 large plum tomatoes, sliced

½ pound provolone cheese, shredded

½ teaspoon freshly cracked black pepper

Shrimp Freshness

You want shrimp with a clean, ocean-like smell. Even a hint of ammonia is a bad sign. Frozen shrimp are fine, but buy them frozen and keep them frozen until you're ready to cook them. Never buy and then freeze fresh (or partially thawed) shrimp, and never thaw and refreeze shrimp.

1. Preheat the oven to 350°F. Clean, peel, and devein the shrimp. Thoroughly clean the leeks. Cut off and discard the dark green ends and chop the rest.

2. In a large bowl, beat together the eggs and egg whites. Whisk in the milk.

3. Heat the oil over medium heat in a large ovenproof frying pan. Sauté the leeks and bacon for 5 minutes, stirring occasionally. Drain off at least half the fat.

4. Add the shrimp, tomatoes, cheese, and egg mixture. Stir to mix.

5. Cover the pan and place in the oven. Bake for 15 minutes. Uncover and bake for 5–10 minutes until the egg is set. Serve sprinkled with black pepper.

CHAPTER 11

Risotto and Polenta

Basic Risotto

Riso is the Italian word for "rice." Risotto refers more to a cooking method in which rice is first "toasted" with oil and onions and then liquid is added a little at a time.

INGREDIENTS | SERVES 10

2 tablespoons olive oil

½ bulb garlic, minced

2 shallots, minced

2 cups arborio rice

½ cup dry white wine (not cooking wine)

5½ cups Chicken Stock (see Chapter 4)

¾ cup fresh-grated Parmesan cheese

½ teaspoon freshly cracked black pepper

½ teaspoon Italian seasoning

The Perfect Pan

Risotto should always be cooked in a heavy saucepan with a large, flat bottom so that the flame underneath can be evenly distributed. If the heat is not evenly distributed throughout the risotto, the grains of rice will cook at different rates, leaving you with the occasional crunchy grain.

1. Heat the oil in a large saucepan over medium heat. Add the garlic and shallots. Sauté for about 3 minutes, then add the rice. Stir constantly.

2. Add the wine and stir until fully absorbed. Add the stock ½ cup at a time, stirring frequently and allowing each addition to be completely absorbed before adding the next. Continue until all the stock is absorbed and the rice is tender.

3. Remove from heat and add the cheese, pepper, and Italian seasoning. Stir, and serve.

Roasted Carrot Risotto

When entertaining, to save time, the carrots can be prepared the day before and refrigerated until ready to use.

INGREDIENTS | SERVES 10

1 pound fresh carrots, diced

3 large yellow onions, diced

3 tablespoons olive oil, divided

4 large sprigs rosemary, stems discarded, divided

2 cups arborio rice

½ cup dry white wine (not cooking wine)

5½ cups Vegetable Stock (see Chapter 4)

½ teaspoon freshly cracked black pepper

1. Preheat the oven to 375°F.

2. Toss the carrots and onions with 2 tablespoons of the oil and half the rosemary. Spread out in an even layer on a baking sheet and roast for about 15 minutes. Set aside.

3. Heat the remaining oil over medium heat in a large saucepan. Add the rice and stir for 1 minute. Add the wine and stir until fully absorbed.

4. Add the stock ½ cup at a time, stirring frequently and allowing each addition to be completely absorbed before adding the next. Continue until all the stock is absorbed and the rice is tender.

5. Remove from heat. Add the roasted carrots and onions and the remaining rosemary and season with pepper. Serve in a heated bowl.

Grilled Broccoli Raab and Alfredo Risotto

The classic Alfredo sauce gives this risotto a rich and creamy taste. The bright green of the broccoli raab mounded on the creamy rice contrasts nicely with the white sauce, making for a beautiful presentation.

Rice for Risotto

The best variety of rice for making risotto is arborio rice, an imported Italian rice. Other types of rice cannot absorb as much liquid or hold their shape throughout the constant stirring required when making risotto.

1. Preheat the grill. In a medium bowl, toss the broccoli raab in 4 tablespoons of the olive oil and sprinkle with black pepper. Grill for 2 minutes on each side.

2. Heat the remaining oil over medium heat in a large saucepan. Sauté the shallots and garlic for 5 minutes. Add the rice and stir for 2 minutes.

3. Add the wine and stir until completely absorbed. Add the stock ½ cup at a time, stirring frequently and allowing each addition to be completely absorbed before adding the next. Continue until all the stock is absorbed and the rice is tender.

4. Prepare the Alfredo sauce by heating the cream over medium-high heat in small saucepan until reduced by half the volume. Add the cold butter a bit at a time and stir to incorporate before adding more. Remove from heat and stir in the cheese.

5. To serve, mound the rice in a serving bowl, top with the broccoli raab, and drizzle with the sauce.

Browned Risotto Patties

The Italian version of "potato pancakes," these patties are a great way to use up leftover risotto.

INGREDIENTS | SERVES 10

2 tablespoons olive oil, divided

1 large yellow onion, finely chopped

2 cups arborio rice

6 cups stock of choice (see Chapter 4)

¼ cup shredded fontina cheese

½ cup cold unsalted butter, cut into pats

½ teaspoon freshly cracked black pepper

1. Preheat the broiler. Lightly grease a baking sheet with 1 tablespoon of the oil.

2. Heat the remaining oil over medium heat in a large saucepan. Sauté the onion for about 2 minutes. Add the rice and stir for 2 minutes. Add the stock ½ cup at a time, stirring frequently and allowing each addition to be completely absorbed before adding the next. Continue until all the stock is absorbed and the rice is tender.

3. Remove from heat and stir in the cheese. Let cool, then form into ½-cup patties.

4. Place the patties on the prepared baking sheet, place a pat of butter on top of each patty, and brown lightly under the broiler. Sprinkle with pepper and serve.

Tomato and Parmesan Risotto

This dish is like baked ziti but with risotto instead of pasta.

1 tablespoon olive oil

1 large yellow onion, diced

½ bulb garlic, minced

2 cups arborio rice

6 cups Chicken Stock (see Chapter 4)

4 cups Old World Gravy (Long-Cooking Tomato Sauce) (see Chapter 3), divided

½ cup fresh ricotta

½ cup shredded fresh mozzarella cheese

¼ bunch fresh basil, chopped, divided

¼ bunch fresh oregano, chopped, divided

¼ bunch fresh parsley, chopped, divided

½ teaspoon freshly cracked black pepper

Plenty of Patience

Cooking risotto requires a watchful eye and lots of patience. It is important to let each ingredient be fully incorporated before adding the next one. Careful stirring will achieve the creamy consistency of a perfect risotto, while neglecting the cooking rice will leave you with a burned mess.

1. Preheat the oven to 350°F.

2. Heat the oil over medium heat in a large saucepan. Sauté the onions and garlic for 3 minutes. Add the rice and stir for 1 minute. Add the stock ½ cup at a time, stirring frequently and allowing each addition to be fully absorbed before adding the next. Continue until all the stock is absorbed and the rice is tender.

3. Pour 2 cups of the Old World Gravy into a large baking dish. Spoon the risotto on top in an even layer. Place dollops of the ricotta all over the risotto and sprinkle with the shredded mozzarella and half the fresh herbs. Ladle the remaining Old World Gravy over the top. Cover with foil and bake for 10 minutes. Uncover and bake for 5 more minutes.

4. Sprinkle with black pepper and the remaining herbs and serve.

Spicy Risotto

This spicy risotto makes a great accompaniment to any roast or meatloaf.

INGREDIENTS | SERVES 10

1 tablespoon olive oil

5 Italian peppers, finely diced

2 large yellow onions, diced

½ bulb fresh garlic, minced

2 cups arborio rice

½ cup Pinot Noir or other red drinking wine of choice

5½ cups Chicken Stock (see Chapter 4)

1 cup Old World Gravy (Long-Cooking Tomato Sauce) (see Chapter 3)

2 fresh plum tomatoes, finely diced

4 sprigs fresh marjoram or oregano, chopped

⅓ cup Parmesan cheese

1 tablespoon red pepper flakes

½ teaspoon freshly cracked black pepper

1. Heat the oil over medium heat in a large frying pan. Lightly sauté the peppers, onion, garlic, and rice for 2 minutes. Pour in the wine and stir until absorbed.

2. Add the stock ½ cup at a time, stirring frequently and allowing each addition to be completely absorbed before adding the next. Continue until all the stock is absorbed and the rice is tender.

3. Add the Old World Gravy, tomatoes, and marjoram. Remove from heat and sprinkle with cheese, red pepper flakes, and black pepper. Serve.

Seasoned Beef Risotto

*True to their name, pine nuts, or pignoli in Italian, are the edible kernels of several
varieties of pine. They are an essential ingredient in authentic pesto.*

INGREDIENTS | SERVES 10

1 large leek

1 tablespoon olive oil

1½ pounds lean ground beef

1 shallot, minced

4 cloves garlic, minced

¼ cup pine nuts

4 fresh plum tomatoes, medium-diced

1½ cups arborio rice

½ cup Merlot wine (or other dry red
drinking wine of choice)

4½ cups Beef Stock (see Chapter 4)

3 sprigs fresh thyme, stems discarded

4 sprigs fresh basil, chopped

⅓ cup fresh-grated Asiago cheese

½ teaspoon freshly cracked black
pepper

1. Thoroughly clean and finely chop the white and green parts of the leek.

2. Heat the oil over medium heat in a large skillet. Add the beef, shallot, garlic, and pine nuts. Cook for about 15 minutes until the beef is lightly browned. Drain excess fat from the pan. Add the leeks, tomatoes, and rice and cook for 5 minutes, stirring frequently.

3. Pour in the wine and stir until absorbed. Add the stock ½ cup at a time, stirring frequently and allowing each addition to be completely absorbed before adding the next. Continue until all the stock is absorbed and the rice is tender.

4. Remove from heat. Stir in the thyme, basil, cheese, and black pepper. Serve hot.

Cleaning Leeks

As leeks grow, sand and dirt accumulate between the layers, so it is important to clean them thoroughly. Before slicing them into rounds, trim off the ends, and make deep slits in each end. Soak in a bowl of water with ice cubes for 15 minutes. This will loosen any dirt, which can quickly be rinsed away after soaking.

Chicken Saltimbocca Risotto

*Do not add any salt to this dish, as the prosciutto and cheese
have enough salt in them to flavor the risotto.*

INGREDIENTS | SERVES 10

2½ pounds skinless, boneless
chicken breasts

¼–½ pound thinly sliced prosciutto

1 tablespoon olive oil

1½ cups arborio rice

1 cup Chardonnay (or other dry white
wine of choice)

4 cups Chicken Stock (see Chapter 4)

⅓ cup shredded provolone cheese

¼ bunch fresh Italian flat-leaf
parsley, chopped

½ teaspoon freshly cracked black
pepper

1. Preheat the oven to 375°F. Wrap each piece of chicken with 1 slice of the prosciutto. Roast for 30 minutes on a well-oiled rack in a roasting pan in the oven.

2. Heat the oil in a large saucepan over medium heat. Add the rice and stir for 2 minutes. Pour in the wine and stir until absorbed.

3. Add the stock ½ cup at a time, stirring frequently and allowing each addition to be completely absorbed before adding the next. Continue until all the stock is absorbed and the rice is tender.

4. Remove from heat and stir in the cheese.

5. To serve, mound spoonfuls of the risotto into serving bowls. Slice the prosciutto-wrapped chicken breasts on the bias and fan over the top of the risotto. Sprinkle with the parsley and pepper.

Chicken and Oregano Risotto

Fresh oregano leaves are essential for this dish. They are not as difficult to get as they used to be—most supermarkets keep fresh herbs in the produce section.

INGREDIENTS | SERVES 10

2½ pounds skinless, boneless chicken
2 tablespoons olive oil
2 large yellow onions, finely diced
6 cloves garlic, minced
1½ cups arborio rice
1 cup dry white wine (not cooking wine)
4½ cups Chicken Stock (see Chapter 4)
½ cup fresh-grated Asiago cheese
½ bunch fresh oregano, chopped
½ teaspoon freshly cracked black pepper

1. Cut the chicken into cubes.

2. Heat the oil over medium-high heat in a large saucepan. Add the chicken and cook for 5–8 minutes until lightly browned.

3. Add the onions and sauté for 2 minutes. Add the garlic and sauté for 1 minute. Add the rice and cook for 1 minute longer, stirring to thoroughly combine the ingredients.

4. Pour in the wine and stir until completely absorbed. Add the stock ½ cup at a time, stirring frequently and allowing each addition to be completely absorbed before adding the next. Continue until all the stock is absorbed and the rice is tender.

5. Remove from heat and add the cheese, oregano, and pepper. Serve hot.

Seafood Risotto

Chock-full of juicy shrimp, lobster, and scallops, this dish impresses guests and family alike.

INGREDIENTS | SERVES 10

1½ pounds cooked shrimp, scallops, and lobster (or any seafood combination of choice)

2 leeks

1½ tablespoons olive oil

1½ cups arborio rice

½ cup dry white wine (not cooking wine)

4½ cups Fish Stock (see Chapter 4)

½ cup fresh-grated Asiago cheese

2 tablespoons cold unsalted butter

1 bunch fresh parsley, chopped

½ teaspoon freshly cracked black pepper

Risotto Patties

Don't throw away your leftover risotto. It can be mixed with eggs and grated Parmesan cheese, formed into patties, and fried for a quick and tasty side dish. Risotto patties make a great accompaniment to roasted meat dishes.

1. Clean and shell the seafood and cut it into bite-sized chunks. Thoroughly clean the leeks and cut into a small dice, using both the white and green parts.

2. Heat the oil over medium heat in a large saucepan. Add the leeks and sauté for 2 minutes. Add the rice and stir for 1 minute.

3. Pour in the wine and stir until fully absorbed. Add the stock ½ cup at a time, stirring frequently and allowing each addition to be completely absorbed before adding the next. Continue until all the stock is absorbed and the rice is tender.

4. Remove from heat and stir in the seafood, cheese, and butter. Serve on a heated platter sprinkled with the parsley and pepper.

Basic Polenta

By using ½ to 1 cup less liquid than is called for in polenta recipes, you can produce a semifirm loaf of polenta that can be cooled and cut into serving portions. Reheat in the oven before serving.

INGREDIENTS | SERVES 10

5 cups water

¼ cup unsalted butter

1¼ cups cornmeal

½ teaspoon freshly cracked black pepper (optional)

½ teaspoon kosher salt (optional)

Keep It Simple

Polenta is delicious just served hot and dotted with butter and sprinkled with freshly grated Parmesan cheese. Slice the polenta, arrange it in a baking dish, dot with butter and Parmesan, and bake for a hot, savory side. Leftover polenta can be sliced, fried in oil, or lightly grilled, and served as a side dish as well.

1. Heat the water and butter to a simmer over medium to medium-high heat in a large saucepan.

2. Slowly whisk in the cornmeal, stirring constantly to avoid lumps.

3. Reduce heat to low. Cook for 20–25 minutes uncovered, stirring frequently until thick and creamy.

4. Season with pepper and salt as desired.

Polenta with Stock

To slightly vary the flavor of this polenta, you can substitute any type of stock. See Chapter 4 for other stock recipes.

INGREDIENTS | SERVES 10

5 cups Chicken Stock (see Chapter 4)
¼ cup unsalted butter
1¼ cups cornmeal
½ teaspoon freshly cracked pepper (optional)
½ teaspoon kosher salt (optional)

1. Bring the stock and butter to a simmer over medium to medium-high heat in a large saucepan.

2. Slowly whisk in the cornmeal, stirring constantly to avoid lumps.

3. Reduce heat to low. Cook for 20–25 minutes uncovered, stirring frequently until thick and creamy.

4. Season with pepper and salt as desired.

Creamy Polenta

For a special treat, you can use heavy cream instead of whole milk in this recipe. This substitution will give you a "Decadently Creamy Polenta."

INGREDIENTS | SERVES 10

3 cups stock of choice (see Chapter 4)
2 cups whole milk
¼ cup unsalted butter
1½ cups cornmeal
½ cup fresh-grated Parmesan cheese
½ teaspoon freshly cracked black pepper (optional)
½ teaspoon kosher salt (optional)

1. Bring the stock, milk, and butter to a simmer over medium to medium-high heat in a large saucepan.

2. Slowly whisk in the cornmeal, stirring constantly to avoid lumps.

3. Reduce heat to low. Cook for 20–25 minutes uncovered, stirring frequently until thick and creamy.

4. Sprinkle with the cheese and season with pepper and salt as desired.

Polenta with Roasted Corn

The combination of fresh corn with the cornmeal intensifies the flavor of the polenta.
This dish is strong enough in flavor to be served with any hearty stew or roast.

INGREDIENTS | SERVES 10

3 ears corn

2 tablespoons olive oil, divided

1 teaspoon freshly cracked black pepper, divided

2½ cups Chicken Stock (see Chapter 4)

2½ cups whole milk

1¼ cups cornmeal

½ cup shredded fontina cheese

Instead of Bread

In Italy, polenta is usually served as a starchy accompaniment to a meal, in place of bread. In this case, it is not sauced, but made into a loaf and cut with a string. This is a nice practice as it allows you to incorporate more ingredients into the polenta (herbs, vegetables, etc.), whereas bread usually only contains a few basic ingredients.

1. Heat the oven to 375°F. Remove the outer husks from the corn. Rub the corn with 1 tablespoon of the oil and season with ½ teaspoon black pepper. Bake right on the oven rack until tender, about 20 minutes. Let cool slightly; then cut the kernels off the cobs. Set aside.

2. Bring the remaining oil, the stock, and the milk to a simmer over medium to medium-high heat in a large saucepan. Slowly whisk in the cornmeal, stirring constantly to avoid lumps.

3. Reduce heat to low. Cook for 20–25 minutes uncovered, stirring frequently until thick and creamy.

4. Remove from heat. Add the corn kernels, cheese, and remaining black pepper.

Grilled Portobello Mozzarella Polenta

Mushrooms should be cleaned without water because they absorb moisture.
Wipe them with a paper towel or dust clean with a pastry brush.

INGREDIENTS | SERVES 10

10 whole portobello mushrooms

2 tablespoons olive oil, divided

½ teaspoon freshly cracked black pepper

3 shallots, minced

½ bulb garlic, minced

5 cups Vegetable Stock (see Chapter 4)

1¼ cups cornmeal

1 cup whole milk or light cream

2 tablespoons unsalted butter

½ bunch fresh parsley, chopped

½ cup shredded mozzarella cheese

1. Preheat the grill to medium temperature. Separate the mushroom stems and caps. Brush the mushroom caps with 1 tablespoon of the oil and season with pepper. Grill for 2 minutes on each side or until the mushrooms are tender. Keep warm.

2. Mince the mushroom stems.

3. Heat the remaining oil over medium heat in a large saucepan. Add the mushroom stems, shallots, and garlic. Sauté for 5 minutes, stirring constantly. Add the stock and bring to a simmer. Slowly whisk in the cornmeal, stirring constantly to avoid lumps.

4. Reduce heat to low. Cook for 20–25 minutes until thick and creamy.

5. Stir in the milk and cook for 5 minutes. Remove from heat. Add the butter.

6. To serve, spoon the polenta onto serving plates. Slice the grilled mushrooms and fan them over the polenta. Sprinkle with the parsley and cheese.

Stewed Fish with Polenta

This polenta makes a great addition to any stew dish. It can also be served on its own or with a light salad or soup as an appetizer.

INGREDIENTS | SERVES 10

2½ pounds halibut fillets
1 tablespoon olive oil
3 shallots, minced
½ bulb garlic, minced
10 fresh tomatoes, chopped
3 stalks celery, thinly sliced
½ bunch fresh parsley, chopped
3 sprigs thyme, stems discarded
1 cup dry white wine (not cooking wine)
2 bay leaves
½ teaspoon kosher salt
½ teaspoon freshly cracked black pepper
4 cups Fish Stock (see Chapter 4)
1 cup water
3 tablespoons unsalted butter
2 cups cornmeal
¾ teaspoon saffron threads

1. Clean the fish and cut into 10 serving pieces.

2. Heat the oil over medium-high heat in a large skillet. Add the shallots, garlic, and fish. Lightly brown the fish for 2 minutes on each side. Add the tomatoes, celery, parsley, thyme, wine, bay leaves, salt, and pepper. Simmer for 45–60 minutes with the lid ajar.

3. Meanwhile, bring the stock, water, and butter to a medium simmer in a large saucepan. Slowly whisk in the cornmeal, stirring constantly to avoid lumps. Reduce heat to low. Cook for 20–25 minutes uncovered, stirring frequently until thick and creamy.

4. Add the saffron to the polenta just before serving. Serve the fish over the polenta.

Fontina and Parmesan Polenta with Sun-Dried Tomatoes

Fontina is a great cheese to use in many Italian dishes. It melts quickly and tastes great in combination with many other cheeses.

INGREDIENTS | SERVES 10

2 tablespoons olive oil, divided

2 cups dry red wine (such as Merlot or Pinot Noir)

1 cup sun-dried tomatoes

1 recipe Creamy Polenta (see recipe in this chapter)

3 sprigs fresh basil, chopped

3 sprigs fresh oregano, chopped

¼ cup Roasted Garlic Paste (see Chapter 3)

1 cup fontina cheese

½ teaspoon freshly cracked black pepper

1. Preheat the oven to 375°F. Lightly grease a large baking sheet with 1 tablespoon of the oil.

2. Bring the wine to a simmer over medium heat in a saucepan. Add the tomatoes and simmer for 5 minutes. Remove from heat and let stand 15 minutes.

3. Drain the wine from the tomatoes and discard the wine.

4. Spread out the polenta 1"–2" thick in a baking pan.

5. Top the polenta with the tomatoes, herbs, garlic paste, fontina, and pepper. Drizzle with the remaining oil. Bake for 15–20 minutes until lightly browned and the cheese is melted.

Savory Breakfast Egg Polenta

This is a great dish to serve in a brunch buffet alongside other Italian favorites, such as breakfast sausage or a frittata.

INGREDIENTS | SERVES 10

4½ cups Chicken Stock (see Chapter 4)

3 tablespoons unsalted butter

1½ cups cornmeal

8 large eggs

½ cup fresh-grated Parmesan or Romano cheese

½ teaspoon freshly cracked black pepper

1. Bring the stock and butter to a slow simmer over medium heat. Slowly whisk in the cornmeal, stirring constantly to avoid lumps. Reduce heat to low. Cook for 20 minutes uncovered, stirring frequently until thick and creamy.

2. Beat the eggs in a small bowl and stir them into the polenta. Cook for about 5 more minutes.

3. Remove from heat. Stir in the cheese and pepper. Serve hot.

Sweet Breakfast Egg Polenta

You can top this polenta with dried or fresh fruit and nuts to add extra flavor, color, and texture.

INGREDIENTS | SERVES 10

5 cups water

1 cup milk

2 tablespoons unsalted butter

1¼ cups cornmeal

¾ cup honey

1. Bring the water, milk, and butter to a medium simmer in a large saucepan. Slowly whisk in the cornmeal, stirring constantly to avoid lumps. Reduce heat to low. Cook for 20–25 minutes uncovered, stirring frequently until thick and creamy.

2. Remove from heat and stir in the honey. Serve hot.

Citrus Polenta

This dish can be served as a breakfast or dessert, or it can accompany a hearty meat recipe.

INGREDIENTS | SERVES 10

Juice and zest of 2 large oranges
3 cups water
3 tablespoons unsalted butter
¾ cup honey
1¾ cups finely ground white cornmeal
½ cup granulated sugar (optional)
½ cup chopped pecans

1. Bring the orange juice, half the zest, the water, butter, and honey to a simmer over medium to medium-high heat in a large saucepan.

2. Slowly whisk in the cornmeal, stirring constantly to avoid lumps.

3. Reduce heat to low. Cook for 20–25 minutes uncovered, stirring frequently until thick and creamy.

4. Serve sprinkled with the remaining zest, the sugar if using, and pecans.

Cinnamon-Nutmeg Polenta with Dried Fruit and Nuts

*To reduce heavy cream, heat it at a medium to medium-high temperature,
making sure you don't scorch the cream or let it boil over.*

INGREDIENTS | SERVES 10

1½ cups cornmeal

½ cup brown sugar (optional)

1 tablespoon cinnamon (preferably freshly ground)

½ teaspoon ground nutmeg

4 cups water

1 cup whole milk

2 tablespoons unsalted butter

1 cup heavy cream (or substitute plain yogurt)

½ cup honey

½ cup finely chopped pecans or walnuts

½ cup raisins or other dried fruit of choice

Grind Fresh Herbs and Nuts

You can use a coffee bean grinder to grind fresh herbs and spices, or nuts. A tip for cleaning it out before and after using it for anything other than coffee is to grind 3 tablespoons of uncooked rice kernels in it and then wipe it dry with a clean cloth or paper towel. The rice works as an abrasive and cleans the inside of the grinder while it absorbs the flavors and oils of previous ingredients.

1. In a medium bowl, sift together the cornmeal, brown sugar if using, cinnamon, and nutmeg.

2. Bring the water, milk, and butter to a simmer over medium to medium-high heat in a large saucepan. Slowly whisk in the cornmeal mixture, stirring constantly to avoid lumps. Reduce heat to low. Cook for 20–25 minutes uncovered, stirring frequently until thick and creamy.

3. If using heavy cream, reduce by half the volume in a large sauté pan.

4. Spoon out the polenta into individual servings and drizzle with the cream and honey. Sprinkle with the nuts and raisins and serve.

Beef and Polenta Casserole

Similar to lasagna, the ingredients in this dish are spread between layers of polenta.

INGREDIENTS | SERVES 10

2 tablespoons olive oil, divided

2 Vidalia onions, diced

1 shallot, minced

1 bulb garlic, minced

1½ pounds lean ground beef

½ recipe Basic Polenta (see recipe in this chapter)

4 medium tomatoes, sliced

1 bunch steamed escarole (or any bitter greens)

½ cup ricotta

3 sprigs basil, chopped

½ teaspoon freshly cracked black pepper (optional)

½ cup fresh-grated Romano cheese

2 tablespoons melted unsalted butter

1. Preheat the oven to 350°F. Lightly grease a large casserole dish with 1 tablespoon of the oil.

2. Heat the remaining oil over medium heat in a large skillet. Add the onions, shallot, garlic, and beef. Sauté for 10–15 minutes until the beef is browned. Drain off excess grease.

3. Spread a thin layer of the polenta in the bottom of the prepared casserole dish. Spread layers of the beef, tomatoes, escarole, ricotta, basil, and pepper on top. Top with the remaining polenta. Sprinkle with the cheese. Drizzle with the butter.

4. Bake for 20 minutes and serve.

When to Use a Slow Cooker

Slow cookers are excellent appliances if you want to make a meal while you aren't at home or if you want to keep an appetizer warm for several hours. Soups and stews work well, as does any dish that doesn't require the food to brown and doesn't need to be quick-cooked, such as fried foods.

Seafood Polenta

After cleaning and shelling the fish, put the shells in an airtight plastic freezer bag and store in the freezer for use in future stocks.

INGREDIENTS | SERVES 10

Polenta
4½ cups Fish Stock (see Chapter 4)
½ cup dry white wine (not cooking wine)
1 tablespoon unsalted butter
1 cup cornmeal

Seafood Mixture
2 medium lemons
2 pounds fresh seafood (scallops, shrimp, and/or lobster)
2 tablespoons olive oil
½ bulb garlic, minced
½ cup dry white wine (not cooking wine)
¼ cup cold unsalted butter
½ bunch fresh parsley, chopped, divided
½ teaspoon freshly cracked black pepper

1. Prepare the polenta: Bring the stock, wine, and butter to a simmer over medium to medium-high heat in a large saucepan. Slowly whisk in the cornmeal, stirring constantly to avoid lumps. Reduce heat. Simmer for 20–25 minutes uncovered, stirring frequently until thick and creamy. Keep warm.

2. Prepare the seafood mixture: Zest and juice the lemons and reserve a few lemon slices for garnish. Mince the zest. Remove shellfish from the shells.

3. Heat the oil to medium-high temperature in a large sauté pan. Add the garlic and seafood and sauté for about 2 minutes. Add the lemon juice, half the zest, and the wine. Cover, and simmer for 3–5 minutes. Add the butter and half the parsley and stir to mix.

4. Serve the seafood mixture over the polenta. Sprinkle with the remaining zest and parsley and the black pepper.

CHAPTER 12

Panini

Ham, Salami, Pepperoni, and Provolone Panini

These Italian cold cuts stack really nicely. Pile them up at least ¼" high.
Don't worry, the cheese will hold it all together.

INGREDIENTS | SERVES 1

3 slices ham

3 slices salami

5 slices pepperoni

3 slices provolone cheese

2 slices Italian bread

1. Preheat the panini press. Lay the ham, salami, pepperoni, and provolone cheese on 1 slice of bread.

2. Top with another slice of bread and place on the press.

3. Close the lid, and cook for about 2–4 minutes.

4. Cut in half, and serve warm.

Variation

Pesto mayonnaise makes a great addition to this panini. Combine 3 tablespoons Traditional Pesto (see Chapter 3) with 1 cup of mayonnaise and blend well in a food processor. It can be stored in the refrigerator for up to a week.

Salami, Mozzarella, and Red Onion Panini

Good-quality salami from an Italian deli makes supermarket salami look like bologna.

INGREDIENTS | SERVES 1

4–6 slices salami

1 ciabatta roll

¼ cup sliced mozzarella

4 cherry tomatoes, halved

¼ red onion, thinly sliced

Olive oil, to taste

Salt and pepper, to taste

Basil leaves, to taste

1. Place the salami on the bottom half of the roll. Pile the mozzarella and tomatoes on top of the salami. Add the red onion slices.

2. Drizzle the sandwich with olive oil. Add salt and pepper to taste and scatter basil leaves for garnish.

3. Enjoy the sandwich open-faced or close the sandwich with the top of the roll.

4. If pressing, place sandwich on a preheated press, close the lid, and cook for 3–5 minutes. Remove from the press, slice in half, and serve warm.

Italian Combo Panini

The Italian Combo is one of the most popular sandwiches in delis, even though it's made a little differently in each one. Be sure to try many different variations of this panini. You won't be disappointed.

INGREDIENTS | SERVES 1

2 slices Italian bread or roll

3 slices ham

3 slices Genoa salami

3 slices pepperoni

2 slices mozzarella cheese

⅛ cup sliced roasted red peppers

2 slices tomato

2 tablespoons oil and vinegar dressing

Popular Variations

Choose your favorites from the following popular Italian Combo ingredients: capicola ham, mortadella, pepperoni, salami, dried sausage, mozzarella cheese, provolone cheese, sweet peppers, black olives, onion, lettuce, tomato, balsamic vinegar, Italian dressing.

1. Preheat the panini press. If using Italian bread, cut to desired length and then slice lengthwise.

2. Add the ham, salami, pepperoni, and mozzarella cheese to 1 slice of bread. Top the meat with the roasted red peppers and tomato slices.

3. Drizzle the oil and vinegar dressing on the other slice of bread and top the sandwich. Use enough dressing to flavor the bread without soaking it or else your panini will fall apart.

4. Place on the press, close the lid, and cook for 4–6 minutes.

5. Remove from the press and cut in half. Serve warm.

Roast Beef with Caramelized Onion Panini

A long roll or a baguette is the right bread for this panini.

1. Preheat the panini press. In a small bowl, add the olive oil, onion, mushrooms, garlic powder, salt, and pepper and mix to coat the ingredients with the oil. Empty the bowl onto the heated press and drizzle additional olive oil on top as desired. Close the press and cook for 4–5 minutes. After 3 minutes, you may open the press and mix the ingredients with a wooden spoon to ensure that they are evenly cooked. Remove them from the press and set aside.

2. Place the bottom half of the roll or baguette on the counter and add the sliced roast beef onto the bread. Sprinkle with salt and pepper and top with the onion mixture.

3. Add the top of the roll or baguette and place the sandwich on the press.

4. Close the press and cook for 3–5 minutes.

5. Remove panini, slice in half, and serve warm.

Chicken, Prosciutto, and Sun-Dried Tomato Panini

Sun-dried tomatoes are sold by the jar, packed in oil or dry. The sun-dried tomatoes packed in oil are perfect for panini sandwiches.

INGREDIENTS | SERVES 1

1 or 2 thin-sliced chicken breasts
Salt and pepper, to taste
2 slices Italian bread
2 tablespoons sun-dried tomatoes
2 slices prosciutto
1 tablespoon grated Parmesan cheese

Reconstituting Sun-Dried Tomatoes

Sun-dried tomatoes that are packed in oil are panini-ready and can be added straight from the jar. Sun-dried tomatoes that are packed dry will taste like shoe leather, so follow these steps to get them panini-ready. Place sun-dried tomatoes in a heat-proof bowl and pour boiling water over them until they are covered. Let sit for 10–15 minutes until soft.

1. Preheat the panini press.

2. Place the chicken breast on the press. Sprinkle with salt and pepper before closing the lid. Cook for 4–6 minutes, depending on the thickness of the chicken breast. Remove from the press and set aside.

3. On 1 slice of bread, add the chicken, sun-dried tomatoes, prosciutto, and Parmesan cheese. Top the sandwich with another slice of bread.

4. Place on the press and close the lid.

5. Cook for 3–5 minutes. Remove from the press and slice in half. Serve warm.

Tomato and Pesto Grilled Cheese Panini

The addition of pesto turns that regular grilled cheese into an Italian treat.

INGREDIENTS | SERVES 1

3 slices mozzarella cheese
2 slices Italian bread
2 slices tomato
1 tablespoon Traditional Pesto (see Chapter 3)

1. Preheat the panini press. Lay the mozzarella cheese on 1 slice of bread. Add the tomato and pesto sauce and cover with the other slice of bread.

2. Place on the press, close the lid, and cook for 3–5 minutes.

3. Remove from the press, cut in half, and serve warm.

Variation

For even more cheesy flavor, add a few slices of provolone cheese to this panini. It will blend nicely with the mozzarella cheese.

Garlic Shrimp and Arugula Panini

Arugula is also known as rocket, roquette, rucchetta, and rucola. It's very popular in Italian cuisine.

INGREDIENTS | SERVES 1

10 medium shrimp, peeled and deveined
2 tablespoons olive oil
2 tablespoons minced garlic
1 long roll
1 tablespoon grated Parmesan cheese
1 cup shredded arugula

1. Preheat the panini press.

2. In a medium bowl, combine the shrimp, olive oil, and garlic and mix well. Pour the contents of the bowl onto the press, close the lid, and cook for 2–3 minutes.

3. Cut open a long roll and add the shrimp, Parmesan cheese, and arugula. Place on the press, close the lid, and cook for 2–4 minutes.

4. Remove from the press, cut in half, and serve warm.

Variation

Sometimes arugula is hard to find at your local supermarket. If you have trouble finding it, you can replace it with endive, escarole, or dandelion greens.

Chicken Caesar Panini

Many popular salads make for nice panini sandwiches. Use thickly sliced bread if you want to load up on the dressing.

INGREDIENTS | SERVES 1

1 or 2 chicken cutlets

2 tablespoons Caesar dressing

2 slices whole-wheat bread

1 tablespoon grated Parmesan cheese

2 or 3 leaves romaine lettuce

2 slices tomato

1. Preheat the panini press. Place the chicken cutlets on the press, close the lid, and cook for 4–6 minutes. Remove from the press and set aside.

2. Add the Caesar salad dressing to 1 slice of bread. Add the Parmesan cheese, romaine lettuce, and tomato slices. Cut the chicken into slices and add to the panini, then close the sandwich.

3. Place on the press, close the lid, and cook for 2–4 minutes.

4. Remove from the press, cut in half, and serve warm.

Pear, Goat Cheese, and Prosciutto Panini

Feel free to add more prosciutto to this panini if it's sliced really thin. If using Italian bread for this recipe, cut it thin.

INGREDIENTS | SERVES 1

1 pear, cut into ¼" slices

2 slices Italian bread

3 tablespoons goat cheese

3 slices prosciutto

3 slices red onion

1 teaspoon balsamic vinegar

1. Preheat the panini press. Lay the pear slices on top of 1 slice of bread. Add the goat cheese, prosciutto, and red onion.

2. Drizzle another slice of bread with balsamic vinegar and top the sandwich. Place on the press.

3. Close the lid and cook for 3–5 minutes. Remove from the press and slice in half. Serve warm.

Variations

Bresaola is an Italian specialty that is made by air-curing beef. If you don't eat pork, then substitute the prosciutto with bresaola.

Eggplant and Roasted Pepper Panini

Grilled eggplant and roasted peppers are good enough to eat by themselves. Add bread and garlic mayonnaise and put it all in the panini press and you've got something even better.

INGREDIENTS | SERVES 1

4 slices eggplant, sliced about ¼" thick
1 tablespoon olive oil
2 slices Italian bread
4 slices roasted red pepper
1 tablespoon garlic mayonnaise

Focaccia

Here is another recipe that you'll want to try on focaccia. See if your bakery has any olive, roasted red pepper, or other varieties of focaccia that will complement this eggplant panini, or make your own using the recipes in Chapter 9.

1. Preheat the panini press. Place the eggplant on the press and drizzle with the olive oil. Close the lid and cook for 3–5 minutes. Remove the eggplant from the press and place on 1 slice of bread. Add the roasted pepper slices on top of the eggplant.

2. Spread the garlic mayonnaise on the other slice of bread. Close the sandwich.

3. Place on the press, close the lid, and cook for 3–5 minutes.

4. Remove from the press, slice in half, and serve warm.

Broccoli Raab and Provolone Panini

Broccoli raab is an acquired taste, but once you acquire it, it'll be hard to get enough.

INGREDIENTS | SERVES 1

2 tablespoons olive oil
2 tablespoons minced garlic
1 cup steamed broccoli raab
2 slices Italian bread, or a ciabatta roll
3 slices provolone cheese

Broccoli Raab

The "raab" in "broccoli raab" can be spelled a few different ways, including "rabe" or even "raap." It is a bitter green that is in season from fall to spring. Broccoli raab is a good source of vitamins A and C as well as potassium, calcium, and iron.

1. Preheat the panini press.

2. In a medium bowl, combine the olive oil, garlic, and broccoli raab. Mix to coat evenly with the oil. Pour contents on the press, close the lid, and cook for 3–5 minutes. Remove from the press and arrange on 1 slice of bread or half of the sliced roll.

3. Add the provolone cheese and top with another slice of bread or the other half of the roll.

4. Place on the press, close the lid, and cook for 3–5 minutes.

5. Remove from the press, slice in half, and serve warm.

Portobello Mushroom and Arugula Panini

Chewy ciabatta bread will help you soak up all of the garlic and oil. You won't want to waste it.

INGREDIENTS | SERVES 1

1 portobello mushroom cap
1 tablespoon olive oil
1 teaspoon minced garlic
1 small bunch arugula
2 slices ciabatta bread

1. Preheat the panini press. Place the mushroom cap on the press and drizzle with olive oil. Add the minced garlic on top and close the lid. Cook for 3–5 minutes. Remove the mushroom from the press and set aside.

2. Add the mushroom and arugula to 1 slice of bread and cover with the other slice of bread.

3. Place on the press, close the lid, and cook for 3–5 minutes.

4. Remove from the press, slice in half, and serve warm.

Basil, Mozzarella, and Tomato Panini

This panini is great with garden-fresh basil. Alternately, try making it with sliced zucchini. You won't give away as many zucchini to neighbors after you've tried it.

INGREDIENTS | SERVES 1

1 bunch basil, gently cleaned
3 slices mozzarella cheese
3 slices tomato
2 slices Italian bread
1 tablespoon Traditional Pesto (see Chapter 3) (optional)

Variation

Try this recipe using yellow pattypan squash. Its mellow flavor makes a great substitute for zucchini, and it's so fun to look at. Leave a few uncooked to show off to your friends.

1. Preheat the panini press. Add the basil, mozzarella, and tomato to 1 slice of bread.

2. For a stronger basil flavor, spread the pesto onto the second slice of bread and place the bread on top of the sandwich with the pesto side down.

3. Place on the press, close the lid, and cook for 3–5 minutes.

4. Remove from the press, slice in half, and serve warm.

Sausage Parmesan Panini

This panini can get messy if you overstuff it. For neater results, try slicing the sausage in half lengthwise. This will help stop it from rolling out of the panini and onto your lap.

INGREDIENTS | SERVES 1

½ pound Italian pork sausage

1 long roll

4 slices mozzarella cheese

3 tablespoons tomato sauce

1. Preheat the panini press. Add the sausage to the press and cook for 5–7 minutes. Remove from the press and slice in half if desired.

2. Cut open the long roll and add the sausage, mozzarella cheese, and tomato sauce.

3. Place on the press, close the lid, and cook for 2–3 minutes.

4. Cut in half and serve warm.

Bruschetta Panini

You'll be surprised at how much flavor is transferred to the bread when you rub it with garlic. If you really love garlic, then chop up the clove when you're done with it and add it to the panini.

INGREDIENTS | SERVES 1

1 sandwich-sized piece of baguette

1 clove garlic

4 slices tomato

2 teaspoons olive oil

1 teaspoon balsamic vinegar

Salt and pepper, to taste

Cocktail Party Options

You can make this panini in bite-sized form for your next cocktail party. Instead of the baguette, use an Italian panella loaf that is sliced ¼" thick. When it's done cooking, use a pizza cutter to slice it into three or four pieces.

1. Preheat the panini press. Slice the baguette lengthwise and place on the press for about 1 minute to warm. Cut the garlic clove in half. Remove the baguette from the press and rub the inside of the baguette with the garlic. Add the tomato slices, then drizzle with olive oil and balsamic vinegar. Add salt and pepper to taste.

2. Place the baguette back on the press, close the lid, and cook for 2–4 minutes.

3. Remove from the press and cut in half. Serve warm.

Italian Sausage and Egg Panini

What better way to start your day than with some hearty Italian sausage? The fantastic scents from the kitchen should wake everyone up in your house. This panini also makes a delicious lunch.

INGREDIENTS | SERVES 1

⅓ pound Italian sausage
2 large eggs
1 long roll
4 strips roasted red peppers

1. Preheat the panini press. Add the sausage to the press and cook for 5–7 minutes. Remove from the grill and slice in half if desired.

2. In a frying pan that has been sprayed with nonstick cooking spray, scramble or fry the eggs.

3. Cut open the long roll and add the sausages, eggs, and roasted red peppers.

4. Place on the press, close the lid, and cook for 2–3 minutes.

5. Cut in half and serve warm.

CHAPTER 13

Homemade Pasta

Basic Pasta

When making pasta dough, use your judgment about how much flour to add. You may need to add more or less flour depending on the level of humidity.

INGREDIENTS | SERVES 10

3 cups durum wheat (semolina) flour
⅛ teaspoon iodized salt
3 large eggs
¼ cup olive oil
¼ cup water (room temperature)

Semolina

Semolina flour is the basis of most types of pasta and Italian breads. It is made from hard durum wheat and has a fine texture. It contains more protein and vitamins than regular white flour and many essential amino acids. Semolina also has a low calorie count and a very low fat content.

1. Sift together the flour and salt into a large mixing bowl.

2. Whisk the eggs in a small bowl. Mix the olive oil and water into the eggs.

3. Make a well in the center of the flour and pour in the egg mixture. Mix together the wet and dry ingredients by hand or in a mixer with a dough hook until the dough forms into a ball. Wrap the dough in plastic wrap and let it rest in the refrigerator for at least 1 hour or up to 1 day. Allow the dough to return to room temperature if it has rested in the refrigerator for more than 1 hour.

4. Roll out the dough on a floured surface, then form or shape the pasta as desired.

5. To cook, bring a large pot of water to a slow boil. Add the pasta and stir to prevent sticking. Cook until al dente. (Cooking times will vary depending on the size of the pasta formed.) Drain and serve as desired.

Spelt Pasta

Chickpea flour may be substituted for spelt flour if you prefer or if it is what you have on hand.

INGREDIENTS | SERVES 10

2 cups spelt flour

1 cup all-purpose flour

⅛ teaspoon iodized salt

3 large eggs

1 egg white

¼ cup olive oil

1 tablespoon water

Separating Eggs

If you don't have an egg separator in your kitchen, break the egg neatly in half and transfer the yolk back and forth from one side of the shell to the other, catching the whites in a small bowl underneath. In some recipes, even the smallest amount of yolk in an egg white can cause the recipe to fail. So, don't break that yolk!

1. Sift together the spelt flour, all-purpose flour, and salt into a large mixing bowl.

2. Whisk the eggs and the egg white in a small bowl. Mix the olive oil and water into the eggs.

3. Make a well in the center of the flour and pour in the egg mixture. Mix together the wet and dry ingredients by hand or in a mixer with a dough hook until the dough forms into a ball. Wrap the dough in plastic wrap and let it rest in the refrigerator for at least 1 hour or up to 1 day. Allow the dough to return to room temperature if it has rested in the refrigerator for more than 1 hour.

4. Roll out the dough on a floured surface, then form or shape the pasta as desired.

5. To cook, bring a large pot of water to a slow boil. Add the pasta and stir to prevent sticking. Cook until al dente. (Cooking times will vary depending on the size of the pasta formed.) Drain and serve as desired.

Whole-Wheat Pasta

You can use any grain flour in this recipe. Different flours will impart different flavors and textures to the pasta.

INGREDIENTS | SERVES 10

2½ cups whole-wheat flour
½ cup all-purpose flour
⅛ teaspoon iodized salt
2 large eggs
2 egg whites
¼ cup olive oil
2 tablespoons water

Drying and Storing Pasta

If you want to make fresh pasta ahead of time, you have a few storage options. If you want to cook the pasta within a day or so, place the noodles on a baking sheet for 2 minutes, sprinkle with flour to prevent sticking, and fold them or twirl them into small nests. Dry for 30 minutes; wrap and store in the refrigerator for a maximum of 2 days. If freezing, follow this same process; frozen pasta will last 2 weeks. When drying egg-based pastas, use a food dehydrator on a low-temperature setting for 2–3 hours. All types of pasta will dry if hung on a floured pasta-drying rack, wooden spoons draped across larger pans, or placed flat on floured baking pans. Be sure to dry thoroughly before storing, as damp pasta can foster mold growth.

1. Sift together the wheat flour, all-purpose flour, and salt into a large mixing bowl.

2. Whisk the eggs and egg whites in a small bowl. Mix the olive oil and water into the egg mixture.

3. Make a well in the center of the flour and pour in the egg mixture. Mix together the wet and dry ingredients by hand or in a mixer with a dough hook until the dough forms into a ball. Wrap the dough in plastic wrap and let it rest in the refrigerator for at least 1 hour or up to 1 day. Allow the dough to return to room temperature if it has rested in the refrigerator for more than 1 hour.

4. Roll out the dough on a floured surface, then form or shape the pasta as desired.

5. To cook, bring a large pot of water to a slow boil. Add the pasta and stir to prevent sticking. Cook until al dente. (Cooking times will vary depending on the size of the pasta formed.) Drain and serve as desired.

Eggless Pasta

This is the perfect pasta for those who need to watch their cholesterol intake. The olive oil adds flavor so you won't miss the eggs.

INGREDIENTS | SERVES 10

2 cups durum wheat (semolina) flour
2 cups all-purpose flour
⅛ teaspoon iodized salt
⅓ cup virgin olive oil
⅓ cup water

Cutting Pasta by Hand

Cutting pasta by hand does not have to be a time-consuming endeavor; just make sure you have a super-sharp knife on hand. Roll your sheets of pasta into a flat jellyroll-shaped log. Cut through the roll with your sharp knife into the desired shape/width of your strands.

1. Sift together the flours and the salt into a large mixing bowl.

2. Whisk together the oil and water in a small bowl.

3. Make a well in the center of the flour and pour in the oil and water mixture. Mix together the wet and dry ingredients by hand or in a mixer with a dough hook until the dough forms into a ball. Wrap the dough in plastic wrap and let it rest in the refrigerator for at least 1 hour or up to 1 day. Allow the dough to return to room temperature if it has rested in the refrigerator for more than 1 hour.

4. Roll out the dough on a floured surface, then form or shape the pasta as desired.

5. To cook, bring a large pot of water to a slow boil. Add the pasta and stir to prevent sticking. Cook until al dente. (Cooking times will vary depending on the size of the pasta formed.) Drain and serve as desired.

Egg White Pasta

Enjoy this lighter take on traditional pasta with New World Fresh Sauce (see Chapter 3) and grilled chicken for a delightful summer meal.

INGREDIENTS | SERVES 10

2½ cups grain flour
½ cup all-purpose flour
⅛ teaspoon iodized salt
6 large egg whites
½ cup olive oil
¼ cup water

Testing Egg Freshness

To test whether or not an egg is fresh, immerse it in a pan of cool, salted water. If it sinks to the bottom, it is fresh. If it rises to the surface, it is spoiled. If the eggs in your refrigerator are approaching or have passed their freshness date, always perform this test before using the eggs.

1. Sift together the grain flour, all-purpose flour, and salt into a large mixing bowl.

2. Whisk together the egg whites, olive oil, and water in a separate bowl.

3. Make a well in the center of the flour and pour in the egg mixture. Mix together the wet and dry ingredients by hand or in a mixer with a dough hook until the dough forms into a ball. Wrap the dough in plastic wrap and let it rest in the refrigerator for at least 1 hour or up to 1 day. Allow the dough to return to room temperature if it has rested in the refrigerator for more than 1 hour.

4. Roll out the dough on a floured surface, then form or shape the pasta as desired.

5. To cook, bring a pot of water to a slow boil. Add the pasta and stir to prevent sticking. Cook until al dente. (Cooking times will vary depending on the size of the pasta formed.) Drain and serve as desired.

Spinach Pasta

If you don't like spinach, any cooked vegetable can be substituted here. Try carrots, beets, or red peppers for a different color and flavor.

INGREDIENTS | SERVES 10

2 cups durum wheat (semolina) flour
2 cups all-purpose flour
⅛ teaspoon iodized salt
½ cup raw spinach
2 large eggs
¼ cup olive oil
1 tablespoon water

1. Sift together the flours and salt into a large mixing bowl.

2. Cook and purée the spinach.

3. In a separate bowl, whisk the eggs, then thoroughly blend the eggs with the spinach, olive oil, and water.

4. Make a well in the center of the flour and pour in the egg mixture. Mix together the wet and dry ingredients by hand or in a mixer with a dough hook until the dough forms into a ball. Wrap the dough in plastic wrap and let it rest in the refrigerator for at least 1 hour or up to 1 day. Allow the dough to return to room temperature if it has rested in the refrigerator for more than 1 hour.

5. Roll out the dough on a floured surface, then form or shape the pasta as desired.

6. To cook, bring a large pot of water to a slow boil. Add the pasta and stir to prevent sticking. Cook until al dente. (Cooking times will vary depending on the size of the pasta formed.) Drain and serve as desired.

Fresh Basil Pasta

If you like, you can try another fresh herb in this recipe. Also, you can use the leaves of the herb, as this recipe calls for, or you can purée the herb.

INGREDIENTS | SERVES 10

1 large bunch basil
1½ cups durum wheat (semolina) flour
2½ cups all-purpose flour
⅛ teaspoon iodized salt
2 large eggs
2 large egg whites
¼ cup plus 1 tablespoon olive oil, divided

Don't Drown Your Pasta

The correct way to eat pasta, according to Italians, is to have it *alla macchiato*, or with just enough sauce on it to "stain it." Avoid lots of heavy sauces; instead, use just enough sauce to complement the delicate flavor of the pasta, without drowning it.

1. Thoroughly clean and dry the basil. Remove the leaves (reserve stems for another recipe if desired).

2. Sift together the flours and salt into a large mixing bowl.

3. Whisk the eggs, egg whites, and ¼ cup oil in a separate bowl.

4. Make a well in the center of the flour and pour in the egg mixture. Mix together the wet and dry ingredients by hand or in a mixer with a dough hook until the dough forms into a ball. Wrap the dough in plastic wrap and let it rest in the refrigerator for at least 1 hour or up to 1 day. Allow the dough to return to room temperature if it has rested in the refrigerator for more than 1 hour.

5. Separate the dough into 2 balls. Roll out 1 ball on a floured surface into a sheet about ⅛"–¼" thick. Brush it very lightly with 1 tablespoon oil and spread the basil leaves evenly over the dough. Roll out the other ball into a sheet the same size as the first and place it on top of the first sheet. Roll to ensure that the 2 sheets are stuck together. Cut the pasta into desired shapes.

6. To cook, bring a large pot of water to a slow boil. Add the pasta and stir to prevent sticking. Cook until al dente. (Cooking times will vary depending on the size of the pasta formed.) Drain and serve as desired.

Fagioli Pasta (Bean Pasta)

Serve this as you would regular pasta—with butter and cheese, red sauce, or garlic and oil. If you use canned beans, make sure to rinse and drain them well before using.

INGREDIENTS | SERVES 10

½ cup cooked cannellini beans (or substitute another legume of your choice)

2 cups whole-grain flour

1 cup all-purpose flour

⅛ teaspoon iodized salt

3 large eggs

¼ cup olive oil

¼ cup water or Vegetable Stock (see Chapter 4)

1. Purée the cooked beans.

2. Sift the flours and salt into a large mixing bowl.

3. In a separate bowl, whisk the eggs. Mix the beans, oil, and water (or stock) into the eggs.

4. Make a well in the center of the flour and pour in the egg mixture. Mix together all the ingredients by hand or in a mixer with a dough hook for about 3 minutes until the dough forms into a ball. Wrap the dough in plastic wrap and let it rest in the refrigerator for at least 1 hour or up to 1 day. Allow the dough to return to room temperature if it has rested in the refrigerator for more than 1 hour.

5. Knead the dough for a few minutes before rolling it out on a floured surface. Form or shape the pasta as desired.

6. To cook, bring a large pot of water to a slow boil. Add the pasta and stir to prevent sticking. Cook until al dente. (Cooking times will vary depending on the size of the pasta formed.) Drain and serve as desired.

Roasted Garlic Pasta

*To help balance the strong flavor of the garlic, serve this pasta
with thick slices of plain, warm Italian bread.*

INGREDIENTS | SERVES 10

1 cup durum wheat (semolina) flour

1 cup whole-wheat flour

2 cups all-purpose flour

⅛ teaspoon iodized salt

2 large eggs

¼ cup virgin olive oil

¼ cup water

1 tablespoon olive oil

¼ cup Roasted Garlic Paste (see Chapter 3)

Testing for Doneness

Different types of pasta cook at different rates, so there is no set length of time for cooking. The only way to be sure your pasta is cooked enough is to taste and feel it. Pasta should be "al dente," or just firm to the bite. Also, pasta continues to cook a bit as you take it off the heat and drain it, so take this into account when testing for doneness.

1. Sift together the flours and salt into a large mixing bowl.

2. Whisk the eggs in a small bowl. Whisk the ¼ cup virgin olive oil and the water into the eggs.

3. Make a well in the center of the flour and pour in the egg mixture. Mix together the wet and dry ingredients by hand or in a mixer with a dough hook until fully incorporated and the dough forms into a ball. Wrap the dough in plastic wrap and let it rest in the refrigerator for at least 1 hour or up to 1 day. Allow the dough to return to room temperature if it has rested in the refrigerator for more than 1 hour.

4. Separate the dough into 2 balls. Roll out 1 ball on a floured surface into a sheet about ⅛"–¼" thick. Brush very lightly with 1 tablespoon oil and spread the garlic paste on the dough. Roll out the other ball into a sheet the same size as the first and place it on top of the first sheet of dough. Roll to ensure that the sheets are stuck together. Cut or form the pasta into desired shapes.

5. To cook, bring a large pot of water to a slow boil. Add the pasta and stir to prevent sticking. Cook until al dente. (Cooking times will vary depending on the size of the pasta formed.) Drain and serve as desired.

Acini di Pepe

This tiny round pasta, Italian for "peppercorn," is perfect for use in soups or pasta salads.

INGREDIENTS | SERVES 10

1½ cups durum wheat (semolina) flour
¼ cup fresh-grated Parmesan cheese
2 large eggs
2 tablespoons olive oil
1 tablespoon water

1. In a medium bowl, mix together the flour and cheese.

2. In a separate bowl, whisk the eggs, then whisk in the oil and water.

3. Make a well in the center of the flour and pour in the egg mixture. Mix together the wet and dry ingredients by hand or in a mixer with a dough hook until fully incorporated and the dough forms into a ball. Wrap the dough in plastic wrap and let it rest in the refrigerator for at least 1 hour or up to 1 day. Allow the dough to return to room temperature if it has rested in the refrigerator for more than 1 hour.

4. Cut the dough into tiny pieces and roll into tiny pea-sized balls.

5. To cook, bring a large pot of water to a boil. Add the pasta and stir to prevent sticking. Cook until al dente, approximately 3–5 minutes. Drain and serve as desired.

Cornmeal Pasta

Serve this pasta with a hearty, spicy meat dish. It will hold up well with heavy gravies, too.

INGREDIENTS | SERVES 10

1½ cups cornmeal
2½ cups all-purpose flour
⅛ teaspoon iodized salt
3 large eggs
¼ cup olive oil
2 tablespoons water

Tip for Cooking Pasta

After putting the pasta in the boiling water, put a tablespoon of olive oil into the water to prevent the pasta from sticking together. You can also add a pinch of salt to the water to help speed up the cooking, but don't do this when you're making an already salty dish.

1. Sift together the cornmeal, all-purpose flour, and salt into a large mixing bowl.

2. Whisk the eggs in a separate bowl. Whisk the olive oil and water into the eggs.

3. Make a well in the center of the flour and pour in the egg mixture. Mix together the wet and dry ingredients by hand or in a mixer with a dough hook until fully incorporated and the dough forms into a ball. Wrap the dough in plastic wrap and let it rest in the refrigerator for at least 1 hour or up to 1 day. Allow the dough to return to room temperature if it has rested in the refrigerator for more than 1 hour.

4. Roll out the dough on a floured surface, then form or shape the pasta as desired.

5. To cook, bring a large pot of water to a slow boil. Add the pasta and stir to prevent sticking. Cook until al dente. (Cooking times will vary depending on the size of the pasta formed.) Drain and serve as desired.

Tomato Pasta

It is okay to use canned puréed tomatoes in this recipe instead of fresh. Try to find the imported ones from San Marzano.

INGREDIENTS | SERVES 10

2 cups durum wheat (semolina) flour

1½ cups all-purpose flour

⅛ teaspoon iodized salt

3 large eggs

½ cup puréed fresh tomatoes (or substitute canned tomato purée)

¼ cup olive oil

2 tablespoons water

1. Sift together the flours and salt into a large mixing bowl.

2. Whisk together the eggs and tomato purée in a separate bowl. Whisk the olive oil and water into the egg mixture.

3. Make a well in the center of the flour and pour in the egg mixture. Mix together the wet and dry ingredients by hand or in a mixer with a dough hook until fully incorporated and the dough forms into a ball. Wrap the dough in plastic wrap and let it rest in the refrigerator for at least 1 hour or up to 1 day. Allow the dough to return to room temperature if it has rested in the refrigerator for more than 1 hour.

4. Roll out the dough on a floured surface, then form or shape the pasta as desired.

5. To cook, bring a large pot of water to a slow boil. Add the pasta and stir to prevent sticking. Cook until al dente. (Cooking times will vary depending on the size of the pasta formed.) Drain and serve as desired.

Eggplant Pasta

To make the eggplant purée called for in this recipe: Slice an eggplant lengthwise, lightly brush with olive oil, roast in a 375°F oven for 20 minutes, and purée.

INGREDIENTS | SERVES 10

1 cup durum wheat (semolina) flour
1 cup whole-wheat flour
1½ cups all-purpose flour
⅛ teaspoon iodized salt
3 large eggs
½ cup eggplant purée
¼ cup olive oil
2 tablespoons water

1. Sift together the flours and salt into a large mixing bowl.

2. Whisk together the eggs and eggplant purée in a separate bowl. Whisk the olive oil and water into the egg mixture.

3. Make a well in the center of the flour and pour in the egg mixture. Mix together the wet and dry ingredients by hand or in a mixer with a dough hook until fully incorporated and the dough forms into a ball. Wrap the dough in plastic wrap and let it rest in the refrigerator for at least 1 hour or up to 1 day. Allow the dough to return to room temperature if it has rested in the refrigerator for more than 1 hour.

4. Roll out the dough on a floured surface, then form or shape the pasta as desired.

5. To cook, bring a large pot of water to a slow boil. Add the pasta and stir to prevent sticking. Cook until al dente. (Cooking times will vary depending on the size of the pasta formed.) Drain and serve as desired.

Saffron and Shallot Pasta

Roast the shallots by tossing them in olive oil and placing them in a 375°F oven for approximately 15 minutes before puréeing them.

INGREDIENTS | SERVES 10

1 cup durum wheat (semolina) flour

2 cups all-purpose flour

⅛ teaspoon iodized salt

2 large eggs

2 large egg whites

3 roasted shallots, puréed

½ teaspoon saffron threads

¼ cup olive oil

2 tablespoons water

Dried Pasta: The Good and the Bad

Not all pasta is created equal. If your pasta comes out gummy or has a sour, bitter, or floury taste, try switching brands. There can be a significant difference between the quality of pasta brands and only a slight difference in price. If you like the brand a friend uses, try it out in your own kitchen.

1. Sift together the flours and salt into a large mixing bowl.

2. Whisk together the eggs, egg whites, puréed shallots, and saffron in a separate bowl. Whisk the olive oil and water into the egg mixture.

3. Make a well in the center of the flour and pour in the egg mixture. Mix together the wet and dry ingredients by hand or in a mixer with a dough hook until fully incorporated and the dough forms into a ball. Wrap the dough in plastic wrap and let it rest in the refrigerator for at least 1 hour or up to 1 day. Allow the dough to return to room temperature if it has rested in the refrigerator for more than 1 hour.

4. Roll out the dough on a floured surface, then form or shape the pasta as desired.

5. To cook, bring a large pot of water to a slow boil. Add the pasta and stir to prevent sticking. Cook until al dente. (Cooking times will vary depending on the size of the pasta formed.) Drain and serve as desired.

Walnut Pasta

This is great served with a pesto sauce, as a side with a main dish, or all on its own.

INGREDIENTS | SERVES 10

2 large eggs
2 large egg whites
2 tablespoons heavy cream
¼ cup melted unsalted butter
½ cup walnuts, finely chopped
3 cups all-purpose flour

1. Whisk together the eggs, egg whites, cream, butter, and walnuts in a bowl. Sift the flour into a large mixing bowl.

2. Make a well in the center of the flour and pour in the egg mixture. Mix together the wet and dry ingredients by hand or in a mixer with a dough hook until fully incorporated and the dough forms into a ball. Wrap the dough in plastic wrap and let it rest in the refrigerator for at least 1 hour or up to 1 day. Allow the dough to return to room temperature if it has rested in the refrigerator for more than 1 hour.

3. Roll out the dough on a floured surface, then form or shape the pasta as desired.

4. To cook, bring a large pot of water to a slow boil. Add the pasta and stir to prevent sticking. Cook until al dente. (Cooking times will vary depending on the size of the pasta formed.) Drain and serve as desired.

Gnocchi

The word gnocchi *literally translates as "lumps." These are potato dumplings that are served the same way as pasta.*

INGREDIENTS | SERVES 10

2 cups durum wheat (semolina) flour
1 teaspoon iodized salt
3 large eggs
1 cup cooked mashed potatoes
¼ cup olive oil
2 tablespoons water

Gnocchi

A tip for making your gnocchi come out perfectly is to cook the mashed potato at least 1 or 2 hours ahead of time. Set it aside in a glass bowl and cover with a cloth. Letting the potatoes stand like this for a few hours helps them lose some of their moisture, thereby producing the perfect texture.

1. Sift together the flour and salt into a large bowl.

2. Whisk the eggs in a separate bowl. Add the potatoes, oil, and water and stir to mix.

3. Make a well in the center of the flour and pour in the egg mixture. Mix together the wet and dry ingredients by hand or in a mixer with a dough hook until fully incorporated and the dough forms into a ball.

4. Use 2 spoons to form the dough into ovals about ½ teaspoon in size.

5. To cook, bring a large pot of water to a slow boil. Add the pasta and stir to prevent sticking. Boil for 10–15 minutes until al dente. Drain and serve.

Roasted Potato and Garlic Gnocchi

*When cooking gnocchi—or any fresh pasta—you should use a slower boil, as
opposed to the strong rolling boil you use when cooking dry pasta.*

INGREDIENTS | SERVES 10

3 large baking potatoes, baked until
fork-tender

½ bulb roasted garlic (see Roasted
Garlic Paste recipe in Chapter 3)

2 cups durum wheat (semolina) flour

⅛ teaspoon iodized salt

2 large eggs

2 tablespoons olive oil

1 tablespoon water

1. Thoroughly purée the potato and garlic together in a food processor or blender.

2. Sift together the flour and salt into a large bowl.

3. Whisk the eggs in a small bowl. Whisk the oil and water into the eggs and stir in the potato and garlic purée.

4. Make a well in the center of the flour and pour in the egg mixture. Mix together the wet and dry ingredients by hand or in a mixer with a dough hook until fully incorporated and the dough forms into a ball. Wrap the dough in plastic wrap and let it rest in the refrigerator for 1 hour or up to 1 day. Allow the dough to return to room temperature if it has rested in the refrigerator for more than 1 hour.

5. Use 2 spoons to form the dough into ovals about ½ teaspoon in size.

6. To cook, bring a large pot of salted (optional) water to a slow boil. Add the pasta and stir to prevent sticking. Boil for 10–15 minutes until al dente. Drain and serve.

Traditional Lasagna

Be creative with lasagna—almost anything can be stuffed between the flat noodles. Layers of seafood, different vegetables, or meats can be used.

INGREDIENTS | SERVES 10

1 recipe Basic Pasta (see recipe in this chapter), unformed and uncooked

8 cups tomato sauce of choice (see Chapter 3)

1 pound hamburger, cooked

1 pound sweet Italian sausage, cooked

¾ cup ricotta

1 cup shredded mozzarella cheese

¼ cup fresh-grated Parmesan cheese

3 sprigs fresh basil, chopped

3 sprigs fresh oregano, chopped

½ teaspoon freshly cracked black pepper

Using Premade Lasagna Pasta

If you don't have time to make your own pasta for this recipe, simply swap out the homemade sheets for store-bought ones. Cook the lasagna noodles according to package directions until al dente, then shock in ice water. Proceed with the recipe instructions as follows.

1. Preheat the oven to 350°F. Roll out the pasta dough into long lasagna sheets about ¼" thick. Bring a large pot of water to a slow boil, add the pasta, and partially cook for approximately 4 minutes, then shock in ice water.

2. Spoon a thin layer of the tomato sauce into the bottom of a large baking pan. Layer pasta sheets over the sauce, then top with a layer of the hamburger, sausage, cheeses, basil, oregano, and pepper. Ladle sauce over the top. Repeat layering until the pan is almost full, finishing with a top layer of pasta, sauce, and cheese.

3. Cover and bake for 45 minutes. Uncover and bake for 15 minutes or until lightly browned and bubbling.

4. Remove from the oven and let stand for 5–10 minutes before serving.

Vegetarian Lasagna

If you prefer, you can substitute other greens for the kale in this recipe, such as spinach or escarole.

INGREDIENTS | SERVES 10

½ recipe Whole-Wheat Pasta (see recipe in this chapter), unformed and uncooked

½ recipe Spelt Pasta (see recipe in this chapter), unformed and uncooked

1 tablespoon olive oil

1 large yellow bell pepper, diced

2 shallots, finely sliced

4 cups New World Fresh Sauce (see Chapter 3)

1 cup Roasted Garlic Paste (see Chapter 3)

1 cup cooked red lentils

1 cup steamed kale

1 cup shredded fontina cheese

½ small bunch fresh parsley, chopped

½ teaspoon freshly cracked black pepper

1. Preheat the oven to 350°F. Bring a large pot of water to a slow boil. While the water heats, combine the 2 types of pasta dough and roll out into lasagna sheets ¼" thick. Partially cook the pasta in boiling water for approximately 4 minutes, then shock in ice water.

2. Heat the oil in a medium skillet over medium heat. Sauté the bell pepper and shallots in the oil until soft.

3. Ladle enough sauce into a large baking pan to coat the bottom. Layer pasta sheets over the sauce, then top with layers of the garlic paste, lentils, kale, peppers and shallots, cheese, parsley, and black pepper. Ladle sauce over the top. Repeat layering until the pan is almost full, finishing with a top layer of pasta, cheese, and sauce.

4. Cover and bake for 30–45 minutes until heated through and the cheese is melted. Uncover and bake for another 10–15 minutes. Remove from the oven and let stand for 5–10 minutes before serving.

Lobster Ravioli

When making homemade dough for ravioli, the dough should be a bit thicker than for regular pasta shapes because it must endure more manipulation.

INGREDIENTS | SERVES 10

2 pounds fresh uncooked lobster meat

2 bunches leeks

½ bunch fresh parsley, chopped

½ teaspoon freshly cracked black pepper

1 recipe Roasted Garlic Pasta (see recipe in this chapter), uncut and uncooked

4 cups Mascarpone Cheese Sauce (see Chapter 3)

Cooking Ravioli

To prevent ravioli from sticking, stir them gently after dropping them into the boiling water. If you remove them with a slotted spoon as soon as they rise to the surface of the water, they will not overcook. Spooning them out instead of draining into a colander helps keep the delicate ravioli intact.

1. Roughly chop the lobster meat into bite-sized pieces. Thoroughly wash and dry the leeks. Thinly slice both the white and green parts.

2. In a large bowl, mix together the lobster, leeks, parsley, and black pepper.

3. Roll out the pasta dough on a floured surface into sheets about ½" thick. Cut into circles 3" in diameter.

4. Spoon teaspoonfuls of the lobster mixture onto the centers of the circles. Lightly paint the outer edge of the pasta circles with a tiny amount of water, fold the circles in half, and seal by pressing closed with your fingers.

5. Bring 2 gallons of water to a slow boil. Add the ravioli and cook until al dente, approximately 10 minutes. While the ravioli cooks, heat the cheese sauce in a small saucepan over low heat.

6. Serve the ravioli with the cheese sauce.

Pasta-Wrapped Shrimp with Pesto

This pasta-wrapped shrimp makes an impressive presentation, and the taste is equally fantastic.

INGREDIENTS | SERVES 10

3 shallots, minced

½ bulb garlic, minced

½ teaspoon freshly cracked black pepper

2 pounds large fresh shrimp

1 recipe Basic Pasta (see recipe in this chapter), unformed and uncooked

1 recipe Walnut Pesto (see Chapter 3)

1. Combine the shallots and garlic in a bowl with the black pepper. Peel, devein, and clean the shrimp (remove the tails, too).

2. Roll out the pasta dough into a sheet as thin as possible, taking care not to tear the dough. Cut into 3" squares.

3. Place 1 shrimp in the center of each square. Add approximately ¼–½ teaspoon of the garlic and shallot mixture. Wrap and seal the shrimp in the pasta.

4. Bring a large pot of water to a boil. Add the pasta and cook for 3–5 minutes until the pasta is al dente and the shrimp are cooked through. Drain and serve with the pesto. (Do not heat the pesto.)

Baccalà with Pasta and Fresh Peas

Baccalà is whole, small cod that is cured in brine and air-dried. Dried cod is commonly used in Italian cuisine and is usually cooked in sauces with tomato and milk or cream.

INGREDIENTS | SERVES 10

1 pound *baccalà* (dried, salted cod)

1 recipe Basic Pasta (see recipe in this chapter), unformed and uncooked

1 pound fresh peas

1 teaspoon olive oil

4 cups heavy cream

½ teaspoon freshly cracked black pepper

1. Pound on the dried cod with a wooden spoon or pestle and then soak in cool water in the refrigerator for 4–5 days (2 days at the very least) prior to preparation. Change the water at least 2 or 3 times a day and gently rinse the fish each time. After soaking, drain the fish and cut it into large squares. Set aside.

2. Roll out the pasta dough on a floured surface into a sheet about ¼" thick and cut into the desired shapes.

3. Shuck the peas and steam until al dente.

4. Heat the olive oil over medium heat in a large sauté pan. Add the *baccalà* and sauté for 8 minutes. Add the cream and reduce by half the volume over medium to medium-high heat.

5. Bring a large pot of water to a slow boil and add the pasta. Cook until al dente and drain. Add the pasta and peas to the pan with the *baccalà* and remove from heat. Season with the pepper, stir to combine, and serve.

Pork-Filled Pasta Shells

Many Italian recipes call for bread to be soaked in wine or water. Use day-old Italian bread slices.

INGREDIENTS | SERVES 10

1 tablespoon olive oil

4 slices toasted Italian bread

¼ cup robust red wine, mixed with ½ cup water

2 pounds lean ground pork

1 large egg

⅓ cup fresh-grated Parmesan cheese, divided

3 medium yellow onions, finely diced

6 fresh plum tomatoes, finely diced

½ bunch fresh oregano, minced

1 recipe Basic Pasta (see recipe in this chapter), unformed and uncooked

8 cups New World Fresh Sauce (see Chapter 3)

½ teaspoon freshly cracked black pepper

1. Preheat the oven to 375°F. Grease a large Dutch oven or heavy ovenproof pan (with a lid) with the oil.

2. Soak the toast in the wine mixture, then squeeze out excess liquid.

3. In a large mixing bowl, combine the pork, egg, half the cheese, onion, tomato, oregano, and bread. Roll into ovals about 3" long and ¼" thick.

4. Roll out the pasta dough on a floured surface into a sheet about ¼" thick. Cut into 4" circles. Place a meat oval into the center of each pasta circle. Gently fold up 2 sides and pinch the ends together to form a shell.

5. Ladle sauce into the prepared pan to coat the bottom. Place the stuffed shells in the pan and ladle more sauce on top. Sprinkle with the remaining cheese and the black pepper.

6. Cover and bake for 45–60 minutes until the pork is thoroughly cooked.

Pasta Stuffed with Fresh Cod in Saffron Broth

You can make the cod-filled pasta a day ahead and refrigerate.

INGREDIENTS | SERVES 10

1½ pounds fresh cod
1 bunch green onions, finely sliced
6 cloves garlic, minced
¼ cup black olives, sliced
1 recipe Basic Pasta (see recipe in this chapter), unformed and uncooked
1 bunch leeks
1 teaspoon olive oil
½ cup dry white wine (not cooking wine)
8 cups Fish Stock (see Chapter 4)
1 teaspoon saffron

1. Cut the fish into a medium dice.

2. In a large bowl, mix together the fish, green onions, garlic, and olives.

3. Roll out the pasta dough on a floured surface into 3" × 6" rectangles. Place 1½–2 tablespoons of the fish mixture on each rectangle. Dampen the edges of the pasta with water, fold in half, and press closed. Seal by pressing the edges with fork tines.

4. Thoroughly clean and thinly slice the white and green parts of the leeks. Heat the oil over medium heat in a large stockpot. Add the leeks and sauté for about 5 minutes. Add the wine and reduce by half. Add the stock and saffron and simmer for 45 minutes, uncovered.

5. Bring a large pot of water to a slow boil. Add the pasta and cook for about 6 minutes until al dente (the pasta will float to the top).

6. Ladle the leek broth into serving bowls, add the cod pasta, and serve.

Classic Fettuccine Alfredo

This butter, cream, and cheese sauce was made famous by a restaurateur named Alfredo in Rome in the 1920s when he served it with fettuccine.

INGREDIENTS | SERVES 10

1 recipe Basic Pasta (see recipe in this chapter), unformed and uncooked

8 cups heavy cream

½ cup (1 stick) unsalted butter, chilled

¼ cup fresh-grated Romano cheese

¼ cup fresh-grated Parmesan cheese

½ teaspoon dried parsley

½ teaspoon freshly cracked black pepper

1. Roll out the pasta on a floured surface into a sheet about ¼" thick. Cut into fettuccine about ¼" wide and 12"–18" long. Bring a large pot of water to a slow boil. Add the pasta and cook until al dente, approximately 6 minutes. Drain, shock in cold water, and drain again.

2. In a large saucepan, reduce the heavy cream to ¾ quart (3 cups) over medium to medium-high temperature. Add the cold butter a little at a time, stirring after each addition until melted and incorporated into the cream. Remove from heat.

3. Add the pasta and both cheeses to the reduced cream and gently toss for 1–2 minutes to mix and reheat the pasta.

4. Serve on a heated platter sprinkled with the parsley and pepper.

Fettuccine Alfredo *con Capesante*

Although scallops are usually sold already cleaned and shelled, they can be served in their shells. Heat them in a sauté pan with oil, garlic, salt and pepper, lemon juice, and parsley until they are steamed open.

INGREDIENTS | SERVES 10

1½ pounds *capesante* (sea scallops), cleaned and shelled

1 recipe Basic Pasta (see recipe in this chapter), unformed and uncooked

2 quarts heavy cream

3 tablespoons cold unsalted butter

½ cup fresh-grated Asiago cheese

1 teaspoon olive oil

3 shallots, finely diced

4 medium red bell peppers, finely sliced

½ cup dry white wine (not cooking wine)

½ bunch fresh parsley, chopped

½ teaspoon freshly cracked black pepper

1. Remove the muscle (the small, tough piece) from each scallop.

2. Roll out the pasta on a floured surface into a sheet about ¼" thick. Cut into fettuccine about ¼" wide and 12"–18" long. Bring a large pot of water to a slow boil. Add the pasta and cook until al dente, approximately 6–8 minutes. Drain, shock in cold water, and drain again. Set aside.

3. In a large saucepan, reduce the cream to about 1¾ quarts over medium heat. Add the butter and cheese and immediately remove from the heat.

4. While the cream is reducing, heat the oil in a large saucepan over medium heat. Add the shallots and red peppers and toss until the shallots just begin to wilt, about 2 minutes. Add the scallops and cook for about 2 minutes. Add the wine, cover, and simmer for 3 minutes.

5. Add the cream mixture to the scallop mixture, which should still be on the heat. Add the pasta into the scallop mixture and stir for a minute to reheat. Remove the resulting mixture from the heat. Serve on a heated platter sprinkled with the parsley and black pepper.

Stuffed Shells

Most people think of stuffing these pasta shells with ricotta and mozzarella cheese, but try this version with mascarpone and Gorgonzola.

INGREDIENTS | SERVES 10

1 cup mascarpone cheese
½ cup Gorgonzola cheese
3 large eggs
1 teaspoon red pepper flakes
½ bunch fresh basil, chopped
4 cups New World Fresh Sauce (see Chapter 3), divided
1 recipe Spelt Pasta (see recipe in this chapter), unformed and uncooked

1. Preheat the oven to 350°F.

2. In a large bowl, mix together the mascarpone, Gorgonzola, eggs, red pepper flakes, and basil.

3. Ladle ½ cup of the New World Fresh Sauce into a large baking pan to coat the bottom of the pan.

4. Roll out the pasta dough on a floured surface into a sheet about ½" thick. Cut into 4" ovals. Place 2 heaping tablespoons of the cheese mixture in the center of each oval. Fold up 2 edges and pinch the ends together to form shells. Place in the pan. Ladle the remaining sauce over the top of the shells.

5. Cover and bake for 20 minutes. Uncover and bake for 5 more minutes until lightly browned and bubbling.

Baked Spaghetti Tart

Though this is an unusual way to prepare spaghetti, you will find the result very delicious.

INGREDIENTS | SERVES 10

4 tablespoons olive oil, divided

½ recipe Roasted Garlic Pasta (see recipe in this chapter), uncut and uncooked

2 Vidalia onions, finely sliced

1 bunch fresh arugula

1 cup Chicken or Vegetable Stock (see Chapter 4)

¼ cup melted unsalted butter

½ cup fresh-grated Romano cheese

½ teaspoon freshly cracked black pepper

2 slices crusty Italian bread, toasted and chopped

1. Preheat the oven to 375°F. Lightly grease a large, round casserole pan with 1 tablespoon of the oil. Roll out and cut the pasta into spaghetti.

2. In a large bowl, mix together the pasta, the remaining oil, the onions, arugula, and stock and place in the prepared casserole dish. Cover and bake for 30 minutes.

3. Meanwhile, in a medium bowl, mix together the butter, cheese, pepper, and bread.

4. Top the tart with the bread mixture. Bake for 5 more minutes, uncovered.

Pasta Dumplings

This is an easy way to make gnocchi without the potatoes. These drop dumplings can be eaten the same way, with tomato or Alfredo sauce.

INGREDIENTS | SERVES 10

1 gallon stock of choice (see Chapter 4)

1 recipe Basic Pasta (see recipe in this chapter), unformed and uncooked

In a large stockpot, bring the stock to a slow boil and drop in teaspoonfuls of the pasta dough. Boil until al dente or fully cooked, about 15–20 minutes. Drain and serve as desired.

Pasta *con Ragu Bolognese*

Oregano and marjoram can be used interchangeably—the flavors are similar. Commonly believed food lore is that Bolognese sauce originated from someone using a leftover meatloaf to fortify a sauce.

INGREDIENTS | SERVES 10

4 slices toasted Italian bread

½ pound lean ground beef

½ pound ground veal

½ pound lean ground pork

1 large egg

¼ cup fresh-grated Romano cheese

3 shallots, minced

½ bulb garlic, minced

¼ bunch fresh marjoram or oregano, chopped

½ teaspoon freshly cracked black pepper

6 plum tomatoes, diced

3 bell peppers (any color), medium-diced

1 recipe Basic Pasta (see recipe in this chapter), unformed and uncooked

2 cups heavy cream

¼ bunch fresh parsley, chopped

1. Preheat the oven to 350°F. Soak the bread in water and immediately squeeze out the liquid.

2. In a large loaf pan, mix together the ground meats, egg, cheese, shallots, garlic, marjoram, bread, and pepper. Bake for 45 minutes.

3. Finely break up the meat in a large saucepan, add the tomatoes and peppers, and simmer for 1 hour, uncovered.

4. While the sauce simmers, roll out the pasta on a floured surface and cut into desired shapes. Bring a large pot of water to a boil. Add the pasta, and cook until al dente. Drain, and set aside.

5. In a small saucepan, reduce the cream by half the volume, then whisk it into the tomato-meat mixture.

6. Add the pasta to the sauce and toss to mix. Serve on a heated platter, sprinkled with the parsley.

Bowtie Pasta with Braised Beans and Greens

Escarole or spinach can be substituted for the kale in this recipe.

INGREDIENTS | SERVES 10

1 cup dried garbanzo or cannellini beans
¼ cup olive oil
2 large yellow onions, diced
2 medium carrots, diced
2 stalks celery, diced
½ bulb garlic, minced
2 bay leaves
8 cups Chicken Stock (see Chapter 4)
4 sprigs thyme, stems discarded
½ recipe Basic Pasta (see recipe in this chapter), unformed and uncooked
2 bunches kale, chopped
½ teaspoon freshly cracked black pepper

1. Soak the beans overnight in 8 cups water. Drain.

2. Heat the oil over medium heat in a large stockpot. Add the onions, carrots, celery, and garlic. Cover and let sweat for about 8 minutes, stirring occasionally.

3. Add the beans, bay leaves, stock, and thyme and reduce the heat. Simmer for 3–4 hours with the lid ajar until the beans are thoroughly cooked.

4. Meanwhile, roll out the pasta dough on a floured surface into a sheet about ¼" thick. Cut into 1" × 3" rectangles. Pinch each rectangle in the center to form a bowtie. Bring a large pot of water to a slow boil. Add the pasta and cook until al dente. Drain.

5. Add the kale to the bean sauce, stir, and cover. Let braise for 5 minutes. Add the pasta to the sauce and toss to mix.

6. Remove the bay leaves. Serve in soup bowls and sprinkle with the pepper.

Deep-Fried Pasta

"Deep-fried" is a scary term, but that shouldn't stop you from enjoying this. Using olive oil will reduce the cholesterol in this dish.

INGREDIENTS | SERVES 10

¼ recipe Basic Pasta (see recipe in this chapter), unformed and uncooked

4 cups cooking oil

Great Garnish

Deep-fried pasta is not intended to be eaten as a main dish. However, it makes a fantastic garnish for many different foods. Try sprinkling some deep-fried pasta on soups, stews, or salads for a crunchy, fun twist.

1. Roll out the dough on a floured surface and form as desired. (A spaghetti noodle works well and makes an interesting garnish.) The pasta doesn't need to be cooked unless it has dried. If it has dried, it should be cooked al dente and then drained.

2. Heat the oil over medium-high heat in a large, deep pan.

3. Fry the pasta until lightly golden brown.

Cheese Tortellini

Tortellini literally translates as "stuffed straight hat with a hole." In Italy, stuffed pastas originated from the necessity to use good leftovers.

INGREDIENTS | SERVES 10

¾ cup ricotta

¼ cup mascarpone cheese (optional)

¼ cup shredded mozzarella cheese

¼ cup fresh-grated Romano cheese

1 large egg

1 bunch fresh parsley, finely chopped

4 cloves garlic, minced

½ teaspoon freshly cracked black pepper

1 recipe Basic Pasta (see recipe in this chapter), unformed and uncooked

1. In a medium bowl, mix together the cheeses, egg, parsley, garlic, and pepper.

2. Roll out the pasta dough on a floured surface into a sheet about ⅛"–¼" thick. Cut into 2" squares.

3. Place ¼–½ teaspoon of the cheese mixture on each pasta square. Dampen the edges and fold up the opposite corners to form a triangle, then seal together the edges. Gently pull down the base ends of the triangle and bring them together until they overlap, forming a ring-like shape. Press the ends together to secure them. (The top of the triangle will stand up a bit, like a hat.)

4. Bring a large pot of salted (optional) water to a slow boil. Add the pasta and cook for about 10 minutes. Drain and serve as desired.

Meat Ravioli

These can be made larger and called tortelli. *Ravioli or tortelli can be stuffed with a variety of fillings, so experiment with flavors and ingredients you love!*

INGREDIENTS | SERVES 10

4 thick slices crusty Italian bread (either stale or toasted)

¾ pound lean ground beef

¾ pound lean ground pork

¼ cup fresh-grated Asiago, Parmesan, or Romano cheese

½ teaspoon freshly cracked black pepper

6 cloves fresh garlic, minced

1 fresh shallot, minced

¼ bunch fresh oregano, leaves chopped

1 recipe Basic Pasta (see recipe in this chapter), unformed and uncooked

1. Soak the bread in water, then squeeze out all excess water.

2. In a large mixing bowl, mix together the beef, pork, cheese, pepper, garlic, shallot, oregano, and bread.

3. Roll out the pasta dough on a floured surface into a sheet about ⅛"–¼" thick. Cut into 3" squares.

4. Place 1–1½ teaspoons of the meat mixture in the center of each square. Lightly wet the edges with water using a small pastry brush or your finger. Fold over 1 corner to form a triangle and seal together the edges.

5. Bring a large pot of water to a slow boil. Add the pasta and cook for about 20 minutes. Drain and serve as desired.

CHAPTER 14

Salads

Fresh Tomato Salad

Use beefsteak tomatoes or plum tomatoes for this recipe, and only prepare this dish when tomatoes are in season. Also, use only fresh herbs. If you cannot find fresh basil, you can substitute ½ bunch oregano for a different but still delicious flavor.

INGREDIENTS | SERVES 10

2½ pounds fresh tomatoes, cut into wedges

1 pound Vidalia onions, finely sliced

About 20 fresh basil leaves, sliced

2 tablespoons fresh basil tops

2 tablespoons extra-virgin olive oil

1 teaspoon freshly cracked black pepper

Mix together all the ingredients. Serve chilled.

Fresh Mozzarella and Tomato Salad

Sliced fresh basil leaves sprinkled on top make a wonderful garnish for this popular salad. This addition will also make the salad more fragrant.

INGREDIENTS | SERVES 10

1 pound fresh mozzarella cheese (in water)

2 pounds tomatoes

½ cup extra-virgin olive oil

½ teaspoon freshly cracked black pepper

½ bunch whole basil leaves

1. Remove the mozzarella from the water and pat dry. Slice into approximately ¼"–½" slices. Slice the tomatoes the same way, so slices are the same size.

2. Alternate cheese and tomato slices on a serving platter. Drizzle with the oil and sprinkle with the pepper. Scatter basil leaves across the plate to serve.

Buying and Storing Leafy Greens

When buying greens such as escarole, kale, lettuce, and spinach, look for leafy parts that are tender but crisp. Store greens unwashed in sealed plastic bags. Rinse greens in cold water and pat dry with a paper towel right before use.

Caesar Salad

*For "authentic" Caesar salad, use only romaine lettuce. But if you prefer,
you may use another green or mix several different types.*

INGREDIENTS | SERVES 10

Croutons

1 loaf crusty Italian bread

⅓ tablespoon olive oil

Salad

1 tablespoon extra-virgin olive oil

2 tablespoons well-beaten pasteurized egg or pasteurized egg product

2 tablespoons balsamic vinegar

4 anchovy fillets

½ cup fresh-grated Parmesan cheese

½ teaspoon freshly cracked black pepper

¼ bunch fresh parsley, chopped

3 heads romaine lettuce, chopped and kept chilled

1. Preheat the broiler. To make the croutons, thinly slice the bread and cut each slice into 2 rectangles. Paint the bread with the olive oil and lightly brown under the broiler. (You can do this ahead of time.)

2. In a small bowl, whisk together the extra-virgin olive oil, egg, vinegar, anchovies, cheese, pepper, and parsley.

3. Toss the romaine with the dressing, top with croutons, and serve.

Pasteurization Is Important

When using raw egg in a dish, such as the dressing in Caesar Salad, it is very important that you use pasteurized eggs. Pasteurization is not as important when cooking eggs in recipes, as any harmful bacteria will be killed during the cooking process. Raw eggs can carry *salmonella* and *E. coli*, which can make you very ill.

Antipasto Salad

Antipasto literally translates as "before the meal." In an authentic Italian restaurant, a whole section of the menu will be devoted to antipasto selections.

INGREDIENTS | SERVES 10

½ pound capicola or prosciutto

½ pound Genoa salami or soppressata

½ pound provolone cheese, sliced

¼ pound pepperoni, sliced

2 cups fresh mesclun greens

5 tomatoes, medium-diced

1 red onion, finely sliced

2 hard-boiled eggs, sliced

6 pepperoncini

¼ pound black olives

¼ pound green olives

3 anchovy fillets (optional)

½ cup salad dressing of choice

1. Cut the capicola, salami, provolone, and pepperoni into thin strips.

2. Mound the greens in the center of a serving plate or platter. Arrange the meat, cheese, and other ingredients on top and serve the salad dressing on the side at the table.

Antipasti

The Italian word for "appetizer" is *antipasto*. Although an antipasto course is not commonly found in Italian homes, it is a necessary element to all holiday meals and formal dinners.

Aunt Gloria's Italian Green Bean Salad

This simple dish is great to take on picnics. It can be served chilled, slightly warm, or at room temperature.

INGREDIENTS | SERVES 10

2 pounds red potatoes

5 cups Italian flat green beans

2 medium red onions, finely sliced

⅔ cup extra-virgin olive oil

⅓ cup red wine vinegar

1 tablespoon dried oregano

½ teaspoon freshly cracked black pepper

Red Onions

Red onions are sweeter than white or yellow, but the taste is still very strong. If you are eating them raw—on sandwiches, for example—the taste will be mellower if you soak the slices in cold water for 10 minutes, then drain and pat dry before using.

1. Place the potatoes in a large pot and add enough water to cover. Simmer the potatoes until just fork-tender (do not overcook them). Drain well and dry in a hot (400°F) oven for 2 minutes. Let cool.

2. Fill a large pot with about 1" of water and bring to a simmer. Add the beans and cook until just tender but still crisp. Drain well, shock in ice-cold water to stop the cooking process, drain again, and let cool.

3. Peel and large-dice the potatoes.

4. Toss together all the ingredients in a large bowl, mixing well to distribute the spices and oil evenly.

Cannellini Bean Salad

If you use canned beans for this recipe, be sure to drain the beans, rinse them, and dry them thoroughly before mixing with the other ingredients.

INGREDIENTS | SERVES 10

1 small onion, minced

½ cup minced scallions

⅓ cup extra-virgin olive oil

Zest and juice of 1 large lemon

½ teaspoon freshly cracked white pepper

3 cups cooked cannellini beans

1. In a large bowl, mix together the onion, scallions, oil, lemon zest, lemon juice, and pepper.

2. Add the beans to the oil mixture and combine thoroughly. Serve immediately.

Oil on Salads

When using olive oil for salads, it is best to use extra-virgin olive oil. Since it comes from the first pressing of the olives, it is more expensive but also more flavorful. Do not use extra-virgin olive oil for regular cooking, as it burns easily.

Wilted Kale Salad with Roasted Shallots

If you don't have kale, or you'd just like to try something different, you can substitute escarole or even spinach.

INGREDIENTS | SERVES 10

10 cups whole shallots

⅓ cup olive oil

3 large bunches kale

2 tablespoons balsamic vinegar

½ teaspoon coarse salt

½ teaspoon freshly cracked black pepper

1. Preheat the oven to 375°F. Peel the shallots and leave whole.

2. In a bowl, toss the shallots in the oil. Place in a roasting pan and roast in the oven until fork-tender, about 20 minutes. Remove from the oven and slice the shallots in half.

3. While the shallots roast, quickly wilt the kale in 2 gallons of boiling water for 1 minute. Remove from heat, drain, and set aside to cool.

4. Serve by mounding the cooked kale in the center of a plate or platter. Top with the shallots, drizzle with the vinegar, and sprinkle with salt and pepper.

Lobster Salad

Everyone loves the classic steamed lobster with melted butter, but this salad gives lobster a whole new twist. The herbs and spices create a fresh flavor.

INGREDIENTS | SERVES 10

2 (2½-pound) live lobsters

3 gallons water

2 cups white wine (such as Pinot Grigio)

2 bay leaves

Juice of ½ large lemon

1 tablespoon fresh lemon zest

2 bunches fresh parsley

3 leeks, finely sliced

⅓ cup extra-virgin olive oil

½ teaspoon kosher or coarse salt

½ teaspoon freshly cracked black pepper

1. Rinse the lobsters in ice-cold water.

2. In a large stockpot, bring the water, wine, bay leaves, lemon juice, lemon zest, parsley, and leeks to a boil. Add the lobsters and cook for approximately 10 minutes until the shells are red and the lobsters are thoroughly cooked. Remove the lobsters from the liquid with a slotted spoon. Allow the lobsters to cool, remove the meat from the shells, and cut into bite-sized chunks. Remove and discard the bay leaves and strain leek and parsley mixture.

3. Toss together the lobster and the wilted leek and parsley mixture. Drizzle with the oil and sprinkle with salt and pepper.

Bread Salad

This is one of those recipes that will really benefit from top-shelf extra-virgin olive oil. Reserve inexpensive olive oil for other dishes.

INGREDIENTS | SERVES 10

2 large loaves crusty Italian bread

⅔ cup extra-virgin olive oil

⅓ cup balsamic vinegar

2 tablespoons Roasted Garlic Paste (see Chapter 3)

¼ bunch fresh parsley, chopped

¼ bunch fresh basil, chopped

⅓ cup fresh-grated Locatelli Romano cheese

½ teaspoon freshly cracked black pepper

1. Slice and toast the bread. Cut into a large dice.

2. In a medium bowl, mix together the oil, vinegar, garlic paste, herbs, cheese, and pepper.

3. Toss with the bread and serve.

Grilled Tuna Salad

Most grilled tuna salad recipes call for lemon or orange zest, but other citrus fruits work just as well. This recipe calls for tangerines, but you can use lime or grapefruit, too.

INGREDIENTS | SERVES 10

¼ cup olive oil, divided

2 pounds fresh tuna steaks

½ teaspoon coarse salt

½ teaspoon freshly cracked black pepper

20 tangerines

2 pomegranates

¼ bunch fresh parsley, chopped

½ teaspoon capers, rinsed

1. Preheat the grill. Lightly oil the fish and season with salt and pepper.

2. Zest 5 of the tangerines using a citrus zester or vegetable peeler. Peel and section all of the tangerines. Remove the seeds from the pomegranates.

3. Grill the tuna to desired doneness. Let cool, then thinly slice on the bias (at an angle).

4. Arrange the tuna and tangerines on a serving platter or plates. Drizzle with the remaining oil and sprinkle with the tangerine zest, pomegranate seeds, parsley, and capers.

Savoy Cabbage Salad

Fennel and anise seed can be used interchangeably. Make this dish at least 8 hours ahead of time. You can prepare it the night before and refrigerate until time to serve.

INGREDIENTS | SERVES 10

½ cup extra-virgin olive oil

⅓ cup white wine vinegar

3 anchovy fillets (optional)

1 head Savoy cabbage, shredded

3 bulbs fennel, shredded

3 Vidalia onions, shredded

3 cloves garlic, minced

½ teaspoon freshly cracked black pepper

1 teaspoon fennel seeds

1. In a blender, mix together the oil, vinegar, and anchovy.

2. In a large bowl, toss the cabbage, fennel, onions, and garlic with the oil mixture, the pepper, and fennel seeds.

3. Chill for at least 8 hours before serving.

Try Savoy

A head of Savoy cabbage is softer and more compact than the cabbage you are used to seeing in the market. The leaves are curlier, more wrinkled, and darker green in color. You can eat it raw by cutting it into very thin strips and seasoning it with balsamic vinegar, virgin olive oil, salt, and pepper.

Celeriac Misto

Celeriac has a pretty mild flavor, but the extras in this salad really make it tangy.
You can add more or fewer walnuts and currants according to your taste.

INGREDIENTS | SERVES 10

3 celeriac (celery root), shredded

Zest and juice of 1 large lemon, divided

2 large leeks, finely sliced

½ cup walnuts, finely chopped

½ cup Gorgonzola cheese

¾ cup apple juice

½ cup extra-virgin olive oil

½ cup dried currants

½ teaspoon freshly cracked black pepper

1. In a medium bowl, soak the celeriac in cold water with 1 tablespoon of the fresh lemon juice for 2 minutes.

2. Drain the celeriac and mix it with all the other ingredients in a large bowl. Serve.

Fennel

Available in winter, fennel (*finocchio* in Italian) has a delicate anise flavor and can be eaten raw; sliced and seasoned with virgin olive oil, lemon juice, pepper, and salt; or cooked in various ways. You can boil, broil, or fry fennel. It makes a great side dish to meat and can be the main ingredient in a salad.

Fresh Crab with Arugula Salad

You can buy lump crabmeat in containers in the fresh fish section of the market. Just be sure you don't pick up artificial crabmeat—it is processed whitefish that is pressed and colored red.

INGREDIENTS | SERVES 10

2½ pounds fresh cooked crabmeat
2 bunches arugula
5 medium plums, cut in half
½ cup extra-virgin olive oil
¼ cup white wine vinegar
½ teaspoon coarse salt
½ teaspoon freshly cracked black pepper

1. If shelling the crab, make sure all bits of shell are removed from the meat. If not precut, cut the crabmeat into bite-sized cubes.

2. To serve, mound the arugula on a serving platter and top with the crab and plums. Drizzle with the oil and vinegar and sprinkle with salt and pepper.

Baby Greens with Apple and Mascarpone

Sunflower seeds are good on this salad, but you may substitute any other seed or nut (walnuts and slivered almonds work well), or omit them entirely if that is your preference.

INGREDIENTS | SERVES 10

5 tart apples, thinly sliced
Zest and juice of 1 large lemon
2 tablespoons extra-virgin olive oil
½ teaspoon freshly cracked black pepper
5 cups baby salad greens
¼ cup shelled sunflower seeds
½ cup mascarpone cheese

1. In a large bowl, mix together the apples, lemon zest and juice, oil, and pepper.

2. Mound the greens on serving plates and top with the apple mixture, sunflower seeds, and dollops of the cheese.

Fig and Gorgonzola Salad

Do not use dried figs for this recipe. If you cannot find fresh figs, make another salad. Figs come in white and black, and you can use either for this recipe.

INGREDIENTS | SERVES 10

2 toasted flatbreads of any flavor (see Chapter 9)
¾ cup extra-virgin olive oil
½ cup orange juice
¼ bunch fresh parsley, chopped
½ teaspoon freshly cracked black pepper
10 fresh figs, sliced into wedges
5 cups baby salad greens or mesclun
½ cup crumbled Gorgonzola cheese

1. Tear the toasted flatbread into bite-sized pieces.

2. In a large bowl, whisk together the oil, orange juice, parsley, and pepper.

3. Toss the figs, greens, and cheese with the oil mixture. Cover and refrigerate for 1 hour. Serve with the toasted flatbread pieces.

Cheese Tortellini Salad

To prepare the tortellini for this salad, rinse with cold water after cooking, and lay it out in a single layer on wax paper to dry.

INGREDIENTS | SERVES 10

2 shallots, minced
4 sprigs marjoram, chopped
½ recipe cooked Cheese Tortellini (see Chapter 13)
1 cup Roasted Eggplant Purée (see Chapter 3)
2 tablespoons extra-virgin olive oil
4 tablespoons red wine vinegar
½ teaspoon freshly cracked black pepper

In a large bowl, mix together all the ingredients. Serve.

Christmas Eve Salad

Cook the shrimp ahead of time to enable thorough chilling. The eggplant can be prepared a few days early as well.

INGREDIENTS | SERVES 10

10 fresh extra-large shrimp, peeled and deveined

2 tablespoons ketchup

1 teaspoon lemon zest

1 teaspoon (or more to taste) prepared horseradish

¼ pound Parmesan cheese

2 medium grapefruit or oranges

5 cups mixed baby greens

2 medium red onions, finely sliced

1 cup thickly sliced pepperoni

1 cup *Melanzane Marinate* (Pickled Eggplants) (see Chapter 2)

¼ cup extra-virgin olive oil

½ teaspoon freshly cracked black pepper

1. Peel the shrimp and slice in half lengthwise. Cook quickly in boiling water. Drain and chill completely in the refrigerator or in ice-cold water (drain again if water is used).

2. In a medium bowl, mix together the ketchup, zest, and horseradish. Coat the shrimp with the ketchup mixture.

3. Use a vegetable peeler to cut the Parmesan into fine curls. Peel the grapefruit and cut the fruit into sections.

4. Mound the greens on a serving platter. Top with the onions and place the pepperoni on one side and the eggplant on the other. Fan the grapefruit sections over the onion, then top with the shrimp and Parmesan curls. Drizzle with the oil and sprinkle with black pepper.

Hearty Cold Antipasto Salad

This is the perfect salad to serve at a picnic. It's full of delicious ingredients and makes a colorful addition to your picnic table. Just be sure it can rest in a cool, shaded spot.

INGREDIENTS | SERVES 10

¼ cup pasteurized egg, or Egg Beaters

2 tablespoons Roasted Garlic Paste (see Chapter 3)

½ cup extra-virgin olive oil

¼ cup balsamic vinegar

3 anchovy fillets

½ teaspoon freshly cracked black pepper

1 head romaine lettuce

¼ pound capicola, thinly sliced

¼ pound Genoa salami, thinly sliced

½ cup thinly sliced pepperoni

2 medium red onions, sliced

2 hard-boiled eggs, sliced

12 Roasted Red Peppers (see Chapter 15), diced

¼ cup black olives

1. Prepare the Caesar dressing by emulsifying the egg, garlic paste, oil, vinegar, anchovy, and black pepper in a food processor or blender.

2. Clean the lettuce and remove the outer leaves and heart. Discard the heart and set aside the outer leaves. Gently chop the remainder into bite-sized pieces. Cut each slice of meat into quarters.

3. Lay out the large romaine leaves on a platter. Mix the chopped lettuce with the dressing and mound on top of the base leaves. Arrange the onion, egg, red peppers, meats, and olives decoratively on top. Serve.

Tired of Romaine?

To add variety to your salads, experiment with the many types of greens that are available in most markets. Oak leaf, frisée, arugula, spinach, and dandelion are just a few. You can use one type or mix a few different varieties together for more color and texture.

Eggplant Arugula Salad

Don't use a highly flavored dressing on this salad—it will overpower the delicate mix of flavors. A simple vinaigrette of extra-virgin olive oil and a good balsamic vinegar, like the one here, is perfect.

INGREDIENTS | SERVES 10

3 medium eggplants
5 ounces Parmesan cheese
2 tablespoons olive oil
⅓ cup pine nuts
½ cup extra-virgin olive oil
¼ cup balsamic vinegar
3 shallots, diced
½ bulb garlic, minced
2 bunches arugula
3 ripe peaches or nectarines, cut into wedges
½ teaspoon freshly cracked black pepper

1. Preheat the oven to 375°F. Slice the eggplants in half lengthwise. Shave the Parmesan into thin curls using a vegetable peeler.

2. Rub the eggplant with the 2 tablespoons olive oil. Place the eggplant halves face down in a baking pan and roast for approximately 45 minutes until soft. Let cool.

3. Toast the pine nuts in the oven on a baking sheet until lightly brown. Allow the pine nuts to cool.

4. To prepare the vinaigrette, blend the extra-virgin olive oil and vinegar in a small bowl.

5. Scoop out the eggplant flesh and toss with the shallots and garlic in a medium bowl. Mound on serving plates. Arrange the arugula and cheese on one side and the peaches on the other. Drizzle with the vinaigrette and sprinkle with the toasted pine nuts and black pepper.

Citrus Green-Bean Salad

The Italian cooking term al dente, which normally refers to pasta, can also be used when cooking vegetables for salads. The green beans in this recipe should be cooked until just al dente, or until there is a bit of a crunch when you bite into them.

INGREDIENTS | SERVES 10

5 cups fresh green beans

½ cup hazelnuts, crushed

½ bunch fresh chives or scallions, sliced

½ cup fresh-grated Asiago cheese

½ cup extra-virgin olive oil

¾ cup orange juice

½ teaspoon freshly cracked black pepper

1. Clean and cut off the ends of the green beans. Blanch the green beans, then shock in ice water.

2. In a large bowl, mix together all the ingredients. Serve.

CHAPTER 15

Vegetables

Cavolfiore Fritto (Fried Cauliflower)

You can also use the batter in this recipe for frying a number of other vegetables, such as blanched broccoli, mushrooms, peppers, and asparagus.

INGREDIENTS | SERVES 10

1 head fresh cauliflower, blanched and shocked

4 large eggs

¼ cup fresh-grated Asiago cheese

¼ cup whole milk

½ cup all-purpose flour

½ cup fresh bread crumbs

¼ cup olive oil

½ bunch fresh parsley, chopped

½ teaspoon freshly cracked black pepper

Blanch and Shock

To blanch and shock vegetables, quickly cook in boiling water to al dente. Then immediately remove from the water and shock in ice water until completely cold. Drain the vegetables, season, and serve, or prepare as the recipe directs.

1. Cut the cauliflower into bite-sized florets.

2. In a medium bowl, beat the eggs. Mix in the cheese and milk.

3. In a shallow dish, combine the flour and bread crumbs.

4. Heat the oil over medium heat in a large frying pan with a lid. Dip the florets in the egg mixture, then dust with the bread crumb mixture. Place in the hot oil. Sauté on all sides until lightly brown and fork-tender, about 10 minutes.

5. Drain on a rack lined with paper towels. Sprinkle with parsley and pepper. Serve hot.

Wilted Kale with Dried Currants and Walnuts

The slightly bitter taste of the kale is offset by the sweetness of the currants. The nuts create a nice crunchy texture.

INGREDIENTS | SERVES 10

3 bunches fresh kale (or substitute any other fresh green)

2 cups balsamic vinegar

1 cup dried currants

1 cup chopped walnuts

¼ cup honey

¼ cup extra-virgin olive oil

½ teaspoon kosher salt

½ teaspoon freshly cracked black pepper

1. Rinse the kale in cold water and pat dry.

2. Place the kale, vinegar, currants, and walnuts in a large stockpot. Cover and bring to a low simmer. Cook for 5–10 minutes or until the greens are just wilted.

3. Immediately remove from heat and drizzle with the honey and oil. Sprinkle with salt and pepper and serve.

Broccoli with Romano Bread Crumbs

Blanching and shocking the broccoli helps maintain its green color. If a vegetable isn't shocked with cold water when it comes out of the boiling pot, it will continue to "cook" even after it's been drained.

INGREDIENTS | SERVES 10

¼ cup olive oil, divided

2 heads fresh broccoli

¼ cup melted unsalted butter

⅓ cup bread crumbs

⅓ cup fresh-grated Romano cheese

½ teaspoon freshly cracked black pepper

1. Preheat the oven to 375°F. Grease a large casserole dish with 1 tablespoon of the oil.

2. Clean the broccoli and cut lengthwise. Quickly blanch the broccoli in boiling water until just al dente, then drain. Shock in ice water and drain thoroughly. Place the broccoli in the prepared casserole dish.

3. In a large bowl, mix together the remaining oil, the butter, bread crumbs, and cheese. Sprinkle the bread crumb mixture on top of the broccoli.

4. Bake for 15 minutes or until the bread crumbs are lightly browned and the broccoli is warm. Serve sprinkled with pepper.

Roasted Garlic Smashed Potatoes

Cooking potatoes whole instead of cutting them up decreases absorption of water.
Quick-drying in a hot oven after boiling them helps remove water, too.

INGREDIENTS | SERVES 10

2 pounds potatoes

¼ cup Roasted Garlic Paste (see Chapter 3)

¼ cup unsalted butter

¼ cup heavy cream

½ teaspoon kosher salt

½ teaspoon freshly cracked black pepper

1. Clean and peel the potatoes. Fill a large ovenproof pot with water and bring to a boil. Add the potatoes and boil for 5 minutes. Lower heat to a simmer and continue to cook for 40 minutes or until tender. Drain, return the whole potatoes to the pot, and return the pot to the stovetop for a few minutes for the potatoes to dry out (or place in a hot oven for 5–10 minutes).

2. Mash the potatoes, then fold in the remaining ingredients until well mixed. Serve.

Mashing Potatoes

Mashing potatoes in a standing mixer seems like an easy way to break up most lumps and evenly incorporate butter, seasonings, and milk. However, it's all too easy to overmash them, which quickly turns starches into gluey gluten. The key is to "smash" (or whip) them by hand or with a mixer just enough to break up the lumps, then fold in the butter, milk, and seasonings by hand.

Roasted Butternut Squash Stew

Butternut squash is the closest equivalent to the native Italian zucca, a round, bumpy-skinned squash with flesh resembling that of a pumpkin in texture and color.

INGREDIENTS | SERVES 10

2 large butternut squash, peeled and chopped

2 medium yellow onions, chopped

3 medium carrots, chopped

2 stalks celery, chopped

2 sprigs fresh thyme, stems discarded

¼ bunch fresh parsley, stems discarded

¼ cup olive oil

2 tablespoons ground cumin

½ teaspoon ground mace or nutmeg

1 bay leaf

½ teaspoon freshly cracked black pepper

6 cups Chicken Stock (see Chapter 4)

1. Preheat the oven to 375°F.

2. In a large bowl, toss the vegetables and fresh herbs in the oil. Place in a roasting pan and roast for 45 minutes, uncovered.

3. Remove from the oven and place all the ingredients in a large stockpot. Simmer for 1½ hours, uncovered. Let cool. Remove bay leaf and purée until smooth.

4. Serve with steamed greens, if desired.

Celeriac Alfredo

Sometimes called Verona celery, celeriac (celery root) can be eaten raw; cut into sticks and sautéed with oil, vinegar, pepper, and salt; or fried, plain or with breading.

INGREDIENTS | SERVES 10

1 tablespoon olive oil

2 bulbs fresh celeriac, thinly sliced

½ bulb garlic, minced

2 cups Easy Alfredo Sauce (see Chapter 3)

½ cup Sage Pesto (see Chapter 3)

½ teaspoon freshly cracked black pepper

1. Preheat the oven to 375°F. Grease a large baking dish with the oil.

2. Bring a large pot of water to a boil and cook the celeriac until fork-tender (al dente).

3. Layer the celeriac, garlic, and Alfredo sauce in the prepared pan. Sprinkle with the pesto and pepper.

4. Cover and bake for 15 minutes. Uncover and bake for 15 more minutes. Serve hot.

Broccoli Raab Parmesan

This bitter variety of broccoli is very popular in southern Italy. It is often boiled prior to other preparation to cut the bitter taste. It is commonly sautéed in oil and garlic and seasoned with lemon juice, salt, and pepper.

INGREDIENTS | SERVES 10

2 heads fresh broccoli raab

2 tablespoons olive oil, divided

2 Vidalia onions, thickly sliced

½ teaspoon freshly cracked black pepper, divided

1½ cups Old World Gravy (Long-Cooking Tomato Sauce) (see Chapter 3)

½ pound provolone cheese, shredded

1. Preheat the oven to 375°F. Clean and trim the broccoli raab and discard the very ends of the stems. Pour 1 tablespoon of the oil into the bottom of a large oven-proof pan.

2. Place the broccoli and onion in the prepared pan and season with half of the pepper. Stir thoroughly. Roast for 12 minutes, uncovered, and remove from the oven.

3. Pour half of the sauce in the bottom of a separate baking dish. Arrange the broccoli and onion in the bottom of the dish. Sprinkle with the provolone. Drizzle with the remaining sauce, then drizzle with the remaining oil.

4. Sprinkle with the remaining pepper. Bake for 10 minutes, uncovered, and serve.

Patate Fritti (Fried Potatoes)

Enjoy these potato pancakes hot and crispy, immediately after cooking. Sprinkle with Parmesan cheese, if desired.

INGREDIENTS | SERVES 10

5 large potatoes, peeled and shredded
½ bulb garlic, minced
¼ cup olive oil
½ teaspoon kosher salt
½ teaspoon freshly cracked black pepper

1. In a large bowl, mix together the potatoes and garlic. Form the mixture into oval pancakes about 4" long and 2" wide.

2. Heat the oil over medium-high heat in a large sauté pan. Fry the pancakes until golden brown and crisp on each side. Fry in batches if necessary to avoid overcrowding the pan.

3. Season with salt and pepper and serve.

Roasted Red Peppers

Homemade roasted red peppers taste so much better than store-bought canned or jarred varieties—and they're extremely simple to make!

INGREDIENTS | 4 PEPPERS

4 large whole red peppers
¼ cup olive oil

Pleasing Peppers

Making your own roasted red peppers is a great idea. They're a common ingredient in many different types of cooking, and they store well in the refrigerator. If you set aside some time to make a batch—even on a day when you won't be using them—they'll be ready for you when you need them.

1. Preheat the oven to 400°F (or preheat the grill on high). Toss the whole peppers (stem and all) in the olive oil. Roast on a baking sheet pan until the skin starts to blister.

2. Immediately place the peppers in a bowl of ice water, or place in a plastic bag and seal immediately (this makes it easy to peel them).

3. After 5 minutes, peel off and discard the skins. Use or store in the refrigerator for later use.

Grilled Vegetables

This one-dish vegetable "lasagna" is the Italian version of a French recipe.
It makes a great side to any roast chicken or meat entrée.

INGREDIENTS | SERVES 10

3 large baking potatoes

4 medium red bell peppers, seeded and cut

2 large onions (any type), cut into ½" rings

¼ cup olive oil

2 cups Old World Gravy (Long-Cooking Tomato Sauce) (see Chapter 3)

2 cups steamed spinach

½ cup Roasted Garlic Paste (see Chapter 3)

1 cup ricotta cheese

½ teaspoon freshly cracked black pepper

1. Preheat the oven to 350°F. Preheat the grill to medium-high. Clean and slice the potatoes lengthwise into ½"-thick slices.

2. Lightly "grease" the potatoes, peppers, and onions by brushing with the olive oil. Grill until fork-tender.

3. While the veggies grill, preheat the Old World Gravy in a small saucepan.

4. Layer all the ingredients in a casserole dish, starting with a few ladlefuls of the sauce on the bottom and alternating layers of vegetables, spinach, garlic paste, ricotta, and sauce. Sprinkle with black pepper.

5. Bake for 20 minutes or just until heated through and bubbling. Serve.

Rolled Squash

Only cook the squash until it is just tender enough to roll—if overcooked, it will fall apart when handled. Leaving peels on the eggplant, zucchini, and yellow squash will help them hold their shape.

INGREDIENTS | SERVES 10

1 large eggplant

2 large zucchini

1 large yellow squash

1 medium butternut squash

1 teaspoon coarse salt

1½ cups cheese sauce of choice (see Chapter 3)

1 cup Traditional Pesto (see Chapter 3)

1. Preheat the oven to 375°F. Clean and slice the eggplant, zucchini, and yellow squash lengthwise. Place on a greased baking sheet and roast for 10–15 minutes or just until tender.

2. Peel and slice the butternut squash, scoop out the insides, and rinse the seeds. Toss the seeds in the salt and toast lightly on another greased baking sheet for about 10 minutes.

3. Partially steam the butternut squash on the stovetop or in the microwave until just fork-tender. Drain off liquid.

4. Coat the inside of a loaf pan with half of the cheese sauce. Then layer the eggplant, zucchini, yellow squash, and butternut squash in the pan. Top with more cheese sauce (leave a little for the end) and ½ cup of the pesto.

5. Carefully fold over the sliced squash to form a roll and top it with the remaining pesto and cheese sauce. Cover and bake for 20 minutes.

6. Uncover and cook for 10 minutes. Serve sprinkled with the toasted seeds.

Pecan Broccoli

For this dish, it is important that the broccoli is cooked al dente, or just firm to the bite. Soggy or limp broccoli will be overwhelmed by the crunchiness of the pecans.

INGREDIENTS | SERVES 10

3 tablespoons olive oil, divided
4 heads broccoli
1 cup shelled pecans
¼ cup honey
1 teaspoon freshly cracked black pepper
¼ cup balsamic vinegar (optional)

1. Preheat the oven to 375°F. Lightly grease a large, oblong baking pan with 1 tablespoon of the oil. Clean and split the broccoli and cut into long spears.

2. Roughly chop the pecans and toss in a small bowl with the remaining oil, the broccoli, honey, and black pepper.

3. Spread the broccoli mixture in an even layer in the prepared baking pan. Roast for 15–20 minutes uncovered until the broccoli is cooked al dente.

4. Place the cooked broccoli spears on a serving platter. Drizzle with the balsamic vinegar, if desired, and serve.

Green Bean Bundles

The preparation of these green beans raises a simple vegetable side to a great dish for entertaining. It makes the portions easy to serve and creates an attractive presentation.

INGREDIENTS | SERVES 10

3 tablespoons olive oil, divided

1½ pounds fresh green beans

½ teaspoon kosher salt

½ teaspoon freshly cracked black pepper

¼ recipe Basic Flatbread (see Chapter 9), unformed and uncooked

1 cup Cannellini Bean Purée (see Chapter 3)

1. Preheat the oven to 375°F. Lightly grease a sheet pan with 1 tablespoon of the oil.

2. Clean the green beans and snap off the stem ends. Blanch the green beans, then shock in ice water. Drain.

3. In a large bowl, toss the green beans in the remaining olive oil and season with salt and pepper.

4. Roll out the flatbread dough into a sheet ½" thick. Cut into strips about 1" wide and 6" long. Gather the green beans into bundles of 6–8 beans, wrap them in the dough strips, tie, and press to seal.

5. Place the bundles on the prepared baking sheet and bake for 15 minutes. While the green bean bundles roast, heat the Cannellini Bean Purée in a small saucepan.

6. To serve, spoon the purée onto a serving platter and top with the green bean bundles.

Sautéed Beets with Shallots

The bright color in this dish gives it a great presentation. It makes a good accompaniment to any roasted meat entrée.

INGREDIENTS | SERVES 10

1½ pounds fresh beets
2 tablespoons olive oil
4 pounds fresh shallots, finely chopped
½ teaspoon kosher salt
½ teaspoon freshly cracked black pepper
½ cup light-bodied red table wine
¼ cup seedless red grapes, cut in half

Shallots

Shallots are onion-like vegetables that can be substituted in many recipes for onions and scallions. Shallots generally have two sections, or "lobes," which should be separated before peeling. Shallots can be cooked various ways, just like onions.

1. Peel and thinly slice the beets.

2. Heat the oil over medium heat in a large sauté pan. Add the beets and shallots and season with salt and pepper. Cover and cook for 20 minutes, stirring frequently.

3. Pour in the wine and cook for 10 minutes, stirring continuously.

4. Add the grapes and reduce heat to low. Cover, and cook for 5 minutes. Serve hot.

Asparagi alla Milanese (Milan-Style Asparagus)

This dish is a dressed-up version of basic steamed asparagus. The butter, egg, and cheese add extra color and flavor.

INGREDIENTS | SERVES 10

2 cups water
2 pounds asparagus
1 large egg
3 tablespoons unsalted butter
¼ cup fresh-grated Parmesan cheese

1. Bring the water to a boil in a large saucepan. Break off the "woody" ends of the asparagus (holding each spear at each end and bending until the asparagus spear breaks). Place the asparagus in the water, cover, and steam until al dente.

2. While the asparagus is steaming, fry the egg in a skillet over medium heat.

3. Remove the asparagus from the water, drain, and place on a serving platter. Place pats of the butter on top and evenly distribute the butter over the asparagus as it melts. Place the fried egg over the asparagus tips. Serve sprinkled with the cheese.

Parsley Peas

To create your own variations of this recipe, try it with other herbs in place of the parsley, such as mint or basil.

INGREDIENTS | SERVES 10

1½ pounds fresh peas
4 cups Vegetable Stock (see Chapter 4)
¼ bunch fresh parsley, chopped
½ teaspoon freshly cracked black pepper
½ teaspoon kosher salt

1. Shuck the peas.

2. Bring the stock to a slow simmer on the stovetop. Add the peas and cook until al dente.

3. Remove from heat and add the parsley, pepper, and salt. Serve hot.

Aw, Shucks!

Wondering what *shuck* means? As a noun, a shuck is a husk, pod, or shell. To shuck, as a verb, is to remove the husk, pod, or shell. So, when you shuck peas, you simply remove the peas from the pods. Easy, right?

Baked Sweet Potatoes with Pear

This tasty side dish goes very well with smoked meats or other salty main dishes.

INGREDIENTS | SERVES 10

1 tablespoon olive oil
2 pounds sweet potatoes, thinly sliced
4 pears (any type), thinly sliced
1 teaspoon fennel seeds
3 tablespoons unsalted butter
½ teaspoon freshly cracked black pepper
1 cup pear nectar

1. Preheat the oven to 375°F. Lightly grease a large, oblong pan with the oil.

2. Spread a layer of the sweet potatoes and then a layer of the pears in the prepared pan. Sprinkle the fennel seeds over the top. Dot with pats of the butter and sprinkle with the pepper. Pour the pear nectar over the top.

3. Cover and bake 1 hour. Serve hot.

Escarole Stew

Escarole is a leafy green that is frequently used in Italian cooking.
Serve this stew with crusty Italian bread for dipping.

INGREDIENTS | SERVES 10

4 heads escarole

3 large Idaho potatoes, cut into wedges

3 medium white onions, cut into wedges

2 medium carrots, cut into wedges

2 stalks celery, chopped

½ bulb garlic, minced

¼ cup walnuts, chopped

6 sprigs fresh thyme, stems discarded

1 cup cooked or canned chickpeas

8 cups Vegetable Stock (see Chapter 4)

2 bay leaves

½ teaspoon freshly cracked black pepper

1 teaspoon extra-virgin olive oil

1. Clean the escarole and separate the leaves.

2. Place all the ingredients except the escarole and olive oil in a large stockpot and simmer at medium heat for 1 hour, uncovered.

3. Add the escarole and simmer for 5 minutes.

4. Adjust seasoning to taste. Drizzle with the olive oil, remove the bay leaves, and serve.

The Right Pot

When a recipe instructs you to use a "heavy-bottomed" pot, that's your clue that a thin pot may result in a burned flavor. Thick bottoms conduct heat more evenly and retain heat better, causing fewer "hot spots" where the flame or electric element contacts the pan. Hot spots burn certain foods, no matter how carefully you stir.

Zucchini Patties

This can be served as an appetizer or a side dish. It also makes a great entrée if you are having vegetarians over for dinner.

INGREDIENTS | SERVES 10

1½ pounds fresh zucchini, shredded

2 shallots, minced

3 cloves garlic, minced

4 large eggs, beaten

½ cup fresh-grated Parmesan cheese

½ cup whole milk

½ cup all-purpose flour

½ teaspoon freshly cracked black pepper

½ cup olive oil

1. In a large bowl, mix together the zucchini, shallots, garlic, eggs, cheese, milk, flour, and pepper. Form the mixture into small oval patties.

2. Heat the oil over medium-high heat in a large skillet. Fry the patties on each side.

3. Drain the patties on paper towels and serve.

Carrot and Citrus Casserole

This slightly sweet casserole is colorful and nutritious. Serve as an appetizer or accompaniment to a roasted meat entrée.

INGREDIENTS | SERVES 10

2 tablespoons unsalted butter, divided

2 pounds fresh baby carrots

½ cup dried currants (or substitute raisins)

Juice and zest of 3 large oranges

¼ cup brown sugar

½ cup long-cooking oats

1. Preheat the oven to 375°F. Lightly grease a casserole dish with ½ tablespoon of the butter.

2. Layer the carrots, currants, orange juice, zest, remaining butter, brown sugar, and oats in the prepared casserole dish.

3. Cover and bake for 1 hour. Uncover and bake for 15 minutes. Serve hot.

Grilled Fennel

*Fennel is a good source of vitamin A. This grilled version is delightful
as a side dish, or try adding some in a salad or soup.*

INGREDIENTS | SERVES 6

3 large bulbs fennel

1 tablespoon olive oil

½ teaspoon freshly cracked pepper, or
to taste

½ teaspoon kosher salt, or to taste

Fennel Tops

Don't throw out the tops! Fennel tops can
be used in stocks, but don't forget about
their distinctive licorice flavor. Take that
into consideration when adding them to
a stock.

1. Remove the tops from the fennel and cut the bulbs into
   1½"-thick slices from bottom to top (*not* across the
   bulb).

2. Heat the grill to medium-high. Dip the fennel slices in
   the oil, shake off excess, and season with pepper and
   salt; place on the grill for 2 minutes, then turn position
   to create an X-shaped mark from the grill rack. Grill
   2 minutes longer, then turn over. Repeat process until
   the fennel is tender, then serve.

Roasted Asparagus

*Use thicker asparagus to withstand the heat of the grill. Be sure
to remove the woody end of the stalk first.*

INGREDIENTS | SERVES 6

2 bunches asparagus

1 tablespoon extra-virgin olive oil

½ teaspoon kosher salt, or to taste
(optional)

½ teaspoon freshly cracked black
pepper, or to taste

Preheat the grill to medium. Toss the asparagus in the oil,
then drain on a rack and season with salt and pepper. Grill
the asparagus for 1–2 minutes on each side (cook to
desired doneness). Serve immediately.

CHAPTER 16

Desserts

Cinnamon Almond Cake

This traditional cake is always a favorite. Add it to your next Thanksgiving meal as a striking variation on the usual string of desserts.

INGREDIENTS | SERVES 12

1 cup sugar
¼ teaspoon grated lemon rind
6 egg yolks
½ pound finely ground almonds
½ teaspoon cinnamon
6 egg whites
½ cup heavy cream
¼ teaspoon granulated sugar
1 teaspoon brandy
Chopped almonds, for garnish

1. Preheat the oven to 350°F.

2. In a large bowl, cream the sugar, rind, and yolks until light and fluffy. Stir in the finely ground almonds and cinnamon.

3. In a separate bowl, whip the egg whites until stiff. Stir a few tablespoons of whites into the almond mixture and then fold in the rest.

4. Pour into 2 greased 8" pans; bake for 45 minutes. Let cool briefly and remove from pans.

5. Whip the cream with the ¼ teaspoon sugar and brandy. Spread between cake layers and then on the top and sides. Garnish with chopped almonds.

Blueberry Ricotta Tart

This tart has a lemon-and-honey-flavored ricotta cheese base. The ricotta filling provides a creamy counterpoint to the juicy berries.

INGREDIENTS | SERVES 8

1 cup ricotta cheese
2 teaspoons lemon zest
1 teaspoon vanilla
2 tablespoons honey
2 tablespoons sugar
1 egg yolk
¼ teaspoon salt
1 (12") round pastry crust, chilled
1 cup fresh blueberries
½ recipe Butter Crumble (see sidebar)

Butter Crumble

In a medium bowl, blend ½ cup all-purpose flour, ½ cup sugar, and ¼ teaspoon salt. Using your fingers, rub ⅓ cup cubed and chilled unsalted butter into the mixture until the mixture resembles coarse sand. Chill the crumble for 30 minutes before use.

1. In a large bowl, whisk together the ricotta, lemon zest, vanilla, honey, sugar, egg yolk, and salt. Cover and chill for 30 minutes.

2. Heat the oven to 350°F and line a baking sheet with parchment paper.

3. Place the chilled pastry crust on the prepared baking sheet. Spread the ricotta mixture onto the crust, leaving a ½" border. Arrange the blueberries over the ricotta mixture, then fold the crust just over the edge of the filling. Top with the Butter Crumble.

4. Bake for 45–55 minutes or until the fruit is bubbling and both the crumble and pastry are golden brown. Cool to room temperature before serving.

Tiramisu Pie

If you prefer, you can use mascarpone cheese instead of the cream cheese in this recipe.

INGREDIENTS | SERVES 8

6 ounces cream cheese, softened

1 cup powdered sugar

3 tablespoons cold, strongly brewed coffee, divided

½ teaspoon powdered gelatin

1 cup heavy cream

½ teaspoon vanilla

1 (9") graham cracker crust

1 recipe Stabilized Whipped Cream (see sidebar)

Cocoa powder, for dusting

Stabilized Whipped Cream

In a small bowl, mix ½ teaspoon unflavored powdered gelatin with 1½ teaspoons cold water. Let stand 10 minutes, then melt in the microwave for 10 seconds. Allow to cool for 5 minutes, or until cool to the touch. In a medium bowl, add 1 cup cold heavy whipping cream, 3 tablespoons powdered sugar, and 1 teaspoon vanilla. Whip with a stand mixer or with a hand mixer on medium-high speed until it starts to thicken. Slowly pour in the cooled gelatin and whip until the cream forms medium peaks.

1. In a large bowl, cream together the cream cheese, powdered sugar, and 2 tablespoons of the coffee until thick and creamy.

2. In a small bowl, combine the remaining coffee with the gelatin. Allow to stand for 10 minutes to bloom. Once bloomed, heat it in the microwave for 10 seconds to melt. Cool to room temperature.

3. In a medium bowl, beat the heavy cream with the vanilla until it begins to thicken. Slowly add in the gelatin mixture and beat until medium peaks form. Fold the whipped cream into the cream cheese mixture. Spread into the prepared pie crust; cover and chill for 4 hours.

4. Once chilled, prepare the Stabilized Whipped Cream. Spread it over the pie. Chill for 1 hour. Dust the pie with cocoa powder before serving.

Tordillas

Though called something different in every family, these are classic Italian Christmas pastries. Of course, they're a delicious treat all year round.

INGREDIENTS | SERVES 10

3 cups all-purpose flour

2 tablespoons baking powder

Pinch iodized salt

¼ cup granulated sugar

1 cup shortening

6 large eggs, lightly beaten

½ cup port wine

4 cups vegetable or corn oil

4 cups honey

Italian Sweets

Italian cuisine is not really known for its sweet dishes. Most sweet dishes are tied to holy days, feasts, weddings, and other celebrations. Pastries, gelato (ice cream), and biscotti are the most common types of Italian desserts.

1. Sift together the flour, baking powder, and salt in a large mixing bowl.

2. In a separate bowl, cream together the sugar and shortening, then add the eggs and wine.

3. Make a well in the center of the flour mixture and pour in the egg mixture. Mix by hand or in a mixer with a dough hook at medium speed until the dough forms into a ball. Cover the dough with plastic wrap or a clean towel and allow it to rest for at least 1 hour (no longer than 3 hours) in the refrigerator.

4. Pull off pieces of the dough in portions equal to about 2 tablespoons. Roll into little ovals using your hands. Continue until all the dough is used up.

5. Heat the oil over medium-high heat in a deep, heavy-bottomed skillet. Fry each oval until light golden brown. Drain on paper towels.

6. Heat the honey over medium heat in a saucepan. Dip each oval into the honey, carefully shaking off excess, and place on wax paper. Serve slightly warm, but be sure the honey has cooled enough not to burn the mouth.

Classic Biscotti

It is the twice-baked aspect that gives biscotti its characteristic crunch. There are numerous variations of this recipe, but this is the classic almond-and-anisette flavor.

INGREDIENTS | SERVES 10

½ teaspoon plus 1½ cups unsalted butter, divided

¾ cup granulated sugar

¾ cup light brown sugar

2 eggs, lightly beaten

¼ cup anisette liqueur

3½ cups all-purpose flour

½ teaspoon baking powder

½ teaspoon baking soda

½ cup sliced almonds

About Biscotti

Biscotti are baked twice for extra crunch—first as a log and then in slices. You can put any dried fruit or nut in biscotti. Pistachios and hazelnuts work especially well. Use dried cherries or apricots instead of raisins for a nice variation. Biscotti keep well, so they make a great holiday gift for friends and family.

1. Preheat the oven to 375°F. Lightly grease a baking pan with ½ teaspoon of the butter.

2. In a large bowl, cream together the remaining butter and the sugars. Add the eggs and anisette liqueur.

3. In a separate large bowl, sift together the flour, baking powder, and baking soda.

4. Mix together the butter and flour mixtures until they are well mixed and a dough forms. Fold in the almonds.

5. Divide the dough into 2 equal parts and form each into an oval-shaped mound about 2" high. Place the dough mounds on a baking sheet.

6. Bake for 20 minutes. Slice the mounds lengthwise into 2"-thick pieces. Return to the oven and bake for 5 minutes.

7. Remove from the oven and let cool slightly. Store in an airtight container.

Italian Bread Pudding

Many cultures have their own version of bread pudding—everyone seeks a use for day-old bread. This is the Italian version of this popular dessert.

INGREDIENTS | SERVES 10

¼ cup unsalted butter, divided

1 large loaf day-old or toasted Italian bread

6 large eggs

2 cups whole milk

2 cups heavy cream

¼ cup anisette liqueur (optional)

¼ cup honey

¼ cup granulated sugar

1. Preheat the oven to 375°F. Lightly grease an oblong 13" × 9" baking pan with 1 teaspoon of the butter.

2. Melt the remaining butter. Tear the bread into large chunks and combine with the melted butter in a large bowl.

3. Beat the eggs in another large bowl and whisk in the milk, cream, liqueur, honey, and sugar.

4. Place the bread mixture in the prepared pan. Pour the egg mixture over the top and stir.

5. Bake for 30 minutes, uncovered. Stir and return to the oven. Bake for about 15–20 minutes longer until set. Serve warm with whipped cream if desired.

Pear-Filled Calzones

This dessert calzone is a refreshing variation of the standard ricotta cheese calzone you're used to.

INGREDIENTS | SERVES 10

1 (¼-ounce) packet dry active yeast
¼ cup warm water (no hotter than 115°F)
1 pound all-purpose flour, divided
Pinch iodized salt
5 ripe medium pears
¼ cup unsalted butter
2 cups warm milk
Zest and juice of 1 large lemon
¼ cup honey
½ teaspoon ground cloves
Cooking spray
½ cup confectioners' sugar

1. In a small bowl, stir the yeast into the warm water. Let stand for 3–5 minutes until foamy. Mix with a few spoonfuls of the flour.

2. Sift together the remaining flour and salt onto a board or clean countertop, or in the bowl of a mixer.

3. Make a well in the center of the flour and pour in the yeast mixture. Gently mix by hand or in a mixer with a dough hook until a soft ball forms. Knead for 5 minutes. Divide the dough into 10 small balls and place on a floured board. Cover with plastic wrap and let rest for 1 hour.

4. While the dough rests, peel, core, and slice the pears. Cut the butter into 10 portions.

5. Mix together the milk, pears, lemon zest and juice, and honey. Sprinkle with the cloves.

6. Preheat the oven to 375°F. Roll out the dough balls to approximately 1" thick on a floured surface. Fill each with the pear mixture and top with a pat of the butter. Fold over the dough and seal firmly. Let rest on the floured board, covered, for about 1 hour.

7. Lightly grease a baking sheet with the cooking spray. Gently place the calzones on the pan and bake for 30–40 minutes. Remove from the oven, place on a plate, and sprinkle with the confectioners' sugar.

Cinnamon Rolls

Homemade cinnamon rolls are vastly superior to those you can buy in the store. Make these for breakfast, as a snack, or as part of a brunch buffet.

INGREDIENTS | SERVES 10

Dough

1 (¼-ounce) packet dry active yeast
½ cup warm water
3 cups all-purpose flour
¼ cup brown sugar
Pinch iodized salt
3 large eggs
1 cup scalded milk (cooled thoroughly)

Filling

1 cup melted unsalted butter
3 tablespoons ground cinnamon
½ cup granulated sugar

Frosting

1 cup confectioners' sugar
1 teaspoon vanilla extract
1½ cups whole milk

Vanillas of the World

The best-quality vanilla beans and extracts come from Tahiti and Madagascar. Cheaper (and often watery) extracts come from Mexico. Major U.S. brands are not as finessed as most exotic imports, but these provide reliable vanilla flavor. For best results, pay more for higher-quality vanilla.

1. Prepare the dough: Stir the yeast into the water. Let stand for 3–5 minutes until frothy.

2. In a large bowl, sift together the flour, sugar, and salt.

3. In a small bowl, mix together the eggs and cooled milk.

4. Combine the yeast water, flour mixture, and egg mixture and mix until a ball forms. Allow the dough to rest for 1 hour in a greased bowl in a warm place.

5. While the dough rests, combine all the filling ingredients in a small bowl.

6. Mix together all the frosting ingredients in a separate bowl. Store the frosting in the refrigerator. Preheat the oven to 375°F.

7. Punch down the dough once it has doubled in size. On a floured surface, roll it out into a ½"-thick rectangle. Paint the dough with the filling mixture and roll it up into a log. Cut the log into 3" sections. Place on a greased sheet pan.

8. Bake for 45 minutes until brown. Let cool slightly and frost. Serve.

Tangy Lime Tart

Try using key limes for a richer lime flavor. Also, add some lime zest to the crust!

INGREDIENTS | SERVES 6

Crust
¼ cup unsalted butter
¼ cup olive oil
¼ cup whole-wheat flour
½ cup all-purpose flour
1 tablespoon water, or as needed

Filling
Juice and zest of 3 medium limes
3 large eggs, beaten
2 tablespoons cornstarch
½ cup granulated sugar
1 cup water

1. Preheat the oven to 375°F.

2. To make the crust: Blend the butter and oil together in a medium bowl. Sift together the flours in a separate bowl, then combine the 2 mixtures, by hand or in a mixer with a dough hook at low speed, adding the water 1 spoonful at a time. Roll out the dough on a floured surface, then place in a pie pan; bake for 10 minutes.

3. To make the lime filling: Mix together all the filling ingredients; bring the mixture to a slow simmer in a medium-sized saucepan, stirring constantly until it becomes thick. Pour the lime mixture into the par-baked pie shell and bake 15 minutes longer.

Grapefruit and Pomegranate Bars

Always wear an old shirt or apron when working with pomegranates, as the bright red juice can stain.

INGREDIENTS | SERVES 10

2½ cups all-purpose flour

1¼ cups unsalted butter

¾ cup confectioners' sugar

1 ripe pomegranate

5 large eggs

½ cup fresh grapefruit juice

2½ cups granulated sugar

1¼ teaspoons baking powder

Chinese Apple

The pomegranate is a large, round, maroon fruit, sometimes called a Chinese apple. When opened, it is full of edible seeds that are tart and slightly crunchy. Pomegranate is somewhat expensive, but it's worth the cost for special occasions and recipes.

1. Preheat the oven to 350°F. In a large bowl, mix together the flour, butter, and confectioners' sugar. Press into a large, oblong baking pan and bake for 20 minutes. Remove from the oven and let cool slightly.

2. While the crust bakes, cut open the pomegranate and remove the seeds. Discard the skin and other material.

3. Beat the eggs in a bowl and mix in the grapefruit juice, sugar, and baking powder. Fold in the pomegranate seeds. Pour the mixture over the crust. Bake for 20–25 minutes until the top is set. Allow it to cool before cutting it into bars.

Momma Theresa's Zucchini Cake

If you have a lot of zucchini left over at the end of the summer, use it to make this delicious cake. Serve warm with whipped cream.

INGREDIENTS | SERVES 10

3 large eggs

1 cup vegetable oil

3 teaspoons vanilla extract

1½ cups granulated sugar

3 cups all-purpose flour

1 teaspoon salt

1 teaspoon baking powder

1 teaspoon baking soda

1 teaspoon ground cinnamon

2 teaspoons ground cloves

2 medium zucchini, shredded

1 cup chopped walnuts

1. Preheat the oven to 350°F. Lightly grease and flour a large bundt pan.

2. In a small bowl, mix together the eggs, oil, vanilla, and sugar.

3. In a large bowl, sift together the flour, salt, baking powder, baking soda, cinnamon, and cloves.

4. Mix together the wet and dry ingredients, then fold in the zucchini and walnuts.

5. Pour the batter into the pan and bake for 1 hour. Serve warm.

Oatmeal Muffins

Store these hearty muffins in an airtight container and enjoy them toasted with butter for the next few days.

INGREDIENTS | SERVES 10

1 cup all-purpose flour

1¼ tablespoons baking powder

¼ teaspoon salt

¼ cup granulated sugar

¼ cup light brown sugar

1 large egg

¾ cup whole milk

¼ cup melted unsalted butter

1 cup uncooked oatmeal

½ cup chopped dried fruit

½ cup chopped nuts of choice

1. Preheat the oven to 400°F. Grease a muffin tin. In a large bowl, sift together the flour, baking powder, salt, and sugars in a large bowl.

2. In a separate bowl, beat the egg and whisk in the milk and butter.

3. Combine the wet and dry ingredients, then fold in the oatmeal, fruit, and nuts.

4. Pour the batter into the greased muffin tin, filling each about halfway. Bake for about 20 minutes. Serve.

Mustastoy

This sweet bread, called something different in every family, makes a great breakfast or snack. You can substitute other nuts for walnuts, if you prefer.

INGREDIENTS | SERVES 10

2 cups honey

3 large eggs

¼ cup granulated sugar

2 teaspoons baking powder

½ cup whole milk

¼ cup unsalted butter

4 cups all-purpose flour

1 cup chopped walnuts

1. Preheat the oven to 275°F (low-heat oven). Lightly grease a baking sheet.

2. In a large bowl, mix together all the ingredients. Cover the dough with plastic wrap or a clean towel and allow it to rest for ½ hour.

3. Form the dough into small oval loaves and place on the greased baking sheet.

4. Bake for 1 hour. Let cool before serving.

Fig Tart

You can use either the white or dark figs for this recipe—just be sure they're fresh figs.

INGREDIENTS | SERVES 10

2 cups all-purpose flour

1¼ cups cold unsalted butter

¾ cup granulated sugar

2 medium pears, cored and sliced

6 whole fresh figs

Figs

Fresh figs are a wonderful addition to salads. They are expensive, but a few go a long way. White figs, if you can find them, are pretty additions to any salad plate but there is virtually no difference in taste between the black and the white varieties.

1. Preheat the oven to 375°F.

2. In a large bowl, mix together the flour, butter, and sugar. Roll out the dough and place in a large ungreased tart pan. Fill the crust with the sliced pears.

3. Clean the figs and cut them in half; scatter them across the pears.

4. Fold the dough ends up slightly to cover the fruit around the edge of the tart. Bake for 20 minutes.

Almond Loaf

Almonds are common ingredients in sweet Italian dishes. Enjoy
this bread for breakfast or as a snack with tea.

INGREDIENTS | SERVES 10

2¼ cups all-purpose flour
1 tablespoon baking powder
½ cup unsalted butter
1 cup granulated sugar
3 large eggs
¾ cup whole milk
1 tablespoon almond extract
½ cup chopped or slivered almonds

Just a Spoonful of Sugar

When grinding almonds for a sweet recipe, put a spoonful of sugar in with the almonds to be ground. This prevents the almonds from getting too oily and forming a paste while being processed. Just be sure not to add too much sugar, especially if there is other sugar in the recipe.

1. Preheat the oven to 350°F. Lightly grease and flour a loaf pan.

2. In a large bowl, sift together the flour and baking powder.

3. In a separate bowl, cream together the butter and sugar.

4. In a small bowl, beat the eggs, then add the milk and almond extract.

5. Combine the flour, butter mixture, and egg mixture. Fold in the nuts. Pour into the greased loaf pan.

6. Bake for 40–45 minutes. Serve warm.

Anisette Cookies

For frosting: whip together ½ cup unsalted butter, 1 cup whole milk, 2 cups confectioners' sugar, and ½ teaspoon vanilla extract.

INGREDIENTS | SERVES 10

2 cups all-purpose flour
1 tablespoon baking powder
2 large eggs
6 tablespoons unsalted butter
⅓ cup whole milk
½ cup granulated sugar
1 teaspoon anisette liqueur

1. Preheat the oven to 350°F. In a large bowl, sift together the flour and baking powder.

2. In a medium bowl, beat the eggs, then add the butter, milk, sugar, and anisette liqueur.

3. Mix together the dry and wet ingredients to form a dough.

4. Form by rolling into cigar-sized rolls. Using your finger, spiral the dough into a "beehive" shape. Place on an ungreased baking sheet.

5. Bake for 10–12 minutes. Let cool slightly. Frost if desired and serve.

Gelato di Espresso (Espresso Gelato)

When you think of Italy, gelato and espresso may instantly come to mind. Here, they go hand in hand to give a cool and delicious pick-me-up.

INGREDIENTS | MAKES 1 QUART

3 cups whole milk

1 cup sugar

Pinch salt

⅓ cup coarse-ground espresso beans

1 tablespoon espresso powder (do not use instant coffee)

5 large egg yolks

1 cup heavy cream

2 teaspoons vanilla extract

1. In a small saucepan, combine the milk, sugar, salt, ground espresso beans, and espresso powder. Stir over medium heat. Once simmering, remove from heat, cover, and allow to steep for 1 hour.

2. After 1 hour, strain the milk mixture to remove all of the coffee grounds. You may want to do this a few times to ensure that you remove the maximum amount of grounds. Reheat the milk mixture over medium-low heat.

3. In a separate bowl, whisk the egg yolks. Once the milk mixture is hot, temper the yolks by adding half of the mixture into the eggs, whisking constantly. Add the egg mixture to the saucepan, and heat until thickened.

4. Pour ½ cup of the heavy cream into a large mixing bowl over an ice bath. Strain the custard into the cream. Add the remaining ½ cup cream and stir to combine.

5. Add to the ice cream maker and follow the manufacturer's instructions for freezing. Stop the churning as soon as the gelato is just frozen.

Gelato di Limoncello (Limoncello Gelato)

The perfect ending to the perfect Italian meal is limoncello, an Italian lemon liqueur. This gelato variation steps it up and gives you a creamy dessert to boot!

INGREDIENTS | MAKES 1 QUART

3 cups whole milk

1 cup sugar

Pinch salt

Zest of 2 lemons, finely chopped

5 large egg yolks

⅔ cup heavy cream, divided

¼ cup limoncello

Fresh-squeezed juice of ½ large lemon

Limoncello

There are several different stories as to the origin of limoncello. What does remain consistent is that limoncello was first created in the 1900s. It originated on Italy's southwest coast, in either Capri, Sorrento, or Amalfi. In Italy, it is commonly used as an apéritif and a digestive before and after meals.

1. In a small saucepan, combine the milk, sugar, salt, and lemon zest. Stir over medium heat. Once simmering, remove from heat, cover, and allow to steep for 1 hour.

2. If a smooth texture is desired, strain the milk mixture through a fine sieve to remove the lemon zest. (Leave zest in for a tangier lemon flavor.) Reheat the milk mixture over medium-low heat.

3. In a separate bowl, whisk the egg yolks. Once the milk mixture is hot, temper the yolks by adding half of the mixture into the eggs, whisking constantly. Return the mixture to the saucepan and heat until thickened. Pour ½ cup of heavy cream into a large mixing bowl over an ice bath. Strain the custard into the cream.

4. Stir together the limoncello, lemon juice, and remaining cream. Stir into the gelato mixture. Refrigerate 8 hours to overnight.

5. Add to the ice cream maker and follow the manufacturer's instructions for freezing. Stop the churning as soon as the gelato is just frozen.

Gelato alla Nutella (Hazelnut Nutella Swirl Gelato)

Nutella is to Italy what peanut butter is to the United States. It is used in sandwiches, pastries . . . you name it. Made of hazelnuts and cocoa powder, it makes the perfect complement to hazelnut gelato.

INGREDIENTS | MAKES 1 QUART

1½ cups toasted hazelnuts, skins removed

¾ cup sugar

1 cup milk

2 cups heavy cream

Pinch salt

4 large egg yolks

2 tablespoons Frangelico or other hazelnut liqueur

½ cup Nutella

Nutella

Nutella was created by Pietro Ferrero in the 1940s to extend the chocolate supply during the rationing of cocoa. Nutella was originally made in loaves and wrapped in foil (much like butter is today) so that it could be cut and spread on bread. It has since evolved into the much-loved creamy, silky spread that it is today.

1. Combine the hazelnuts and sugar in a blender or food processor and pulse until well chopped.

2. Add the milk, cream, and salt to a medium saucepan. Add the hazelnut mixture and bring to a boil over medium heat. Remove from heat and steep for 1–2 hours.

3. Place a strainer over a medium saucepan and pour the hazelnut milk mixture into it. Wring the juices out of the strained hazelnuts into the saucepan. Discard the nuts and bring mixture to a simmer.

4. In a separate bowl, whisk the egg yolks. Once the milk mixture is hot, temper the yolks by adding half of the mixture into the eggs, whisking constantly. Return the mixture to the saucepan and heat until thickened. Remove from heat and stir in the Frangelico.

5. Chill 4 hours or overnight.

6. Add to the ice cream maker and follow the manufacturer's instructions for freezing. Just before the gelato is frozen, swirl in the Nutella. Stop the churning as soon as the gelato is just frozen.

Gelato di Pistacchio (Pistachio Gelato)

Believe it or not, despite their nutty appearance, pistachios are not nuts. They are actually the seeds of a plum-like fruit, the flesh of which is removed during processing.

INGREDIENTS | MAKES 1 QUART

1 cup unsalted shelled pistachios

1 cup sugar

2 cups milk

Pinch salt

4 large egg yolks

2 teaspoons vanilla extract

1¼ cups heavy whipping cream

1 cup toasted unsalted shelled pistachios, chopped

1. Combine the pistachios and sugar in a blender or food processor and pulse until well chopped. Place into a medium saucepan. Add the milk and salt and bring to a boil over medium heat.

2. In a separate bowl, whisk the egg yolks. Once the milk mixture is hot, temper the yolks by adding half of the mixture into the eggs, whisking constantly. Add the egg mixture to the saucepan and heat until thickened. Remove from heat and stir in the vanilla.

3. Chill 4 hours or overnight. Stir in the cream and chopped toasted pistachios.

4. Add to the ice cream maker and follow the manufacturer's instructions for freezing. Stop the churning as soon as the gelato is just frozen.

Gelato di Mora e Salvia (Sage Blackberry Swirl Gelato)

*With the deep flavors of the blackberries and the refreshing earthy
flavors of the sage, this gelato will have you swooning.*

INGREDIENTS | MAKES 1 QUART

3 cups whole milk

1 cup sugar

Pinch salt

1 vanilla bean, split and scraped

5 large egg yolks

1 cup heavy cream, divided

3 cups fresh sage

2 teaspoons vanilla extract

⅔ cup seedless blackberry jam

3 tablespoons blackberry brandy or dark berry liqueur

Sage

Sage is an astringent, an antiseptic, and a tonic herb, with a camphor-like aroma. Sage is said to prevent spasms, improve liver function and digestion, and have anti-inflammatory, antidepressant, and estrogenic effects. So not only is this sage gelato delicious, some might say it has health benefits as well!

1. In a small saucepan, combine the milk, sugar, salt, vanilla bean seeds, and empty vanilla bean pod. Stir over medium heat. Once simmering, remove from heat, cover, and allow to steep for 1 hour.

2. After 1 hour, remove the bean pod (save for later use). Reheat the milk mixture over medium-low heat.

3. In a separate bowl, whisk the egg yolks. Once the milk mixture is hot, temper the yolks by adding half of the mixture into the eggs, whisking constantly. Return the egg mixture to the saucepan and heat until thickened. Pour ½ cup of the heavy cream into a large mixing bowl over an ice bath. Strain the custard into the cream.

4. Blanch the sage in boiling water for 10 seconds, then shock in an ice bath. Towel the leaves dry. Add the leaves and the remaining ½ cup of heavy cream to the blender and process. Add the sage mixture and vanilla extract to the prepared custard, allowing the sage to infuse into the mixture. Strain after 2 hours and place in the refrigerator until thoroughly chilled, about 5 hours or overnight.

5. Just before churning the gelato, stir together the jam and liqueur thoroughly in a small bowl.

6. Add the gelato to the ice cream maker and follow the manufacturer's instructions for freezing. Stop the churning as soon as the gelato is just frozen. Swirl in the jam mixture before placing into the freezer.

APPENDIX A

Sample Holiday Menus

New Year's Day

Hearty Artichoke Leaves (Chapter 2)
Fig and Gorgonzola Salad (Chapter 14)
Grilled Duck Breast with Fruit Salsa (Chapter 6)
Green Bean Bundles (Chapter 15)
Carrot and Citrus Casserole (Chapter 15)
Spelt Pasta with Sage Pesto (Chapters 13 and 3)
Italian Bread Pudding (Chapter 16)

Easter Sunday

Garlic Soup (Chapter 4)
Fresh Crab with Arugula Salad (Chapter 14)
Wilted Kale Salad with Roasted Shallots (Chapter 14)
Leg of Lamb (Chapter 5)
Easter Pizza Casserole (Chapter 5)
Sausage-Filled Shallots (Chapter 2)
Roasted Potato and Garlic Gnocchi (Chapter 13)
Gorgonzola Browned Pears (Chapter 2)
Easter Egg Bread (Chapter 9)

Thanksgiving

Cheese-Stuffed Prunes (Chapter 2)
Turkey and Fig Balls (Chapter 8)
Roasted Garlic Smashed Potatoes (Chapter 15)
Baked Sweet Potatoes with Pear (Chapter 15)
Herbed Flatbread (Chapter 9)
Broccoli Raab Parmesan (Chapter 15)
Pecan Broccoli (Chapter 15)
Almond Loaf (Chapter 16)

Christmas Eve

Christmas Eve Salad (Chapter 14)
Clam-Stuffed Portobellos (Chapter 2)
Frittura di Paranza (Pan-Fried Smelts) (Chapter 2)
Baccalà in Saffron Marinara Broth (Chapter 7)
Shrimp Scampi (Chapter 7)
Red Snapper with Peppers (Chapter 7)
Aragosta con Burro all'Aglio (Lobster with Garlic Butter) (Chapter 7)
Basic Risotto (Chapter 11)
Seafood Polenta (Chapter 11)
Fresh Vegetable Dip with Crusty Italian Bread (Chapter 2)
Cavolfiore Fritto (Fried Cauliflower) (Chapter 15)
Classic Biscotti (Chapter 16)
Tiramisu Pie (Chapter 16)

Christmas Brunch

Savory or Sweet Breakfast Egg Polenta (Chapter 11)
Sausage and Pepper Frittata (Chapter 10)
Cinnamon Rolls (Chapter 16)
Melon and Prosciutto (Chapter 2)
Garlic and Olive Bruschetta (Chapter 2)
Broccoli with Romano Bread Crumbs (Chapter 15)
Osso Buco with Polenta Dumplings (Chapter 5)
Hearty Cold Antipasto Salad (Chapter 14)
Gelato di Limoncello (Limoncello Gelato) (Chapter 16)
Tordillas (Chapter 16)

APPENDIX B

Standard U.S./Metric Measurement Conversions

VOLUME CONVERSIONS

U.S. Volume Measure	Metric Equivalent
⅛ teaspoon	0.5 milliliter
¼ teaspoon	1 milliliter
½ teaspoon	2 milliliters
1 teaspoon	5 milliliters
½ tablespoon	7 milliliters
1 tablespoon (3 teaspoons)	15 milliliters
2 tablespoons (1 fluid ounce)	30 milliliters
¼ cup (4 tablespoons)	60 milliliters
⅓ cup	90 milliliters
½ cup (4 fluid ounces)	125 milliliters
⅔ cup	160 milliliters
¾ cup (6 fluid ounces)	180 milliliters
1 cup (16 tablespoons)	250 milliliters
1 pint (2 cups)	500 milliliters
1 quart (4 cups)	1 liter (about)

WEIGHT CONVERSIONS

U.S. Weight Measure	Metric Equivalent
½ ounce	15 grams
1 ounce	30 grams
2 ounces	60 grams
3 ounces	85 grams
¼ pound (4 ounces)	115 grams
½ pound (8 ounces)	225 grams
¾ pound (12 ounces)	340 grams
1 pound (16 ounces)	454 grams

OVEN TEMPERATURE CONVERSIONS

Degrees Fahrenheit	Degrees Celsius
200 degrees F	95 degrees C
250 degrees F	120 degrees C
275 degrees F	135 degrees C
300 degrees F	150 degrees C
325 degrees F	160 degrees C
350 degrees F	180 degrees C
375 degrees F	190 degrees C
400 degrees F	205 degrees C
425 degrees F	220 degrees C
450 degrees F	230 degrees C

BAKING PAN SIZES

U.S.	Metric
8 × 1½ inch round baking pan	20 × 4 cm cake tin
9 × 1½ inch round baking pan	23 × 3.5 cm cake tin
11 × 7 × 1½ inch baking pan	28 × 18 × 4 cm baking tin
13 × 9 × 2 inch baking pan	30 × 20 × 5 cm baking tin
2 quart rectangular baking dish	30 × 20 × 3 cm baking tin
15 × 10 × 2 inch baking pan	30 × 25 × 2 cm baking tin (Swiss roll tin)
9 inch pie plate	22 × 4 or 23 × 4 cm pie plate
7 or 8 inch springform pan	18 or 20 cm springform or loose-bottom cake tin
9 × 5 × 3 inch loaf pan	23 × 13 × 7 cm or 2 lb narrow loaf or pâté tin
1½ quart casserole	1.5 liter casserole
2 quart casserole	2 liter casserole

Index

We Have

EVERYTHING®

on Anything!

The Everything® list spans a wide range of subjects, with more than 500 titles covering 25 different categories:

Business	History	Reference
Careers	Home Improvement	Religion
Children's Storybooks	Everything Kids	Self-Help
Computers	Languages	Sports & Fitness
Cooking	Music	Travel
Crafts and Hobbies	New Age	Wedding
Education/Schools	Parenting	Writing
Games and Puzzles	Personal Finance	
Health	Pets	